W9-BVL-435

Offshore Ready

Strategies to Plan & Profit from

Offshore IT-Enabled Services

Stuart Morstead

and

Greg Blount

Foreword by

Rick Beatty

First Edition

ISANI PRESS

Copyright © 2003 by Stuart P. Morstead and Gregory T. Blount.

Published by ISANI Press (www.isanipress.com)
Cover design by Jesika Cook at manipul8, Inc. (www.manipul8.com)
Copy editing by Josephine Roccuzzo
Printed and bound by Branch Smith Printing, Inc., (www.branchsmith.com)

All rights reserved. No part of this book may be reproduced or transmitted in any form, or by any means, electronic, or mechanical, including photocopying, recording, or by any information storage and retrieval system, without permission in writing from the publisher.

Library of Congress Control Number: 2003102049

ISBN 0-9728682-0-8 (paperback)
1. Business. 2. Strategy. 3. Information Technology. 4. Offshore. 5. Offsourcing. 5. IT-enabled Services. 6. Call Center. 7. BPO. 8. Business Process Outsourcing

Printed in the United States of America.

This book is available at quantity discounts for bulk purchases. Please email us at info@offshoreready.com or go to our web site at www.offshoreready.com to contact the publisher.

The purpose of this book is to educate readers on the opportunities and challenges of developing offshore IT-enabled services options. It is not intended to be an endorsement for or a warning against the practice of developing and/or contracting IT-enabled services in geographies outside the United States or Western Europe.

This publication is designed to provide accurate and authoritative information with regard to the subject matter covered. It is sold with the understanding that the publisher is not engaged in rendering legal, accounting or other professional advice. If legal or other expert advice is required, the services of other competent professional organizations should be sought.

> From a *Declaration of Principles* jointly adopted by a Committee of the American Bar Association and a Committee of Publishers and Associations

The reader is encouraged to acquire additional information from other publications and resources, some of which are mentioned in this text, to gain a more complete understanding of the subject matter. The authors will have neither liability for nor responsibility to any person or entity with respect to any loss or damage caused, or alleged, by the information provided in this book.

The terms Offsourcing Roadmap[sm], Total Cost of Offsourcing[sm], TCO[sm], Offsourcing Maturity Model[sm], and OMM[sm] are all service marked by ISANI Group, Inc..

To my parents, whose unquestioning support in my early endeavors made the thought of writing this book less a daunting prospect and more an engaging challenge.

-Stuart

To my parents for their support, values and the work ethic they taught me. To my mother in particular, who passed away in 2002.

-Greg

We are both grateful to our families, who have made great sacrifices during the book's development and production, as well as during our long periods of travel overseas, learning the lessons described herein.

There is a tide in the affairs of men, which, taken at the flood, leads on to fortune; omitted, all the voyage of their life is bound in shallows and in miseries. On such a full sea we are now afloat; and we must take the current, the clouds folding and unfolding beyond the horizon when it serves, or lose our ventures.

Julius Cæsar. Act iv, Sc. 3. – William Shakespeare

Table of Contents

List of Tables

List of Figures

Foreword

The tremendous benefits of having an operational center offshore are no secret to Microsoft, GE, British Telecom, Dell, GM, Ford, American Express and many other well-known corporations that are planning to add thousands of developers and customer service agents in India alone. Executives in these companies know that there is a spectacular competitive advantage in a process that costs less than 60% of a comparable US-based capability. "Sixty percent lower costs" is a phrase that would warm hearts in any board meeting in the United States. Not much of a secret but still a bit of a mystery, establishing an offshore capability is an adventure worth taking—but as with many adventures, you will benefit from having a guide or two. If you are reading this book then you are curious about success offshore, and I can recommend a couple of guides.

I have seen firsthand the truly magical elements of a software development center in Bangalore, India. Requirements for a release of a new J2EE software product were defined by a small team in the states and shipped to a 100-plus–person center in Bangalore. All development and testing was performed in India, and the ready-to-deploy, Internet-based product was shipped back to the states. Magic. Functional equivalence and high quality at less than 50% of costs in the US. A walk in the park. So let's move more of the process offshore.

Not quite.

Moving an onshore process offshore is not a simple step; it's not even a simple project. The rewards for success are greater than any executive productivity strategy that I have ever seen, but the strategy carries unique obstacles. For one thing, if you wake up in California with a burning desire for an in-person discussion with the lead person in your new center, then days (maybe weeks) might pass before you could make it happen. If you think about calling after a briefing at 9:00 AM it will be after 10:00 PM in Bangalore. Communication requirements for offshore operations are unique; much of the valuable experience in this book addresses this issue. You cannot fully succeed offshore with normal attention to effective communications. This holds true for English-speaking resources in India and would only be magnified for a center in regions where people don't speak English.

Communications are just one facet of the unique requirements underpinning offshore success in this book. Organization, policies, methods and process details all will change in the areas chosen for offsourcing. Working offshore also involves immersing yourself in a culture different from your native culture. It represents a colossal change to the people currently performing the functions you want to offsource—a change so dramatic that it can be perceived as a threat or as implied criticism.

The absolute need for unwavering executive sponsorship and active support in the face of this change is another unique and crucial aspect of going offshore. New problems and obstacles are natural side effects of dramatically changing the onshore culture, but they can be resolved with patience and the active engagement of players from upper management on down. Addressing these issues is another valuable aspect of this book.

Still, this journey offshore is a winning strategy for information systems and IT-enabled services, particularly call centers and repetitive business processes. For organizations similar to those where I have spent much of my career, offshore strategies are rapidly becoming core to growth, and at times even survival. The goal state of having a low-cost, high-quality center offshore will add to profits and create competitive advantage.

The authors of this book are vetted guides who can help you on this venture. Stuart Morstead and Greg Blount possess invaluable hands-on experience in creating offshore capabilities. They have been involved in strategic planning, program and project management, process development, communication problem resolution and even cultural integration planning and execution. I have also seen firsthand vendors (or partners, as Stuart and Greg think of them) solicit the authors' involvement in tough issues—even though they represent the client's interest—because of their approach to building relationships and focusing on getting to the best solution. They are proven management consultants, entrepreneurs and executives with global experience. This book lets you stand on their shoulders.

Offshore Ready will serve you well. It will draw your attention to the critical elements of a successful program to create an offshore capability. It will remind you that the benefits of operating offshore are exceptional and well worth the effort. This distillation of experience should save you time and money and give you an invaluable advantage on your quest.

I wish you good luck.

Rick Beatty

Preface

In the National Museum in Mumbai, India, there is an exhibit dedicated to a number of British Man-of-War ships built by Indian companies in the early 1800s. Originally "taken offshore" for reasons of cost, the construction of these vessels in India proved prescient once combat began. They simply performed better than domestic vessels owing to the superior materials used in building and the greater degree of precise and careful workmanship.

Fast forward to the 1970s, '80s and '90s and one finds a steady migration of manufacturing offshore to take advantage of lower-priced labor. Whether in textiles or more durable goods, the combination of cheap labor and ever-increasing pools of skilled workers created a compelling argument for businesses to move production overseas. This migration was slowed at times by legislation or the buoyancy of profits during good times, but the trend remained.

The migration of IT-enabled services[1] offshore has begun because there is now more pressure than ever to ratchet down costs, save money and operate more efficiently. It will grow not out of some grand design of developing countries to capture high-tech industry, though they are certainly happy to do so, but because of the economics. And unlike previous migrations, once the movement begins in earnest, it will be compressed into a matter of years, not decades, owing to the absence of government regulations and organized resistance. The regulators are unlikely to see striking programmer unions protesting for the imposition of quotas and tariffs on services.

My own introduction to offshore IT-enabled services came in the area of application development. In late 1991 while working on a large software implementation project in Mexico City, I was tasked with the delivery of an application only to be told that there may not be adequate resources available. The then-Big 6 firm where I was working was unable to convince sufficient numbers of its bright-eyed, starched-collared young consultants to get on a plane to Mexico City (my friends and I being notorious exceptions to this rule) every week.

The partner suggested that we take a look an Indian offshore group with US operations based in Florida as a way to fill the gap. Internal resources were tight in the US, and the partnership was not averse to making margin on subcontractors so long as the client's and therefore our risk could be adequately managed. A couple of weeks later, after a long day of discussions with the prospective partner during which we were given the grand tour of the facilities and a steady stream of information on process and quality, we found ourselves

---

[1] For purposes of ease of writing this text uses the term IT-enabled services broadly to include application development, monitoring, call centers and repetitive business processes (outsourcing). In other materials you may note a distinction between IT services and IT-enabled services.

signing on to the new model. The basic value proposition was cost savings, but rigorous adherence to process was the deal closer.

What followed was months of hard work, splitting time between Florida and Mexico City to manage a dedicated group of professionals to deliver high-quality product. Given the time frames involved and the lack of collaborative work tools available in the pre-Web world, our narrow focus was on programming. In retrospect, the work was so successful that we could have taken advantage of the enormous cost savings made possible by moving the work truly offshore to India.

This all happened ten years ago. Why then is this book being written several years later and thirty years after the birth of the offshore industry?

The story of application development is a little complex ...

First, to understand why we were successful in 1991 and '92 is to know that we were working on mainframes with established methodologies, stable technologies and proven approaches. The traditional relationship of the IT organization to the business community had been one of gathering requirements, writing program specifications and delivering code to a nervous, but grateful, business community.

The emergence in the early 1990s of widespread adoption of client-server computing, with its rapid prototyping and heavy focus on user interaction in requirements gathering, led to a paradigm shift in the way that business requirements were driven into application development. The glowing green screens of the seventies and eighties were giving way to the more attractive graphical user interfaces of the nineties. Suddenly we began hearing terms like *ergonomics* being applied to software development. New positions like Information Architect, someone who assesses the way in which users interact with the information on a screen, were being bandied around. Anything and everything was possible: businesses could get what they wanted, when they wanted, and the code would look cool—or so it seemed.

Thrown into the context of going offshore, the challenges of successful delivery now exploded. Business users and developers working on prototypes were separated by thousands of miles. Communication bandwidth, still expensive, became an issue, and the collaboration on ergonomically appropriate applications between different cultures doomed many projects to failure.[2]

---

[2] This was true for purely US-based projects, not just those between the US and an international location.

This systemic shock was quickly superseded by the explosive growth of the Web. Expectations were further heightened as the gap between proven approaches, expectations and delivery capabilities widened.

Fortunately, work continued in the background. Methodologies improved, communications costs plummeted, collaborative tools were refined and approaches to organizing the work (recognizing the distributed nature of the workforce) were enhanced.

Now, with a post–dot-bomb focus on "back to the basics," long-term strategies to increase productivity and manage costs are back in vogue. What began as a ripple of activity with Texas Instruments, General Electric (GE), Microsoft and others is becoming the accepted way to achieve cost saving as high as 60%. A recent survey of chief information officers (CIOs) noted that although only 9% of CIOs were currently doing offshore development, some 42% would consider it. This ripple of interest is poised to become a tidal wave of activity.

The history of the rest of the IT-enabled services value chain, including call centers and business processing, is shorter and less complex.

During the past ten years, communications bandwidth costs have plummeted, while infrastructure has reached a critical mass. The cost savings now possible are in the 35%–65% range. It is that simple.

And yet, taken collectively the benefits of offshore IT-enabled services are still somewhat unexplored by many who have the most to gain. This is due in part to the educational, change management, operational and business continuity issues surrounding the opportunity and in part to a lack of reference material for practitioners who are responsible for making their offshore initiatives truly work. **Going offshore is hard work, but it is a real and very achievable goal, as this text will demonstrate.** Until case development tools, voice recognition software and other automation mechanisms become far more advanced than they are currently, there will be no substitute for human beings—meaning that offshore approaches will be the dominant approach to step changes in cost and quality for IT-enabled services.

This book does not address the moral or ethical correctness of moving program initiatives offshore. IT-enabled services are simply part of the next wave of migration, albeit with more focused geographic destinations including India, the Philippines and (at some point in the not-so-distant future) China. That this migration is coming, I am sure; that it should be done well, if and when the time comes, is the mandate here. History has shown that when countries take advantage of economic comparative advantage, everyone is a winner in the long run. Nevertheless, there are many public policy implications that need to be explored with respect to this migration, its speed and the long-term security of our economy. But I will save that discussion for another book.

My coauthor and colleague Greg Blount and I do, however, advocate strongly in this text that a portion of savings derived from moving offshore be reinvested in retraining and assistance for those who are displaced by this change. It is not a foregone conclusion that moving offshore always creates redundancy at home, although this outcome is likely.

Greg and I are indebted to a great number of colleagues and clients with whom we have worked in recent years for their insights and assistance. Shashank Samant, Raja Nagarajan, Dr. Alo Ghosh, Shailendra Ghaste, B. R. Sheaker, Chris Briggs, David Rimmer, Jose Thomas, Arindrajit Ray, Puneet Chadra, Prakash Gurbaxani, Bob Reimer, Joe Duryea, Ted Sarbin, Satish Bangalore, Jack McCarty and Bill McLaughlin have all given extensively of their time to provide introductions and fill in gaps of our understanding of current macro trends, industry players and operational approaches. Among this group, Rick Beatty has been inspirational. Rick's visionary conceptualization of the possibilities inherent in moving IT-enabled services offshore and unflagging support have been invaluable in getting us to where we are today.

The next few years herald rapid adoption of offshore IT-enabled services, with a vast array of products, services and business models coming to market. The difference between success and failure for many will be a thorough understanding of the issues. And although this book cannot possibly include all the existing opportunities and challenges, it is perhaps a guide for the serious traveler.

Stuart P. Morstead
Houston
February 2003

Introduction

The Imperative

The modern business climate seems to be a steady progression of belt-tightening with a focus on doing more with less. Businesses have created personnel cost-reduction incentives, branded expense control initiatives and pursued every get-lean scheme possible. Programs like total quality management, business process Re-engineering and Six Sigma have become so widely adopted as to become household names; and yet the pressure for ever-increasing savings continues unabated. Despite this focus, businesses now find themselves in the lean years of the longest ever postwar expansion in US history. Many are experiencing strained financial positions; and some industries, including telecommunications and airlines, are in severe cash crunches. **Where will this next round of savings come from?**

The Approach

For anyone with a manually intensive repetitive business process, a call center or large software development or maintenance needs, the answer is likely to become the adoption of **offshore IT-enabled services**, a practice we call *offsourcing*. Cost savings of between 35% and 65% are possible by offsourcing, while providing functional equivalence of your existing process. Put another way, offsourcing provides an opportunity to get twice as much done with the same budget or to add a significant contribution to the bottom line. Imagine taking a $10 million budget and returning $4 million to the corporate bottom line for reinvestment in growth-related activities like new product development, marketing and sales. How might this be viewed in the organization?

In many cases the service levels supported may actually increase, since more highly trained or educated individuals are available to work the process or because some of the savings may be traded for additional staff.

The Challenge

> *Cost savings of between 35% and 65% are possible by offsourcing, with no degradation in service.*

When the US manufacturing sector began to move offshore en masse, it tended to do so for items of limited complexity. As time passed and the sophistication of the remote location increased, there was a progression to ever more complex goods. Anti–child labor and "Buy USA" campaigns notwithstanding, consumers cared little about where or by whom the products were made since they had no ongoing involvement with the producers. They were interested in the retail cost of goods.

IT-enabled services represent a far more challenging environment. They begin with a high degree of complexity and involve rapid, multidimensional decision-making processes at just about every juncture of development and consumption. Further, the end consumer of a good often must interact with its producer in real time for a product to have any hope of success. Factor into the process the absolute reliance on cross-cultural communication, and you have an environment filled with potential hurdles in change management, methodology, contractual service levels, communications infrastructure and the like.

The pioneers of offshore services have more often than not been the Fortune 100. They have enormous staffs, huge budgets and can afford to diversify their portfolio of initiatives with a combination of low- and high-risk activities. They can also afford the learning curve required in getting to the better cost model that offshore services represent, since the benefits are so large. If they are looking at cutting $20 million out of a $100 million budget by leveraging offshore services, then spending $10 million on a one-time evaluation and buildout process is more than cost justified. In fact it would demonstrate a lack of fiduciary duty not to spend the money. But what about the vast majority of businesses that do not belong to this elite club? Should they ignore the opportunities to reduce unit costs or the potential to invest in new product development or sales and marketing made possible by an offsourcing strategy?

The Answer

We believe that the answer to the above question is a resounding "no." The "bleeding edge" has long since passed. Large companies have paved the way for the midsize and smaller firms by pushing sufficient capacity offshore to establish a critical mass of infrastructure, providers and intellectual capital to reduce the cost of entry—meaning that **offshore IT-enabled services are now within the reach of all large, most middle-market and even some smaller companies.** Success is a matter of education, preparation and commitment. There is an old saw that those who fail to prepare, prepare to fail. It is doubly true with offshore IT-enabled services.

We advocate a process-driven approach—not only to execution, but also to the Business

> *Offshore IT-enabled services are now within the reach of all large, most middle-market and even some smaller companies. Success is a matter of education, preparation and commitment.*

Case development and planning. (See Chapter 10 on Establishing the Business Case.) View challenges in the larger context, even as you plan for specific projects. The manner in which you begin your initiatives could determine not only their success in the short term, but also their long-term flexibility and the ability of the organization to respond quickly to a changing business climate. Plan to succeed from the beginning. Do not assume that you will just learn from your failures while you figure out how to save money.

This book is a roadmap to guide you through the challenges and opportunities of moving your IT-enabled services offshore. It is intended to help you avoid the traps that others have faced, to accelerate your time to implementation and to increase both the scope and degree of your successes. It is broad enough to give you a taste of most of the issues that you will encounter and (we hope) deep enough to offer actionable perspectives and responses. Inevitably, your business will bring a unique set of challenges to the environment, so we have focused where possible on creating frameworks that can accommodate the majority of field situations. If you are left wanting for more information when you complete a chapter, then it is our goal that you are at least equipped with the right questions to ask.

How This Book Is Organized

The content is organized into discrete parts for the simple reason that the reader is apt to have use for different components at different times, and because we recognize that we have a diverse audience. For the conceptual reader and possible change agent, we hope that you read enough to pique your interest and then pass the book on to someone in the organization who can take a crack at implementation. And likewise, for those operations people in the audience, we hope there is enough substance to make you want to tease the organization's visionaries with some of the more conceptual aspects of this work.

With the notion of accessibility in mind, the book's style reflects a focus on explaining concepts in basic, easily understood terminology. Where possible acronyms and technical jargon are avoided, and because specificity sometimes requires that technical terms or words with infrequent usage be applied, a glossary of terms is supplied to provide clarity.

The reader will note that Parts II through V have a heavy focus on India. This is a reflection of the authors' belief that at present and in general, India provides the most attractive offshore environment across many areas of the IT-enabled services value chain. Nevertheless, the Philippines has very strong providers and is possibly a better match for some clients. These ideas are explored in the text, along with a caveat to consider the geographic element in the context of a broader global portfolio strategy in which some diversity may increase the total benefits. In addition, the examples in Parts II through V are drawn primarily from the application development environment, which, again, is a reflection of the authors' greater experiences in this area. However, the examples are genericized where possible to illustrate the offshore opportunities in the entire IT-enabled services value chain.

Regardless of how you come to find yourself with a copy, we trust you will find this book an easy and possibly even entertaining read. We look forward to your feedback.

Sections

Part I: An Overview of Offsourcing

Part 1 provides the reader with a broad overview of the benefits and risks, critical success factors and approaches to adopting offsourcing practices. In doing so it aims to compress the learning curve for practitioners by beginning their education with the possibilities and benefits that offsourcing provides.

Read alone without benefit of the other sections, Part I will provide the reader with an understanding of the variety of offsourcing solutions, the legal structures in which they might be exercised, a summary understanding of the risks and benefits of adopting offsourcing practices (if not a full appreciation of the underlying reasons) and an overview of the major vendors in the space.

Part II: Planning and Preparing for Success

Part II assumes that the reader has progressed beyond the interest level and is either actively pursuing an offsourcing strategy or more likely is working the organization to develop support for the concept. Some content covers the softer aspects of garnering organizational support; however, the primary thrust is to build a numbers-driven approach to developing a comprehensive Business Case, with detailed cost data to support the initiative.

Topics covered include understanding the portfolio of opportunities, prioritizing those opportunities and performing data collection to support the Business Case. This is rounded out with an in-depth discussion of vendor selection in an environment where the qualifying factors should exceed those appropriate for domestic turnkey projects.

Part III: Executing the Plan

With a theme that there are no "silver bullets," Part III delivers a realistic perspective on the challenges of adopting offsourcing practices. Special attention is given to the importance of investing for the long haul and appropriately educating the organization on the level of executive commitment required for success.

Head-count reduction, skill-set mix adjustments and expanded workforce diversity are among the topics discussed. This section also contains background on the tough change management issues to be expected in adopting offsourcing practices. Further, it provides a foundation on the methodology options available and hits hard on the subject of metrics as a means of understanding, controlling and improving your organization's performance and the performance of your vendor, if you have involved a third party in your offsourcing solution.

Part IV: Maintaining and Renewing Your Offshore Initiatives

You have embarked on an offsourcing strategy, but what is your level of maturity? Are you ready to expand the benefits accruing to your organization by moving up the Offsourcing Maturity Model curve?

Part IV provides perspective on the continuum of offsourcing capabilities and what steps you can take to move to full benefits. In addition it considers the nature of the relationship that you may have established with a vendor and provides guidance as to whether you should really be looking for a partnership. Finally, it provides a governance framework for managing either type of relationship, noting the specific organizational constructs and activities required.

Part V: Offsourcing Case Studies

Part V describes three real-life offsourcing environments. Taken in order of strategic commitment, we review case studies reflecting outbound call centers, long-term product development and a joint venture relationship. The cases described are meant to provide a representative selection of the scenarios that the reader may consider for implementation. Although these situations are not exhaustive, taken in the aggregate the case studies should provide the reader with significant applicability for his or her own projected implementation.

Each case involves both a unique vendor and a unique buying organization. Areas of focus include vendor selection, project launch, change management issues, process development and critical success factors.

Part VI: Offsourcing Summary

Part VI brings the book's various themes into full focus. A summary of do's and don'ts and a final review of critical success factors provide a framework for making appropriate selections.

Beyond summarizing the book's main points, this section also endeavors to put offsourcing into the broader strategic perspective of a "mega trend" in outsourcing. We hope to leave the reader with not only an operational guide, but also a baseline to reflect on the broader possibilities of outsourcing to achieve optimal operational efficiencies and competitive advantage.

Part VII: Appendices

The final section of this book is both a user resource and a parking lot. It contains a few items that simply did not fit in the main body of the text, but were nonetheless considered to be valuable to the reader.

The section is both long and short: long in that there is precious little information about offsourcing available in print, so we relied in part on sources from numerous fields outside the immediate discipline; short in that the referenced materials hint at far greater complexity than could be included in this concise guide. Such are the trade-offs in writing an introductory piece on a broad subject.

Who Should Read This Book

In short, anyone who has significant internal IT-enabled services costs should find this book useful.

Chief Executive Officers (CEOs)

Successful offshore enablement is the result of sustained pressure and commitment. It is not a one-off event, but instead occurs within a context of individual and organizational diligence and obligation. As the captain of the ship, the CEO is best positioned to recognize the opportunity and make the commitment to winning the war on costs. As a text targeted at practitioners, this book may focus more than you'd like on the operational level. However, we encourage you to read Part I to understand the issues and constraints associated with this tremendous opportunity for cost savings.

Chief Information Officers (CIOs)

Mainframe maintenance, client-server conversions, Web-app development and XML integration: the list of competing demands for today's IT executive seems to grow by the quarter. Meanwhile the constraints of doing ever more with less and supporting business users' faster competitive cycles make for a daunting job description. How to tackle the beast? In the post–dot-bomb era, there is at least the possibility of recruiting and retaining talent; but what about cost containment and managing the skills matrix required to support the business?

Offsourcing provides an opportunity for the CIO to attack a variety of cost areas while retaining access to an extraordinary pool of talent. For most CIOs, the question of offsourcing has moved beyond viability and into the realm of execution. This book contains real-life success stories and blueprint processes to facilitate the CIOs move to action.

Chief Financial Officers (CFOs)

The traditional CFO outsourcing pitch is simple: the vendor will take the assets and the people off the books and rent them back to the organization over a period of time at a lower cost or, alternatively, will pay the firm for the assets up front and rent them back at the same cost. The vendor is able to do so by being an expert in the area of outsourcing and by leveraging the economies of scale that come from performing the same magical feat over and over again with numerous customers.

In many offsourcing scenarios, the connection between scale and cost savings is a little more tenuous, since automation and purchasing power may not be relevant to building the cost savings. The primary driver is the difference in labor costs, representing in some cases up to 65% savings. The challenge however, is not just to demonstrate that cost per hour is significantly less (it is), but to establish that the productivity per hour is reasonable once travel, communications and project management costs are loaded—and, further, that the delivery risk can be effectively managed. Chapter 10 is especially useful for the CFO looking to build a Business Case to invest in this new approach to delivering corporate IT services.

> *The primary driver is the difference in labor costs, representing in some cases up to 65% savings.*

Onshore and Offshore Information Technology Professionals

Whether you are a technology director in a multinational corporation or an entry-level programmer in an offshore service provider, this book warrants your attention. Mega trends are difficult to stop—and make no mistake: offsourcing is a mega trend. In the next ten years it promises to profoundly transform the way IT organizations are structured to deliver services. As is the case with any step change in business practices, there will be winners and losers. This book does not make any socioeconomic judgments about the nature of these changes or their impacts. It does, however, take a perspective on the onshore and offshore skill sets required to support the offsourcing environment. In addition we hope that it also provides offshore operators with the means to better express to their buyers the critical need for commitment. Educated buyers are demanding, but they are also more likely to be successful and therefore to be with you for the long term.

The objective is to be prepared with tools and skills when offsourcing comes to a neighborhood near you. Get the facts, make a plan and be prepared to ride the wave.

Operational Managers

Operational managers will be on the front lines of the IT-enabled services migration with their IT brethren and will face many of the decisions concerning when and where to go with offsourcing. Those with profit and loss (P&L) responsibility will be driven to offshore methods for the reasons discussed above, and those who are line managers may have active involvement in call center or business process outsourcing offshore activities. This book offers a thorough grounding in the many operations-related issues of moving offshore and is a basic guide for building your plan to make the target environment operational.

Students

The best advice I have heard given to college recruits considering a confusing array of career choices is to pick a growth industry. "Surely information technology is a growth industry," you might say; and you would be right. But steel was a growth industry throughout the 20th century, and as long as people are still making cars and building skyscrapers, or until some replacement material comes along, it will continue to be in this century. The right question is, "Will it be an industry that realizes a growth in employment in the geographic area in which I want to live?" What about when the cost of bandwidth approaches zero? When there are videophones available on every desk? When the cost of hiring a PhD from the top school in the world's most populous country is the same as that of hiring an average college recruit in the US or Western Europe?

These trends are already under way. Wouldn't it be better to understand the paradigm before investing in skills that may fall victim to wage deflation? The flip side of this equation is that offsourcing will also create new growth opportunities and career paths in ways yet unforeseen.

A Note on www.offshoreready.com

At the time of printing, the Web site accompanying this book is undergoing a rapid makeover. Over time we expect that you will be able to order additional copies of the book and much of the base materials including checklists, templates and financial models to which we refer in the text. In the meantime, please e-mail us at info@offshoreready.com with any questions, feedback or to contact the authors.

We look forward to your joining our community on the Web.

Part I: An Overview of Offsourcing

Chapter 1

What Is Offsourcing?

Overview

Offsourcing is the contracting of IT-enabled services internally or externally from a remote geography to take advantage of lower costs and better availability of specialized skill sets. **The savings can range from 35% to 65%, depending on the activity, volume, complexity and approach used to execute the capability.**

For those who look to an external service provider, offsourcing has some of the characteristics of traditional contracting, consulting or outsourcing, including the opportunity to leverage the focus and the unit cost reduction that comes from the scale and independence of the provider. Unlike with domestic outsourcing, however, lower costs do not necessarily come from the advantages of scale, but may instead be a reflection of the geography itself.

For those who seek an equivalent internal capability in the offshore geography, the cost savings and skill sets available create compelling arguments to change the current business model. The objective is functional equivalence at a lower cost, so the offshore operation may in fact be less automated while maintaining a far better cost structure.

> *Organizations today are successfully realizing dramatic savings and quality improvements by moving offshore.*

Results have shown that regardless of whether the approach is through organic investment or use of a vendor, **organizations today are successfully realizing dramatic savings and quality improvements by moving offshore.** Later in the text we introduce the Offsourcing Maturity Model, a framework for managing the investment and complexity (visibility and control, infrastructure, change management, communications, etc.) of this new paradigm; but for now we focus on detailing the areas of potential activity.

35% to 65% Savings is possible	
Area	**Overview**
General	The low end of the savings reflect less labor intensive practices, basic vendor involvement, small number of resources and limited to no leverage. The high end represents more manual processes, larger number of resources, Project environments and leverage for the provider.
Application development	Development is a multi-step process. Savings can be achieved within steps by moving them offshore. Commitment to attack the cost of application development requires significant integrated environmentsbetween the on and offshore centers.
Call center solution	Sizable regional variance. Ireland is in the mid-$20s/hour. Caribbean the low $20s, Philippines the mid to high teens and India in the mid teens (numbers are fully loadedand include communication costs). A large percentage of workers in the Indian call centers are making annual salaries of averaging $5,880.
Business process outsourcing	Highly variable, based upon specific function involved, complexity, size and duration.

Table 1: Offsourcing Solution Savings

Note: All dollar-denominated amounts in this text are in US dollars.

The Options

Offshore IT-enabled services range from unleveraged staff augmentation for X dollars per hour to full IT or business process outsourcing, which takes advantage of the additional economies of scale that come from a third party's spreading its fixed costs over multiple buyers, thereby lowering per-unit costs. The physical delivery of services, while largely centered in the remote geography, may occasionally be conducted on site, a practice referred to as **on-site delivery.**

This text reviews offsourcing in the context of the IT-enabled services value chain, which represents a continuum from lower to higher value-added services—often with tremendous complexity.

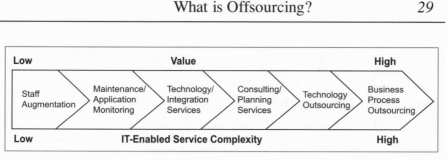

Figure 1: IT-Enabled Services Value Chain

Staff Augmentation

The most common form of leveraging offshore resources is through temporary service engagements to meet specific skill set deficits at low cost. Engagements last from as little as 30 days to several months or even years.

The business relationship can run the gamut from a simple task order for a particular resource for a specified number of consulting hours to a long-term commitment by the vendor to provide a certain number of qualified resources in a consult-to-hire scenario. In this more complex form, the vendor might leverage its recruiting capabilities (or more likely those of professional recruiters that he knows in the geographic area) to bring a number of resources to the table for a trial period. The buyer would in turn commit to covering travel expenses and some fixed costs per hire. Going forward, the buyer would keep the new personnel on temporary contract status, paying the vendor a low contract rate. At the end of some specified period, perhaps 90 days, the buyer would have the right to move the contract hire to full-time status or refuse the hire with the guarantee of a replacement candidate from the vendor within some specified time frame.

Who wins? The vendor makes money on the fixed fee per hire and on the contract rate during the trial period. The buyer can get terrific talent at a one-time hiring cost of $10,000–$12,000 (premium paid on the contractor rate over salaried rate during the 90 day period) in comparison to 15%–30% recruiting fees for domestic placements. In addition, they will likely hire the employee at below market rates (the federal government mandates just how far below market you can go) and have some assurance that the employee will remain with the buyer until his or her green card comes through, should the buyer make that choice. The employee benefits from employment in his or her preferred geographic area and is free to walk away at any time should the arrangement prove unsatisfactory.

US- and Western European–based providers of staff augmentation services have been competing with offshore companies for some time and are likely to continue to do so, with the scales tipping in favor of offshore providers for longer-term contracts. The bottom line is that it is a mature industry segment with eroding margins, tactical value to customers and limited strategic importance.

Application Maintenance and Monitoring

Also a well-developed segment of the offshore market, application maintenance has done well for some time. There are numerous reasons:

- **Stable software code base**—presumably the longevity of the established application software code means that there is less instability and therefore less likelihood of some catastrophic event. This stability also translates into fewer communication cycles that can be managed through formalized procedures and more stable and longer elapsed time for build cycles.

- **Minimal new requirements**—This factor limits the possibility of significant disconnects as a result of cultural miscues, since the new requirements tend to be modifications as opposed to radical changes.

- **Lack of pressure from current resources**—most developers like to focus on new development either because it is more interesting or because it presents opportunities for training that can in turn enhance their own market value. Since someone must be around to support the old applications, offsourcing application maintenance is generally viewed as an opportunity for developers to stay focused on building their skills.

Application monitoring is a newer segment of the market that is believed to hold great potential because of the opportunity to easily leverage skills in a remote geography that has a lower price point. Further, there are opportunities in application monitoring for third parties to enhance the buyer experience through the use of monitoring dashboards and cost reductions that come as a benefit of economies of scale. Some of the monitoring dashboards have become quite robust and are delivered via configurable portal interfaces.

In the Web space, application monitoring holds significant opportunities for large organizations owing to the cost of supporting so many areas of tool expertise. Better to offsource it and use the money saved to build more homogenous architectures.

Application Development and Integration

Application development and integration is currently attracting attention as a strong area of growth for the offsourcing industry. More complex than the two areas covered above, within the context of offsourcing, it has traditionally been the purview of domestic integrators or (aside from the odd job here and there) dominated by the large multinationals or India-based giants.

Again the gamut of scenarios runs from a one-off turnkey project in which detailed specifications are provided to long-term strategic relationships in which providers actually keep a dedicated bench available to the buyer, with unutilized resources shadowing those performing the real work. Often vendors will run a short-term proof-of-concept to demonstrate that the cultural or geographic divide in question can be effectively managed by adhering to a common process. Various segments in this market have emerged to respond to different needs, including:

- **Application development**—relatively straightforward, the domestic equivalent is the system integrator. Project management and a little of the "vision thing" allows application developers to be successful.

- **Package software development**—this phenomenon is gaining widespread adoption in the post–enterprise resource management (ERP) wars era. Independent software vendors (ISVs) are simply under tremendous pressure from the half dozen vendors that have been successful in databases, desktop applications, ERP, financial, supply chain or customer relationship management (CRM) solutions. They are now looking increasingly to broader footprints as a way to continue their revenue growth. The size of the big players means that they are already operating in remote geographies with lower development costs and have probably already moved some significant R&D functions offshore. The ISVs must reduce their development cost per hour if they are to compete.

- **Embedded systems development**—Almost everything containing a microchip these days, which is to say that just about any consumer appliance, industrial component or child's toy has some type of embedded system. Organizations are increasingly looking to cut costs and improve time to market in this expensive area of product development. Offsourcing is an increasingly common scenario.

As discussed in Chapter 20 in the Offshore Maturity Model, the opportunity exists to move much more than simply coding offshore when the relationship is a long-term one. The importance of this potential cannot be overstated, since we estimate that only 20% of the development process actually involves the physical coding effort.

Application development is where some of the most noted failures of the recent years have occurred for the simple reason that unlike with staff augmentation (discussed above), the successful delivery of the service requires risk management, quality assurance and some level of relationship building. And yet the commitment on the part of buyers to make the relationship work has often been the same as in the staff augmentation model. This topic is reviewed in some detail in the discussion of risks in Chapter 4.

Call Center

Call center capacity and demand is increasing sharply in India and the Philippines, with numerous large US companies including Dell, Motorola, American Express, VISA, and MetLife having taken the plunge. The ongoing deregulation of the telecommunications sectors will likely add to this growth as the cost of bandwidth, the life support for these operations, is set to decline.

In tandem with the opportunities for offsourcing call center operations are important characteristics of the underlying activity that can impact the potential for success.

- **Inbound Call Centers**

    o **Repetitive question resolution**—Operations that focus on repetitive questions with limited new information and low room for interpretation offer the best opportunity for cost savings. Here, the focus is on reduction of cost per hour per employee.

    o **Technical assistance**—For product companies and technical vendors, the offsourced call center creates the potential for cost reduction, but also for service level improvement by hiring a more highly educated resource at a lower dollar cost average.

    o **Claim resolution**—Often categorized as business process outsourcing, this area carries significant cultural and collaborative hurdles. In one scenario, perhaps an insurance company is fielding inbound calls soliciting assistance in filing health benefits claims. The agent (in collaboration with other parties) may be in the position of denying certain claims based upon the timing and specific constraints of the coverage. Cultural and communication-related concerns could be challenging.

- **Outbound Call Centers**

    o **Sales**—In this area, less activity is expected in the medium term because of the linguistic and cultural sensitivity required to "close" business. However, there are exceptions: technical sales where the knowledge of the product itself is paramount in reaching a deal are expected to see significant growth.

    o **Appointment setting and lead generation**—Numerous large programs offshore are enjoying significant success in this area. The basic script for these items is straightforward, so the training and ramp-up time is minimal.

- **Blended Facilities**

  o **Inbound and outbound campaigns**—Blended call management requires a level of critical mass to be economical. One scenario might involve a company running a television or radio advertising campaign that generates consumer interest. This interest is reflected in spikes of activity that follow viewing of the media. The blended environment allows outbound agents to receive inbound calls to accommodate a potential customer that has demonstrated interest in a product. This environment requires more training and more technology than the other environments described; therefore offshore call mixing is currently limited. It is occurring, however, and as in other areas, it is simply a matter of time and focus before it becomes a common practice.

Business Process Offsourcing

Business process offsourcing (BPO) is the holy grail of IT-enabled services because of the long-term nature of the contracts, barriers to entry that can be built up over time and the perceived infancy of many sectors of the market. Like the call center domain (which in some instances can be considered a subset of BPO), business process outsourcing has its own, though far more varied, landscape.

On the lower value-added end, there is activity in:

- **Data entry**—This function could run the gamut from the keying of ticket information to direct mail response cards. The value proposition is very simple: cheaper resources than can be found onshore capture, edit and otherwise input information into an electronic format.

- **Medical transcriptions**—Like data entry, medical transcription largely involves capturing human notations in one medium and converting them to another. Technology is slowly addressing this problem, but until there is far more sophisticated voice- or character-recognition software, there will continue to be a market for this service. Indeed, this happens to be a highly evolved area with a couple of large players and a number of smaller groups.

On the higher end of the value spectrum, there is activity in:

- **Support and back office operations**—The accounts payable and accounts receivable departments of large companies are ripe for targeting in this environment, since the work is repetitive and the tracking is system driven. Also, time-intensive sales support activities like demos or client research present extremely attractive targets.

- **Customer-driven processes**—In an organization like a large loan or mortgage management company, or possibly even an insurance processing center, endless forms must be collected, sorted, processed and managed. This work is time-consuming, labor intensive and often requires significant domain knowledge. Many large organizations have either piloted or are actively considering moving these functions to an offshore venue.

These high-value areas hold the most future potential for cost savings from offsourcing, since the other areas are slowly being commoditized by technology and are better understood in the offshore context. These areas are also likely to cause the most noticeable impact on a domestic workforce. Depending on the area of specialization, they may require some level of training sophistication and support a wage that reflects the skill of the offshore resources.

Summary

The range of IT-enabled services that may be moved to a remote geography, or offsourced, to take advantage of dramatic cost savings is broad and getting broader. The question of whether or not to offsource may or may not be tied to that of outsourcing. The authors find that many people directly associate going offshore with outsourcing, but this simply does not have to be the case. Offsourcing does not necessarily mean giving up control to a partner. In fact where strategic core initiatives are involved or where there are only limited economies of scale that can be offered to a third party, offsourcing may be desirable—but only while retaining full or partial ownership of the remote operation.

Chapter 1 Summary
What Is Offsourcing?

Chapter Theme

Many companies today are reaping tremendous benefits by moving IT services and IT-enabled services offshore, a practice we call offsourcing. The scope of potential areas for offsourcing continues to increase as the market matures.

- ❏ **Application development**
- ❏ **Application integration**
- ❏ **Application maintenance**
- ❏ **Call center solutions**
- ❏ **Business process outsourcing (BPO)**
- ❏ **Other back office functions**

Key Points

Offsourcing benefits are staggering when you consider that up to 50% of a company's total costs may be in personnel. Moving some of your IT-enabled services offshore can save an astounding 35% to 65%.

- ❏ **35% to 65% savings**
- ❏ **30 year track record**
- ❏ **Increasing demand**
- ❏ **Maturing industry**
- ❏ **Maturing processes**

Reader Take-Away

You should have an understanding of the breadth of services available in offshore environments and a summary understanding of the tremendous financial benefits that are available. You should also be in position to begin forming opinions as to where offsourcing might play a role in your company.

Questions for Consideration

- ❏ Does the organization have activity in many areas of the IT-enabled services value chain?
- ❏ Have you considered offsourcing as a strategy?
- ❏ How might your organization benefit from the potential savings?
- ❏ Do you have a long-term offsourcing vision for your organization?
- ❏ Have you defined a process to determine the scope of the work or specific functions to offsource?

Chapter 2

Offsourcing Market Evolution and Statistics

You don't need a weatherman to know which way the wind blows.

Bob Dylan, "Subterranean Homesick Blues" (1967)

Overview

Current estimates indicate that 5% of the US IT-enabled services market is operating offshore. Most of this activity comes from the nation's largest companies: some 300 of the Fortune 500 already have some type of relationship with an Indian IT-enabled services company. However, according to one analyst group's projection, *80% of US companies are expected to have considered the offsourcing option by 2004*. At an execution level 40% of these companies are expected to have completed some type of pilot with an offshore vendor and be in an operational mode by that time.[3]

Consider the following statistics:[4]

- GE is currently spends 8%–9% of its IT budget in India.
- IT services and IT-enabled services are expected to grow at a compound annual rate of 38% between 1998 and 2008 in India, increasing from $3.2 billion to $77 billion.
- Between 2001 and 2004, IBM's personnel in Indian offshore development centers will increase from 2,200 to 6,500, Accenture's will grow from 100 to 5,000 and EDS's from 600 to 5,000.

Further, key decision makers are rapidly getting on the bandwagon. In a survey of 50 of the Fortune 100 CIOs currently offsourcing to India, the following results were found.[5]

---

[3] Gartner Group, as quoted in CNET News.com, December 11, 2002, http://news.com.com/2100-1001-976828.html
[4] NASSCOM—McKinsey Report 2002.
[5] NASSCOM—McKinsey Report 2002.

Percentage of offshore activity	Currently budgeted offshore (% of respondents)	Expected to be moved offshore in near future
<5%	73%	2%
6% - 10%	15%	8%
11% - 15%	12%	20%
>15%	0%	70%

Table 2: CIO Disposition to Offsource

On a more somber note, the projections of the speed of migration of these activities does not paint a rosy picture for the US IT services worker. It has been estimated that while only a little over 27,000 jobs were lost to overseas competition in 2000, over 450,000 jobs will be lost in 2005. Based on that trend, a separate analyst group is estimating that by 2015 a total of 3.3 million US jobs and $136 billion in wages will transfer offshore to countries such as India, Russia, China and the Philippines.[6]

History

> *By 2015 a total of 3.3 million US jobs and $136 billion in wages will transfer offshore.*

Offsourcing is not a new phenomenon, though the size and scope of the activities have expanded dramatically in the past three to five years. Some of the more established offshore consultancies began as service bureaus in the late 1960s, expanding (as one might imagine) into contract programming and maintenance services. They grew as their domestic economies grew and eventually branched out to provide low-cost alternatives for US and Western European companies. As time passed, they pushed to verticalize their offerings and even establish an international sales presence.

India, given its large and growing base of educated, English-speaking workers, took a lead, particularly after it began to open its economy to competition in the early 1990s. At the same time, complementary industries and infrastructures began to evolve in many offshore domiciles, which in turn facilitated the emergence of providers, since less equipment, software and expertise were required to be brought in-country from outside to satisfy program needs.

As global telecommunications infrastructure increased markedly in the late 1990s and the Web emerged as a low-cost collaborative medium, so too the possibilities increased for providers in lower-cost geographies to offer other IT-

---

[6] Forrester Research, as quoted in CNET News.com, December 11, 2002, http://news.com.com/2100-1001-976828.html

enabled services to the high-cost markets of developed economies. The call center market began in earnest in 1999, with a few venture capital groups and offshore incumbents beginning to take stakes. Today the market it is teeming with new upstarts, service provider incumbents and US players that are trying desperately to reinvent their cost models or risk being rendered irrelevant.

The BPO market is perhaps harder to characterize, given the diversity of processes that hold the potential to be moved offshore or outsourced or both. Specific examples are given throughout the book, but suffice it to say that this market is garnering enormous interest today. The killer application of business process outsourcing has not yet been identified, but many smart people and large investors are working hard to find it.

Enabling Factors

At a macro level the basic value proposition of reduced costs has not changed in offsourcing, but the enabling elements have undergone significant transformation.

These factors include:

- **Reduction in bandwidth costs**—In India, the amount of fiber in the national telecom backbone will go from a little more than 170 thousand kilometers in 2000 to a projected 430 thousand kilometers in 2003. This represents growth in excess of 250% in less than four years, but it doesn't tell the whole story. With the introduction of the 8.4 Tbps Singapore-to-Chennai international link (Bharti Singtel) in 2002, India has catapulted its global connectivity. This link is the greatest capacity pipe in the world, capable of handling 10 times India's current requirements. The impact of this investment at an investment decision–making level cannot be overstated. To illustrate, the cost of a 2 Mbps leased line in 1997 was close to $1 million per year. In 2002 that cost was close to $100,000, (this number varies based on the negotiated rate with the carrier) and with the further deregulation over the next few years it is expected to drop even further.[7]

- **Availability of rapid transportation**—Although complaints about air travel seems to be perennially on the rise, so too are the number of flights and ever more convenient connections. Once off-the-map destinations are now accessible by jet with a variety of carriers. This means that critical personnel can be moved into and out of remote geographies more quickly and with less difficulty than was possible in the past.

---

[7] NASSCOM (National Association of Software and Services Companies)—McKinsey Report 2002.

- **Regulatory environment**—For developing economies to attract the foreign capital they need to modernize their economies, they must make a credible effort to enforce the rule of law, liberalize their telecommunications sectors and respect intellectual property rights. The net result is more enforceable (if not wholly so) contracts, rapid reduction in communication costs and freer access to the hardware required for running offsourcing operations. In addition, some countries have established favorable tax regimes for companies operating in these offshore geographies.

- **Availability of collaboration tools**—Ten years ago team members were using a combination of telephone calls and shared data files to communicate back and forth. Today, we are able to use a host of collaborative tools to manage these same exchanges—and the exchanges themselves can be carried out in more media than was previously possible. Videoconferencing, instant messaging and discussion boards are all available, either free or as piggyback services to the basic data communications infrastructure.

Micro and market-specific changes have led to additional changes, including:

- **Critical mass of vendors**—The number of providers offering their services has increased dramatically, with some reaching significant size. As we discuss in the providers profile in Chapter 7, numerous new US and Western European companies are now building capabilities. This has led to competition based on service level differentiation rather than simply price, an important element in moving offsourcing from the fringes to the mainstream. Companies wanting to move offshore now benefit from competition, a wider variety of models from which to choose and the investment dollars that are pouring in from large venture capital groups.

- **Track records**—Would-be offsourcing executives can point to the competition and to notable/quotable successes as they move their organizations to commit to the model. There is now a body of case histories that demonstrate the viability of the model.

- **Software and hardware support**—Producers of these goods have stepped up their international commitments as markets have reached penetration levels that warrant on-site support. This means that the cost and availability of support services for commercial goods in these areas continue to improve.

Market Size

The market size for any emerging trend is often difficult to pin down. This is perhaps doubly so in the case of offshore markets, where industry forums are perhaps not as mature as in developed economies. Further, the limited access to capital markets means that many groups remain invisible to the scrutiny of sector analysts whose job it is to compile such statistics.

One exception is India and the National Association of Software and Services Companies (NASSCOM; www.nasscom.org). NASSCOM has been a tireless promoter of the entire IT-enabled services sector in India through its conferences, publications and Web site. In addition it has also worked diligently with other services providers, including McKinsey & Co., to produce reports detailing the size, vigor and direction of the sector.

NASSCOM figures indicate the following:[8]

Global IT Spending in 2000			
Service line	Current global market size (US$B)	Indian export revenues for 2000 (US$B)	India's market share in 2000 (%)
Custom Application Development	$18B	$2.50B	13.60%
Application Outsourcing	$11B	$1.70B	15.80%
Packaged Software Support & Installation	$41B	$0.30B	0.70%
Systems Integration	$72B	$0.15B	0.20%
IT Consulting	$19B	$0.05B	0.30%
Network Infrastructure Management	$20B	$0.05B	0.30%
	$181B	$4.75B	

Table 3: India's Market Share of Global IT-Enabled Services

Source: IDC; NASSCOM; McKinsey analysis.

The main take-away from the table above should be that there is already significant penetration in mainstream areas of IT operations. Further, the depth and experience of talent that has been built in serving these markets can be readily leveraged to gain traction in areas where there is only scant current activity.

---

[8] NASSCOM—McKinsey Report 2002.

Geographic Considerations

For the Swiss, any geography other than Switzerland may seem less expensive. Cost is a relative issue; but it is not the only variable to be considered in selecting the geography for offsourcing. Other variables in no particular order include:

- **Tax benefits**—Is there government support available for organizations pursuing offsourcing investments as a part of a broader set of technology investment incentives? If yours is a software package company, is it possible to put place code in escrow outside the United States, so that royalty payments may be kept offshore? India, for example, has shielded all profits in IT-enabled services companies until 2009.

- **Ease of travel**—It is easy to get people both into and out of the country in question? What is involved in getting the contracted parties' employees into the United States? Rotation of key employees to and from the remote geography is a crucial element to achieving world-class standards.

- **Communications infrastructure**—Is there an adequate communications infrastructure already in place? Do you expect further liberalization in this area that might improve this environment in a regime of lower tariffs? What is the lead time required to put dedicated lines in place?

- **Regulatory environment**—Consider the following elements:

  o **Hardware/software**—What are the restrictions on moving hardware into and out of the geography in question? Are there legal technology transfer issues that must be addressed? Are there agency fees required to move the merchandise through customers?

  o **Intellectual property rights**—What is the current legal environment? And, perhaps more importantly, what is the experience of organizations working in that environment regarding the protection of their intellectual property (IP)?

- **Political stability**—What is the current political climate? What would a change in government mean to the regulatory environment?

- **Quality**—It is one thing to be low cost; it is quite another to be low quality. This issue is particularly important in the face of increased offsourcing activity, since a limited supply of talented labor will quickly turn low-cost resources into higher-cost or lower-productivity talent, both of which impact the Business Case of going offshore. Quality can be manifested in several areas, including experience, education, communication and motivation.

- **Resource availability**—As you examine offshore growth potential, you must consider the availability of resources over time. To assess future resources, look at the number of college graduates produced each year by the top universities. Another measure is the growth in services, and thus competition for those available resources over time. Understanding the turnover rates of companies will give you a good indication of competition and how you can put programs in place to both retain and recruit talent.

- **Friendliness to expatriates**—Frequent rotation of personnel has tremendous impact on productivity and morale. Even under scenarios in which no one is expatriated to the remote geography, regular on-site interaction is highly beneficial in understanding the day-to-day constraints and operational challenges. In the case of expatriation, what is the readiness of the local community to accept US or Western European personnel?

- **Certification capability**—Is the industry sufficiently developed in the geography in question, and does it have self-regulating or professional standards associations? Long-term commitments to a partner should be expected to include the achievement of some independently verifiable process capabilities. Possible standards include ISO9000 or, in the case of application development, Capability Maturity Model (CMM) certification or PMI (Project Management Institute) certified managers.

- **English (or other) language skills**—What is the availability of local, fluent talent—or of training to upgrade these skills for specific vocabulary needs? This is as pertinent for Western European companies considering offsourcing as it is for North American ones, since the remote geographies they select for offsourcing are unlikely to have sufficient numbers of personnel conversant in the appropriate languages to provide support.

- **Industry support groups**—Industry consortiums or trade groups play a pivotal role in promoting not only the growth of local industry, but also the adoption of standards and quality certifications. Companies in countries with established groups have the benefit of easier access to information on best practices and international intellectual property rules and regulations. We have mentioned NASSCOM in India, but there are others, varying by geography and industry. One example from the Philippines is the Call Center Association of the Philippines, or CCAP: www.ccap.ph .

Clearly there are many factors to consider in selecting a location for offsourcing IT-enabled services. Not discussed above is any preexisting relationship or geographic presence that you may have established as a result of your organization's other operations. Don't underestimate the value of building on existing infrastructure and the experiences of expatriates in the field or local personnel with corporate knowledge and affiliations. The time and expense that can be saved by bolting on an IT-enabled operation to an existing infrastructure may be considerable. Therefore, an international subsidiary's location in a remote geography, even with marginal qualifications in a few areas, may tip the scales in favor of that region to begin the vendor candidate selection.

Country Overviews

Many countries have active government sponsorship of offsourcing IT-enabled services, and in particular of application development. The following table puts into perspective both the availability and cost of college-graduate talent in selected geographies.

Country	Average salaries of college graduates in 2001 ($US per year)	Total number of college graduates in 2001
India	$2,400	2,100,000
China	$2,000*	950,000
Philippines	$2,900	380,000
Mexico	$1,400	137,600
Ireland	$19,500	43,200

Table 4: Average Salary and Availability of College Graduates in Offshore Venues

*Salaries vary widely by city; in larger cities they could be double the national average.

Source: Manpower Profile of India; Statistical Abstract of India; Educational Statistics Yearbook of China, 2000; China Population Statistical Yearbook; Bureau of Labour and Statistical Standards Philippines; Malaysia Ministry of Education—Department of Statistics; Anuario Estadistico de la ANUES, Mexico.

- **India**—India has the right combination of size, English language skills, communications infrastructure and deep technical talent. It has been and will continue to be a preferred destination for offsourcing IT-enabled services, thanks to the maturity of its providers and depth and experience of its workforce.

  > *India has the right combination of size, English language skills, communications infrastructure and deep technical talent.*

- **China**—China promises to be a long-term player in this market for a number of reasons, not the least of which is the size and growth of its own domestic market. Government policymakers are actively encouraging the segment as a way to modernize the economy; even then–Chinese Premier Ziang Zhamin made a visit to India's IT capital, Bangalore, in early 2002.

The nagging question with respect to China and offsourcing, as with many other sectors, is one of timing: When to go? Labor costs are less, but the challenges are significant. English skills can be lacking and communications are a long way from being anything but a government monopoly. China is recommended as an offsourcing destination only after organizational experience has been established in more advanced locations. This is expected to occur in the coming years.

- **Philippines**—The Philippines has long been considered an excellent destination for offshore development services. Accenture (formerly Andersen Consulting) has had operations in the Philippines for many years; initially focused on supporting their internal product development activities, these operations are being increasingly leveraged to win customer engagements where cost sensitivity is becoming more of an issue. The Philippines, long regarded as having some of the best English skills, has also been successful in deploying Spanish-speaking resources to serve niche (but growing) US markets.

  > *The Philippines, long regarded as having some of the best English skills, has also been successful in deploying Spanish-speaking resources to serve niche (but growing) US markets.*

- **Mexico**—Mexico is the best known of the "nearshore" offsourcing destinations; the call center operations in particular are benefiting from the ready pool of Spanish speakers to serve similar markets in the US. However, in spite of its proximity to the US and its history of success in establishing low-cost manufacturing environments for cross-border activity, Mexico is not a dominant contender for long-term growth of offsourcing services. Governmental resources have been more aggressively allocated in areas outside of IT-enabled services. In addition, the concurrency of the time zone with the US precludes some of the benefits made possible in a mature offsourcing environment that leverages resources removed by several time zones.

- **Ireland**—Ireland was the beneficiary in the 1990s of a lower-cost environment that made it attractive for companies wanting lower-cost services provided in proximity to Western Continental Europe. A generous regulatory environment (facilitated, interestingly, by its nonmembership in the EU) also provided incentives for businesses to offsource there. Among the many firms that placed either call centers or application development environments were Dell, American Airlines, IBM and Compaq. The limited cost differentiation and resource pool, however, would seem to constrain the long-term attractiveness of this market.

In addition to the venues mentioned above, there are a number of other geographies frequently considered as offshore locations. Because of their smaller labor pools or other challenges, however, they are not generally considered to be premier destinations for large-scale commercial activity.

- **Malaysia**—Malaysia has embarked on an ambitious set of IT infrastructure projects with the creation of two new cities dedicated to supporting the growth of IT-enabled services. With proximate location to an international airport and government policies designed to foster foreign investment, they may be long-term players. However, the current delivery capability and linguistic challenges present significant obstacles to the would-be buyer.

- **Canada**—Canada has high wage rates compared to other offshore venues, making offsourcing there hard to justify. Using Canada is like using domestic contracts with the added burden of dealing with the same remote issues faced with offshore venues. The quality of talent is good but not any better than that of other offshore options.

- **Israel**—Very high wage rates and the ever-present worry of political strife may hurt Israel's chances of becoming a long-term player in the people-intensive business of IT-enabled offsourcing. However, the quality of technical talent may make it an attractive option as a base for regional support of IT operations.

- **Russia**—Russia (and some other members of the former Soviet Union) are somewhat wild cards in this equation. The authors have worked with groups from Lithuania, and one even had a short stint running a consultancy using Russian resources. The talent can be excellent, but the regulatory regime, smaller labor pool and difficult business environment create challenges that are more easily resolved in other locations.

Offsourcing Market Evolution & Statistics

Country	Category	Infrastructure	Operating environment	Skills availability	College graduates (annual #)	Cultural compatability	English proficiency	Political climate	Costs
China	Up-and-comer	Poor to fair	Challenging	Moderate	Moderate	Poor	Poor	Moderate	Low
India	Leader	Poor to good	Challenging	High	High	Good	Good	Moderate	Low
Ireland	Leader	Good	Good	Moderate	Low	Good	Good	Moderate	High
Mexico	Leader	Good	Poor	Moderate	Low	Good	Good	High	High
Philippines	Leader	Fair to good	Fair	Moderate	Moderate	Good	Good	Moderate	Moderate

Table 5: Summary of Top Offshore Venues

The following table shows the average IT labor cost and scale of operations currently in those countries. Keep in mind that these figures are estimates and include both the servicing of domestic demand and offsourced business.

Country	Average IT labor cost ($US per year) (2001)	Estimated number of software companies (2001)	Estimated number of IT employees (2001)
China	$8,952	5,000	200,000
Canada	$28,174	NA	NA
India	$5,880	900	**415,000**
Ireland	$23-34,000	750	23,000
Israel	$15-38,000	400	35,000
Malaysia	$7,200	NA	NA
Mexico	$1,400	NA	NA
Philippines	$6,565	1,000	**290,000**
Russia	$5-7,500	1,000	8,000

NA - Information Not Available

Table 6: Scale of Leading Offshore Venues

Sources: Information in Tables 5, 6 and 7 comes from the following:
- *CIO* Magazine, November 15, 2002, issue.
- Geopolitical risk ratings are based on reports by PRS Group, an East Syracuse, NY–based information provider.
- Most infrastructure ratings are based on Global Technology Index reports from Meta Group and the authors' personal experience.

Companies Offsourcing Today

The list of companies reinventing themselves to take advantage of the opportunities is long, distinguished and growing every day. We highlight a few of the industries below:

- **Industrial concerns**—GE is probably the best-known large company taking advantage of offsourcing to increase the margins in its various lines of business, but it is by no means alone. Numerous other players including GM, Rockwell Automation and Texas Instruments are developing functions ranging from R&D centers to call centers and back office processing facilities.

- **Airlines**—Have you ever wondered where that paper ticket goes when you check in at the airport? Possibly to be scanned for data entry in the Philippines or India and later reconciled with the financial system. American consolidated all five of its European reservations offices to Ireland as early as 1995.

- **Health care**—Health care has been a significant if limited adopter of offsourcing practices. The medical transcript business is quite large, but there are emerging areas that are growing, including contract nursing.

- **Strategic consultants**—Even the strategic consultants are getting in on the action, with McKinsey having recently made a move to offsource (internally) much of its presentation product services to India.

Perhaps the most surprising thing about the offshore market is that more companies are not embracing it aggressively. The information in Table 7 from a study published by NASSCOM and McKinsey indicates the estimated potential cost savings in various industries and the impact on EBITDA for those players. It assumes 40%–60% savings in the areas targeted to affect the overall goals. The results are striking.

Industry	Overall cost savings (%)	EBITDA increase	Key opportunity areas
Insurance	10.0 - 15.0%	3.5X	Claims processiing Call center operations
Banking	8.0 - 12.0%	1.5X	Call center operations Loan processing
Pharmaceuticals	5.0 - 6.5%	1.3X	Research & development
Telecommunications	1.5 - 2.5%	1.1X	Call center operations Billing
Automotive	1.0 - 2.0%	1.1X	Engineering & design Accounts payable/receivable
Airlines	0.8 - 1.8%	1.2X	Revenue acconting Call center operations Frequent flyer programs

Table 7: Impact on EBITDA of Offsourcing in Selected Industries

Summary

Offsourcing is ready for prime time.

The legacy of early adopters including Microsoft, Dell, GE, Texas Instruments, ATT, American Express, JP Morgan, Bank of America, Citibank and IBM plus the years of process experience is coalescing with a maturation of tools, communications infrastructure and government support to rapidly reduce risk and improve the economics of utilizing offsourcing services. A variety of countries meet the baseline criteria to deliver a credible value proposition, but India stands alone with strong players in every field. Other geographies, including the Philippines and, in the longer term, China, are positioned to be strong competitors in this global competition for offsourcing with category specialists.

Review the increased EBITDA of the companies that are using offshore resources compared with those that are not. Could it be just coincidence? We expect this trend to accelerate rapidly in the next 12 to 18 months.

Chapter 2 Summary
Offsourcing Market Evolution and Statistics

Chapter Theme

Select offshore geographies are growing rapidly as global centers for IT-enabled services. Many have reached a level of critical mass and infrastructure that will allow their growth to accelerate over the next few years. Spurred by the sagging US and European economies, companies are moving functions offshore to reduce costs and increase productivity.

- ❐ Used By GE, Microsoft, IBM, Citibank, TI, Oracle
- ❐ 38% CAGR in India alone
- ❐ Improving infrastructure
- ❐ Good education system

Key Points

India and the Philippines have emerged as leaders in the provisioning of offshore IT-enabled services. They offer excellent English-speaking skills coupled with strong technology skills and deep pools of talent. China is positioned well for the long term. All are benefiting from the ongoing reduction in communication costs and maturing technologies.

- ❐ Government sponsored
- ❐ Tax benefits
- ❐ Improving telecom
- ❐ Quality resources
  - Motivated
  - Talented
  - Educated
- ❐ Geographic options

Reader Take-Away

You should have a broad perspective on the most active offshore geographies and the enabling factors that have permitted the increase in work going overseas. In addition you should have an understanding of the relevant criteria in selecting a geography for your own needs.

Questions for Consideration

- ❐ Which venue might be the most attractive for your offsourcing goals?
- ❐ What impact would taking 15% of your IT-enabled services operation offshore have on your company's bottom line? On its market capitalization?
- ❐ Is the board or executive team already discussing this option?
- ❐ What would the board say about migrating IT-enabled services operations offshore?
- ❐ Might you be personally affected by a migration to offsourcing by the organization?

Chapter 3

Offsourcing Benefits

Overview

A historical view of the benefits of moving IT-enabled services offshore would tend to focus on the economics. Today, with the benefit of 30 years of collective industry experience, companies can pursue a variety of benefits with their offshore initiatives, including higher service levels, access to specialized talent and compression of delivery times. In fact a pure focus on cost savings alone may come at the risk of ignoring other important corporate objectives and strategic possibilities.

This chapter introduces you to the generic benefits of offsourcing, the tactical impacts and a hint at the strategic possibilities. However, **the most exciting possibilities and profound strategic implications that offsourcing holds for your business are not in the rote benefits of offsourcing, but in the flexibility that offsourcing creates to revisit the way that you service your customers, manage your business and ultimately make money.** These possibilities are specific to the operations and goals of every enterprise but are based on the benefits reviewed here.

Consider the following:

You manage a software company charged with cutting the cost of software product development by 40% by moving offshore. Would you take that 40% to the bottom line or would you reinvest that money in the development of additional features? More likely you would increase your sales and marketing budgets to stimulate further demand or increase product development budgets in order to get a new product to market. Consider the implication: what began as an offshore cost reduction effort would in fact have the knock-on effect of priming the demand engine by increasing sales and marketing—a hugely important issue in a down or flat market.

> What began as an offshore cost reduction effort would in fact have the knock-on effect of priming the demand engine by increasing sales and marketing.

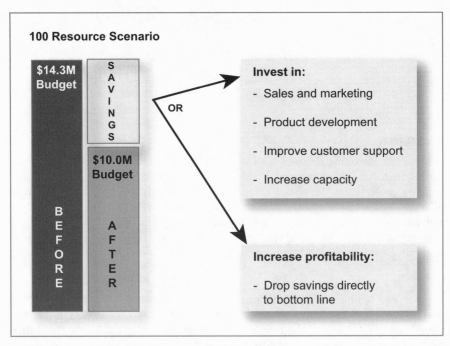

Figure 2: What could you do with the annual savings?

Another option is to take the savings and drop it to the bottom line. The good news is that offsourcing can give you the flexibility to shift the allocation of resources within your organization and get savings while maintaining *functional equivalence.* As you review the benefits below, consider the knock-on impact you might achieve in other areas of your business by reinvesting the benefits that you accrue from offsourcing.

Cost Management

The benefits equation begins with a focus on cost management. Cost management benefits in offsourcing derive from a combination of the following:

- **Cost reduction**—The primary savings come from reduced personnel costs. If you use the appropriate processes and can achieve functional equivalence of 1:1 efficiency or better, you will save a tremendous amount of money.

- **Cost type makeup**—Beyond reducing fixed costs, it is possible also to change some of the fixed costs into variable costs that can scale up and down as the business contracts or grows.

- **Time to saving**— Cost reduction often requires an initial outlay, but if the reduction is sufficient or the staging is well orchestrated, the savings can be sufficient to net out the upfront investment within a single budgeting cycle.

Cost Reduction

Studies by numerous parties indicate that the effective savings of offsourcing in India with a vendor are between 35% and 65%. These savings are potentially even greater when the scale of the operation does not have a big impact on unit costs, and therefore the ownership by the US party makes sense. In owning the "means of production," the US party has greater upfront costs but may achieve a long-term lower operating cost model, since a return on capital for an external vendor is not built in.

Each IT-enabled service is different, with the amount of human intervention involved being the primary driver of lower cost. Even with state-of-the-art collaboration tools, additional time and effort must be spent in having management counterparts on both sides of the team to ensure requirements confirmation and efficient resolution of problems. Fortunately, the cost savings more than compensate for this overlap, leaving a demonstrable surplus in the dollar-by-output equation.

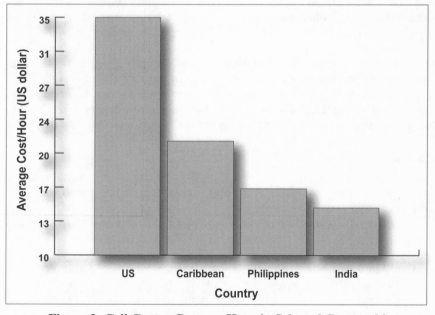

Figure 3: Call Center Cost per Hour in Selected Geographies

Note: Figures are illustrative and inclusive of international and domestic communications costs.

A few additional data points are worth highlighting:

- As of the end of 2002, an estimated 75% of all workers in Indian call centers earned $7,500 or less per year, compared with $25,000 + in the US.

- In India a good junior Java developer earns perhaps $8,000 per year and a senior developer with some architectural skills in the neighborhood of $16,000 per year. Compare this with $60,000–$110,000 per year in the US.
- Many skilled workers have returned to the Indian domestic market as a result of the dot-com shakeout, so project management skills in the region are growing rapidly.

One call center operator went so far as to say that in its domestic operation, 80% of its costs were personnel related, with the balance going to infrastructure, communications and other areas. In the offshore model the reverse was true as a result of the tremendous savings on personnel.

Fixed Cost Reduction

The reduction of fixed costs can also take the form of a conversion to a variable cost. In a domestic US or Western European environment the organization will staff to a long-term demand curve for the services that it will provide. Demand spikes are typically managed by contractors or consultants that are significantly more costly than in-house personnel. Given this significant increased cost for external resources, it often makes good fiscal sense for an organization to keep a buffer of personnel on staff to handle small increased demand variations.

When the cost of contracting external personnel becomes equal to or less than in-house costs, the need for a buffer strictly to manage costs is removed. There are reasons other than cost to keep a buffer, including domain knowledge and continuity of resources; however, if these personnel are marginally productive, wouldn't it make sense to move to the lower-cost environment?

Start-Up Costs

Start-up costs can be significant if you make the decision to offsource without or even with a vendor, but again the savings are sufficiently large to manage the transition within a single budgeting cycle. The type of service anticipated will dictate the setup investment required, including planning, infrastructure and testing.

- **Outbound call center operation**—A reasonable estimate for an operation of 100 agents might be a setup cost of 10% (when working with a vendor) of the annual personnel-related costs with 40% operational savings. This translates into a phenomenal year-one net savings of 30%.

- **Application development**—Assume that you are looking to build a 50 developer offshore bench with the assistance of a vendor. Your annual savings again could approach 50% with a setup cost of roughly 25% in year one. This yields a net savings in year one of 25%, which would increase rapidly in year two.

The above scenarios assume vendor involvement and are conservative with respect to the infrastructure, training, travel, and other investments needed for long-term success. Less conservative numbers or larger amounts of activity would show larger savings. The bottom line is that significant savings are available within a calendar or fiscal cycle and will position you for tremendous savings down the line.

Greater Capacity and Increased Service Levels

"I have to provide more capacity with flat or reduced budgets in 2003."

Source: Interview with software company executive in Dallas, Texas

What would your options be in achieving this goal?

- **Longer hours**—Most staff, and quite often your best staff, will endure this for only so long before moving on, and performance begins to suffer beyond certain thresholds.

- **Low-cost contractors**—This option can often create more problems (regarding learning curves and quality) than it solves. Unfortunately lower-cost contractors typically also have limited skills, and moving to higher-cost contractors/consultants does not solve the budget challenges. In the end this represents only a temporary fix.

- **Compensation adjustments**—Again, the trap of creating an inhospitable work environment will lead to the best people leaving over time. If the budget challenge is only for a short period of time, bonuses or comp time can be used; but that is only a temporary fix.

- **Other**—They have all been tried. The result is often to compel the top 20% of staff to work much longer hours under great duress or to face the alternative of reduced product-delivery expectations for unhappy business units.

Fortunately there is an alternative. The cost savings per unit of productivity discussed in the previous section may also be considered in another light: that of greater capacity. If your organization is fortunate enough not to be under continual pressure to cut costs, or even if it is, you may elect to "reinvest" some of the cost savings that you enjoy from offsourcing on increasing your delivery capacity.

In the software development arena, this means that you may decide to hold your costs steady while providing faster turnaround to the business units or meeting an increased number of commitments to the organization. A commitment on your part to increase your output by 40% over the next two years is certain to gain visibility in the organization.

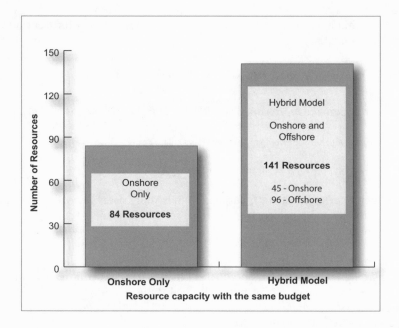

Figure 4: Capacity Increase with Hybrid On- and Offshore Model

Call centers can be managed to trade off and differentiate service levels. Consider reinvesting some of your savings in greater responsiveness to the customer. Do you have an elite (and lucrative) customer group for whom additional personal attention would be appreciated? Or could you reduce waiting time during peak traffic hours for all customers by moving offshore without raising your overall costs? Either approach has a desirable outcome for your internal or external customer. You always have the option to deliver a mix of costs savings and higher service levels.

Offsourcing creates a practical approach for meeting the annual year-end budgeting demands of doing more with the same or less for several years to come.

Access to Talent

The dot-com explosion made acquisition of certain skill sets almost impossible at any price. Mature industries paid the heaviest price, with legions of young, talented professionals leaving their ranks for the lure of stock options and the trappings of "hipper" work environments. The subsequent dot-com implosion has improved the availability of some skill sets, but try to find a senior application or system architect with experience in building J2EE compliant enterprise applications, and you will still be challenged.

India has a large and growing pool of highly trained professionals who can meet these skill deficits either remotely or on site. This means that highly sought-after skills may be acquired at a significant discount, and further that remote "benches" may be built up and carried at a lower cost than would be the case in the United States. This becomes particularly convenient with the establishment of a foreign subsidiary, since once a staff member has been employed for a year, he or she may be brought into the US with little notice on an L1 work visa. Add in the fact that US and Western European companies often have a leg up on local incumbents due to a perception of higher wages and possibly more generous investment in personnel development, and you begin to see the potential for attracting the cream of the crop.

A second impact of the dot-com implosion has been a large repatriation of Indian nationals from the US workforce. Exact numbers are not available, but our experience in helping vendors locate hard-to-find resources suggests that not only have many professionals returned, but many more would be willing to return for the right opportunity. This last point has interesting implications. In the past many of the best and brightest have sought opportunities in the US to exercise their formidable skills, but as more interesting and challenging work is brought to the Indian environment, one might hypothesize that the previous brain drain will be slowed if not reversed.

Quality

Two benefits with respect to quality present themselves. The first, perhaps a restatement of the "Access to Talent" discussion above, is purely centered on availability of higher-quality staff at a lower cost. As an example, take the numbers associated with call center personnel costs mentioned above. These figures can only be truly appreciated in the context of the agents' educational background: they are predominantly college educated. In fact, many Indian call center operators require the minimum of a bachelor's degree for employment and are building career paths for new employees. How might the quality of the service provided by these agents compare to the service provided by someone in a domestic environment with a very different skill profile? These customer experiences, while enormously important within the long-term relationship that organizations try to build with their clients, are difficult to assess empirically.

The second benefit, like the discussion on greater capacity and service levels, is a reflection that cost savings can be traded on to achieve different aims. Here we make apologies to Philip Crosby, who eloquently demonstrated in his book *Quality Is Free: The Art of Making Quality Certain* that with careful planning, good process and collaborative methods, quality could be enhanced with little or no cost. We agree with many of his points; however, a fundamental assumption in the services business must be that a staff member has sufficient training and expertise to deliver the service well. If you have the choice between operating in a venue where base skills are suboptimal at the price point that you can afford versus operating in an environment where base skills are terrific and the cost is significantly less, which venue would you choose? Assume again that you are developing software. Might you take half of your savings in increased sales and marketing and the other half in lower "bug" rates from the stricter adherence to process made possible by the better educated employees and more rigorous testing that you can now afford—all with the same budget?

Productivity Improvements and Compressed Time to Completion

Although productivity takes a hit when activities are split between an onshore location and the remote geography owing to the management overlap required, other aspects of the offsourcing relationship increase productivity through higher utilization. The higher utilization may also have the unintended but highly desirable effect of compressing the delivery time frame in calendar time.

"Follow the Sun" Activity

"Follow the sun" activity is not necessarily a production strategy in which someone works on a task, checks it in at the end of his or her shift and has it picked up by someone else in a remote time zone for further work. More likely, the tasks are different, but tightly coupled. A few examples are given below:

- **Applicant information capture and processing**—Imagine a business process that involves the capture of information about a customer (either through the Internet or via a call center) and back-end processing to validate if the prospect qualifies for the program in question. It could be a credit card, mortgage or affinity program—anything that requires human intervention as some precursor to the final approval. Assume further that most of this activity occurs during US business hours.

  In a traditional paradigm, the processing or verification of the applicant might happen the following day by a back-office staff member. In the offsourcing paradigm, it can be done during the US nighttime with the possibility of acceptance or rejection being delivered by the beginning of the following business day. The new paradigm allows the work to continue even while the customer is unavailable.

  o **Benefits**
      ➢ Cycle time is compressed and customer intimacy is increased.

> Marketing may be able to portray this as a competitive differentiator, thereby increasing sales.

- **Code correction and system testing**—In this application development scenario, system testing of an application during the US business day might result in the identification of several "bugs" or enhancement requests. Those fixes may be investigated and put in place during the next "shift" by the remote resources, allowing the testing team to begin retesting the following day.

  o **Benefits**
    > Testing team resource utilization is increased: a direct gain in productivity.
    > Delivery time frame is compressed: a service level enhancement to the business units.

- **Analysis/design modeling and requirements confirmation**—As your organization moves up the Offsourcing Maturity Model,[9] you will be able to move ever-larger percentages of the work offshore. At the moment that you begin building some of the analysis and design models offshore, you can begin interacting with the subject matter experts and business owners in a more efficient manner. Questions and requests for clarification are written up, delivered through e-mail or collaborative workspace and answered in sequence. Since recommended communication protocol includes the daily interaction of team members via conference call at the beginning or end of the day, the opportunity still exists to resolve minor issues in real time.

  o **Benefits**
    > Analysis and design team utilization is increased: a direct gain in productivity.
    > Delivery time frame is compressed: a service level enhancement to the business units.

For application development practitioners of "paired development" in which two developers work together—one focused on the development of the application and the other on building test scripts or harnesses to validate the correctness of the code—we may be persuaded that the division of these two aspects spread over time zones drives productivity benefits, but we have not yet seen it in practice.

"Around the Clock" Support Model

If your IT organization is like most, the development team is frequently pulled into ad hoc support roles in spite of all best efforts to create clear boundaries

---

[9] See Chapter 20.

between new application development and maintenance. Late night phone calls or, worse, missed phone calls create havoc with the personal lives of support personnel, problems for the user community and a distressing bottleneck in getting back to a normal operating environment.

With an offsourcing capability, the organization is able offload support requirements that come in during odd hours to lower-cost resources that are in the middle of their peak productivity time. Benefits are similar to those described in the "Follow the Sun" section; and where brute force is required to fix a problem regardless of the efficiencies (this resonates loudly with product companies attempting to make general availability dates), someone can be found to focus on the problem at any hour of the day or night.

E-mail is another area where the benefits of around-the-clock support models are making strong showings. **E-mail support is a particular favorite of the offshore call center vendors, since it allows them to effectively double or triple the utilization of a call center terminal.** In one scenario, a call center in India runs all night (daytime in the US), either dialing or answering calls, and then has a second and possibly third shift that is working e-mail support all day (nighttime in the US). Interestingly, this may be an area where China establishes a beachhead in the provision of offshore services, since it does not require real-time or voice-related interaction with a customer, which the current availability of English skills might preclude.

Summary

The corporate drumbeat of achieving more with less is a constant refrain. It is heightened in a slow or slowing economic climate, where there may be stronger pressure to rein in support costs than during the good times. Offsourcing provides one approach to achieving that goal, but its benefits do not stop there. Its scope is far broader and its potential to make deep impacts far greater than simple cost reduction.

Direct benefits include:

- Cost reduction
- Transformation of fixed to variable cost
- Increased capacity
- Improved service levels
- Access to affordable talent
- Quality improvements
- Productivity improvements
- Compressed time to completion
- Follow-the-sun activity: development, troubleshooting and support
- Around-the-clock support

The indirect benefits may include:

- Additional investment dollars into revenue-generating activities such as product development and sales and marketing programs
- Additional investment in R&D for future product offerings
- Key resources focused on more strategic/core business issues

Offsourcing also gives the business unit the luxury of reinvestment flexibility that has long been squeezed from the domestic operation. This flexibility, bought by making a commitment to adopt offshore practices and embracing a lower-cost environment, can be spent on more highly educated workers, customer intimacy programs and differentiated product and service offerings. The rest of the book explores the specifics of achieving the benefits; here we simply state that they are enormous.

Chapter 3 Summary
Offsourcing Benefits

Chapter Theme

The savings from offsourcing are staggering, but cost reduction alone is not the only benefit. The business will benefit from the flexibility that follows a change in the kinds of costs that you have, fixed versus variable, and the intrinsic opportunities created by processes that can "follow the sun."

- ❏ Cost reduction
- ❏ Reduced fixed cost
- ❏ Rapid time to savings
- ❏ Productivity improvements
- ❏ Allows more focus on strategic issues

Key Points

Cost savings can be applied directly to the bottom line or may be traded off in the form of higher service levels or increased capacity. Given the current economy, freeing funds from operational areas while providing functional equivalence can be particularly attractive to those seeking to increase marketing and sales budgets or earnings.

- ❏ Cost savings
- ❏ Other investment options
- ❏ Increased capacity
- ❏ Increased earnings
- ❏ Highly skilled and educated talent

Reader Take-Away

You should internalize that there are more benefits to offsourcing than just low cost resources. You should become attuned to considering offsourcing as a potential approach to increasing service levels and compressing time to delivery by leveraging the time zone differences while delivering up to 50% more capacity at your current budget levels.

Questions for Consideration

- ❏ Is your organization currently investigating cost-saving initiatives?
- ❏ What payback time frame is required for investments in cost saving initiatives?
- ❏ Does the use of more highly educated workers in repetitive tasks create the opportunity for a breakout strategy for your organization?
- ❏ How might the quality of customers' experience with your organization be enhanced by low-cost 24-hour support?
- ❏ How might specific business processes be compressed by establishing onshore/offshore handoffs?

Chapter 4

Offsourcing Risk Management

"Well, everybody in Casablanca has problems. Yours may work out."

Humphrey Bogart

Overview

GE, Dell, Citibank, JP Morgan, Microsoft, Ford, British Telecom, American Express and IBM are only a few of the household names have taken on offsourcing initiatives. For this elite group the risk of offsourcing is mitigated by their financial strength and preexisting international infrastructure. They can truly afford to experiment until they get the model right. Further, their size means that they have well-developed program management and quality assessment capabilities, important assets in the world of offsourcing, where complex work activities arrive with a set of interrelated risks that require careful study and ongoing focus to address adequately.

Does that mean that if yours is not a Fortune 500 company, the risks of offsourcing are too great? Is the learning curve too long or the required investment too high? Have we piqued your interest in the previous chapter only to tell you here that this staggering opportunity is beyond your grasp? The answer is a resounding "no"—provided that you adequately plan and commit to offsourcing as a strategic initiative.

This chapter summarizes a few of the most significant risks of offsourcing. There are many, and the survey nature of this book limits detailed discussion; however, keep in mind that there are reasonable solutions and mitigation steps for each area discussed. Every day, more and more organizations are achieving the dramatic savings and quality improvements that accrue from successful offsourcing.

Commitment

Executive-level commitment is the most important requirement for successful offsourcing. Without it, offsourcing will either provide limited economic benefits or fail completely.

Executive sponsorship and an understanding of the need for senior backing are critical in meeting the challenges inherent in pursuing an

> *Executive-level commitment is the most important requirement for successful offsourcing.*

aggressive offsourcing program. Management, specifically executive management, is the only group that has a sufficient range of control to coordinate an interdisciplinary approach to guaranteeing success.

This level of management is essential to bringing the organization into alignment, as demonstrated in Table 8:

Issue	Executive action	Mid-level action
Personnel compensation	Speak with HR VP and rework the budget	Promise to look into it
Process change required for offsourcing	Sit down with peer or subordinate that is owner of business unit and devise solution	Seek permission to change process
Technology roadblock	Demand work around option or proceed with manual approach until technology is ready (while still saving money off the new process)	Wait until technology is 100%
Complex vendor relationship	Define business requirements and push legal to get the contract finished and signed	Stonewalled by legal team

Table 8: Executive versus Midlevel Sponsorship Example Actions

It is important to note that this is not an indictment of midlevel managers but simply a reflection of the incentives and constraints with which they must live every day. Nor is it advice not to seek midlevel management sponsorship for outsourcing initiatives. But consider the following: A midlevel manager tasked with validating the technology on the offsourcing initiative will likely be encouraged by the organization to delay *everything* until he or she can guarantee perfect performance; whereas an executive in the same position would move to get an initial set of savings for the organization and just continue to work the technology issue down line. Further, a midlevel manager may get fired for not having the technology running perfectly; whereas the executive would be viewed as a "big picture" thinker for pushing ahead with initial savings in spite of the obstacles. This scenario may seem cynical, but we have seen it in practice.

Organizational Resistance

Organization resistance goes in hand in hand with the issue of commitment. Executive commitment is so important to success largely because of the organizational resistance that can be expected.

Offsourcing (like many forms of outsourcing) may create a climate of fear, uncertainty and doubt. We believe that organizational resistance to offsourcing manifests itself in two fundamental ways:

- **Managerial resistance**—What happens when those responsible for making the offsourcing strategy successful do not have a vested interest in its success? In other words, executive management has asked them to look at it as an opportunity for cost savings and to pilot a project to see if it works? Offsourcing works best as a long-term strategy, and rarely as a tactic. So organizational incentives need to be aligned to implement that strategy.

  Imagine you are a midcareer IT manager with a comfortable eight- to ten-hour workday and limited travel requirements. Is it reasonable to expect that you will pull out all the stops to make sure that a project in which you have little vested interest is successful, particularly if success may result in the displacement of many of your colleagues and possibly yourself?

  > *Offsourcing works best as a long-term strategy, and rarely as a tactic.*

- **Demoralization of remaining local employees**—When the first offsourcing pilot project is moved offshore, the question arises, What's next? And when the pilot is successful, who's next? This is a serious issue with behavioral patterns similar to those witnessed during mega-mergers, in which there are destined to be winners and losers.

  Many of the remaining local employees are ones that you will want to keep even as you move up the Offsourcing Maturity Model.[10] You must have a management plan that includes appropriately informing personnel of the strategic direction of the organization even as it focuses retention efforts on high performers.

---

[10] See Chapter 20.

- **Perceived conflict of interest**—On occasion, the IT executive who is charged with vetting out the benefits of offsourcing may be a native of the location that he or she is being asked to consider. It is incumbent on the executive team to work with the executive to create a transparent process at the end of which the IT executive feels comfortable in making the offsourcing recommendation objectively, without being seen as exhibiting misplaced loyalty.

  Likewise, it is wrong for management to assume that just because someone is from a geography that is being considered for offsourcing, he or she is innately more qualified to drive the vendor selection process. The professional in question may have come to North America or Western Europe for his or her secondary education and never actually worked in the geography being considered.

Organizational resistance can derail the best-laid plans and offshore partners. Beyond a commitment to manage issues as they arise, there must be an understanding at the outset of the potential for resistance, so that the challenges can be managed professionally, equitably and (even better) proactively.

Infrastructure Challenges

The good news about infrastructure challenges in the context of a long-term commitment to offsourcing is that once they have been addressed for the first time, they are often far easier to manage going forward. The bad news is that there is a lot of work to do at the front end of offsourcing initiatives to establish a high-performance work environment.

Items that must be addressed include:

- **Software**—What type of restrictions can you expect to see on your software license arrangements when you announce to the vendor that you need remote licenses for your third-party developers?

- **Hardware**—Should you purchase locally or ship? If you ship, how can you expect to expedite customs processing? What happens when you need support for a box loaded and shipped from the US or Western Europe?

- **Communications**—Should you go for a dedicated line? What kind of bandwidth? If the line drops, do you need to plan for contingent connectivity? What is the cost? Should you expect the vendor to pay?

- **Disaster recovery planning (DRP)**—What are the reasonable scenarios that can be expected? How do you plan contingencies for sudden limited access or no access to your remote facility?

From a hardware and software perspective, there are few items that cannot be delivered to most offshore venues within some predictable period of time, but project planning must assume lead time. More problematic is the initial setup of communications links, which require a fairly extensive lead time to install a reasonably sized pipe. (In first quarter 2002, the time required to place a T1 link from Bangalore to the US was 120 days.) Chapter 15 takes a detailed look at the infrastructure requirements for your offsourcing initiatives.

Control, Visibility and Involvement—At Great Distance

Piggybacking the infrastructure discussion is the subject of control, visibility and inevitably involvement. Better infrastructure will allow you to make headway on these issues, but process is critical. Though it may seem Luddite to talk about the risks of long-distance management in an era of unlimited bandwidth, until we have the technology to beam ourselves back and forth like the characters in Star Trek, geographic distance will continue to be a risk factor in successful management of complex projects.

As an example, in a complex, highly integrated application development environment, as the project manager you would need to know:

- Who is making sure that the requirements definition is correct
  - o – that the design models are correct
  - o – that code has been properly tested
  - o – that user needs will be met—and early enough so that if there are disconnects, the users are not delivered an unworkable system
- Which metrics are being captured and by whom, so that baseline data can be established about the productivity of the environment

In moving into the offshore environment, control mechanisms must be established to allow visibility into the underlying activity. Neglecting to do so will leave you blind to both the expected outcomes until it is too late to take action and to the underlying causes of failure once the outcome is established.

If you are working in a vendor environment, you must be prepared (or have people who are prepared) to dig in to the process. Root-cause analysis—looking at spreadsheets and management reports—can only go so far. Do not assume that "things" are being handled as a matter of course unless you have the metrics in place to prove it and your people are actively engaged—at least until a consistent pattern of performance has been established.

Visibility and the control that it makes possible are the result of a combination of process disciplines, tools and training. If short shrift is given to any of these areas, the likelihood of failure is enhanced. Chapter 18 (Process Implementation and Metrics) discusses the approach you should take in defining your hand-offs and instilling the importance of capturing relevant metrics, which will allow you to manage by looking forward rather than behind. You can also refer to the Offsourcing Maturity Model as a reference point for managing risk in this area at different levels of evolution in your offsourcing initiative.

Quality

While you are focusing on the control/visibility/involvement risk you are indirectly addressing the issue of quality. Quality, the measure of excellence against a standard, is a multidimensional subject. In a traditional environment it is centered on elements like management processes, training, testing, customer interaction, user processes and the like. We do not dispute that framework here; but we point out that in the offshore environment, the subject of quality is perceived as such an enormous area of risk that vendors in all sectors have placed enormous emphasis on quality certifications as a way of addressing buyer concerns.

Take software development as an example:

Quality in software development is a risk even under optimal circumstances. It has been shown that the probability of writing a perfect software program on the first go is infinitesimally small. It is easy to understand then the quality challenges that could arise in building a system remotely when the potential for miscommunication and minimal visibility and control are so much greater than in on-site management.

Offshore developers recognize this concern. They also recognize that the credibility that comes with external quality certifications has led to a rush to certification. Fully 50% of the world's Level 5 Capability Maturity Model (CMM)–certified organizations are in India, and many are ISO9000 certified.[12]

External certifications are helpful, but they are not the whole story. Your risk involves whether a vendor can maintain the necessary quality standards in your project. Experience suggests that in projects of medium or even high complexity, offsourcing can hit most quality metrics provided that requirements are effectively, documented and communicated and that the domestic operator is actively involved in delivery.

The story of quality in offsourcing is largely about communications (giving and receiving), realistic expectations, training and committed involvement from the domestic organization.

---

[12] CMM is an industry-recognized standard for the development of quality software. It owes its creation to the Software Engineering Institute (SEI) at Carnegie Mellon.

Intellectual Property Retention and Protection

The US and Western Europe have well-established statutory and common law case history for dealing with intellectual property rights related to software development. But this is not always the case in the most desirable offsourcing locations.

The primary vehicle for insulating your organization from intellectual property risk will be a strong contract with a trusted partner that is guided by the statutes and case history of a venue with which you are comfortable. A number of approaches to insulating yourself from risk are discussed in Part IV, but for now you must understand that this is an area that requires ongoing diligence on the part of the buyer.

Geopolitical Challenges

Political risk is difficult to assess and manage. Assessment of any of the locations mentioned is beyond the scope of this text; however, two items are worth noting:

- **Growing interdependence**—Countries in the developing world are in a competitive market for foreign direct investment. Now more than ever, aggressive actions against neighbors or other members of the world community are subject to tough consequences in the field of finance and trade. Rogue states that eschew capitalist values notwithstanding, this growing interdependence suggests that over time, those nations intent on building and providing offshore IT-enabled services will become gradually less risky places to do business.

- **Portfolio management**—Portfolio theory states that a diversified portfolio can provide the same return with lower risk than an undiversified portfolio. Large companies with major offshore operations are increasingly eyeing the need to manage their risk through not only multiple and alternate vendors, but also multiple geographic presences.

Cultural Integration

Like executive commitment, a lack of cultural integration or sensitivity can relegate an offsourcing initiative to the status of missed expectations and limited benefits.

Consider the following:

You receive as much information every day through body language and cultural cues as you do through written language and oral expression. Imagine you are in a project kick-off meeting. Someone pushes back from the table in response to a comment made by a colleague. Later, someone gestures to make a point, but it goes unnoticed or is ignored.

Both are potentially significant, undocumented, nonverbal events that may profoundly impact a decision-making exercise and ultimately the success of the project. Yet, they may go unnoticed by the untrained eye.

Assume further that the person trying to make the point is a team leader (junior line management) and that the chair of the meeting happens to be the client. What are the odds that this potentially crucial information from the behavioral cues and gestures has been conveyed?[13] Poor. And yet these situational decision points are pivotal to the success of any systems integration project.

You may never reach a level of "certified expertise" on the finer aspects of the culture of the remote geography that you select for your offsourcing venture, but that is not the point. The focus must be on recognizing that there are fundamental differences in approaches to solving problems and that success will be built on a foundation of understanding and respect. You must understand at a minimum the basic cultural cues that allow you to assess when "yes" really means "no," and vice versa. Taking the time at the outset of the project to provide adequate opportunity for team building and an understanding of the basic differences in norms of communications is fundamental to the success of the endeavor and to building a working level of trust and respect between the participants.

---

[13] In his excellent book *Riding the Waves of Culture: Understanding Diversity in Global Business,* Fons Trompenaars cites a definition of culture given by Schein in his work *Organizational Culture and Leadership.* "Culture," Schein says, "is the way a group of people solves problems." Trompenaars goes on to explain cultural differences "under three headings: (1) those which arise from our relationships with other people; (2) those which come from the passage of time; (3) those which relate to the environment." Further, with respect to relationships with people, he cites Parson's "five orientations covering the ways in which human beings deal with each other":

- **Universalism and particularism**—Roughly, is something broadly true all the time or do specific circumstances come into play to change that?

- **Individualism and collectivism**—Which is of paramount importance: the one or the many?

- **Neutral and emotional**—What is acceptable communication in a business environment?

- **Specific and diffuse**—Is it possible to have a successful business relationship at arm's length or is some degree of personal contact required?

- **Achievement and ascription**—How are individuals esteemed? Based upon recent performance or the trappings of privilege that may have little to do with their own labor?

Communication is a two-way exercise. Information must be given and received. Applying these spectrums of behavior to the offshore environment in which you work can give you tremendous insight into the interactions with your colleagues and help you to more effectively meet their communication needs.

Frame of Reference

Inevitably, individual corporate histories and frames of reference will greatly influence the way that risk is perceived and managed as part of any offsourcing initiative:

- **The manner in which your organization perceives and manages risk—** Is it risk averse by nature? Does it have a history of bold initiatives? How is failure managed?

- **International experience—**Does the organization have overseas operational experience? Does it have an international client base? Is the executive team well traveled and open to other cultures?

- **Offsourcing objectives—**What are the goals of your program? A simple program will have limited risks, financial and otherwise. More aggressive programs imply greater risk even in a domestic context, albeit with more potential upside.

As discussed in the section on Building Sponsorship, the more research and planning you do, the better you will understand and manage issues proactively; but be aware of the following:

- **Windows of opportunity—**In a competitive environment, you may have only a limited window of opportunity to move offshore prior to being swallowed by the coming wave of lower-cost competition.

- **Lost savings—**The longer you research and plan, the longer you delay actual savings that accrue from the execution of your program.

Third parties provide a rapid and cost-effective way to help you to rapidly navigate the research and planning phases and thus advance to implementation and savings.

Summary

Offsourcing carries strategic, operational, economic and personnel-related risks; and as with any business risk, you must consider mitigation strategies. **The good news (and there *is* good news) is that the risks of offsourcing can be effectively mitigated or managed** with proper commitment, planning, training and a closed-loop improvement process that delivers feedback for the organization to take action on such challenges. Third parties with real field experience can also give you a tremendous jump-start on risk identification and ongoing management.

Chapter 4 Summary
Offsourcing Risk Management

Chapter Theme

Offsourcing has significant potential challenges, but with proper planning and expert advice, the risks can be aggressively mitigated. The organization's frame of reference, including history and global distribution of operations, will weigh heavily on the perception of risk.

- ❏ **Executive sponsorship**
- ❏ **Active executive support**
- ❏ **Infrastructure plan**
- ❏ **Identify training needs**
- ❏ **Cultural integration plan**

Key Points

Executive sponsorship is the single largest risk factor to understand.

If you have limited to no experience in moving operations offshore, consulting a third party that has done it before can pay great dividends.

There are risks to NOT offsourcing.

- ❏ **Change management**
- ❏ **Extend your disaster recovery plan**
- ❏ **Understand geopolitical ramifications**
- ❏ **Resource planning**

Reader Take-Away

The risks of offsourcing are manageable. Companies like GE, Microsoft, Dell, IBM and Citibank have embraced it as a way to make a material impact on the bottom line and accomplishing more with less. Challenges must be met with education, executive sponsorship and commitment.

Questions for Consideration

- ❏ Do you have executive commitment? Will the organization push through the inevitable obstacles that will arise from time to time?
- ❏ Is line management (where the program will ultimately succeed or fail) adequately informed, trained and motivated to succeed?
- ❏ Do you understand the scope of your infrastructure needs?
- ❏ Is there an appreciation for the cultural differences that must be overcome?
- ❏ Do you have critical intellectual property that must be protected at all costs?

Chapter 5

Total Cost of Offsourcing

Overview

The scope of your objectives and your bias to owning the infrastructure will inevitably dictate the level of investment required to "operationalize" your offsourcing initiative. Limited benefits can be gained quickly with limited investment. Basic data entry operations or even simple programming from detailed specifications are basically commodity exercises that require little in the way of infrastructure. If, however, your vision is grander and the size or scope of benefits you are seeking is larger, successful offsourcing will require a thorough understanding of the investment required (the total cost of offsourcing, or TCO) to reach expected operational performance.

Introducing the Offsourcing Maturity Model

A significant challenge in some offsourcing initiatives is the length of time that it may take to reach a goal state. Investments (costs) will need to be made along the way as you reach for optimal scale and performance. Your challenge at the outset is to understand to which areas and with what degree of commitment you should budget resources to support an evolving offsourcing environment. The Offsourcing Maturity Model gives you that capability.

The Offsourcing Maturity Model (OMM) is a roadmap and risk management framework for reinventing the IT-enabled service functions into a low-cost, high-quality service organization leveraging remote resources. **The OMM is also a framework for conceptualizing the way in which you set goals for, operationalize and manage your offsourcing activity.** The model **provides a reference point in considering the investments required to achieve specific benefits.** Chapter 20 is devoted to a detailed discussion of the OMM, but you may assume that greater investment is required to reach higher levels of actualization within the model.

Level 1, or Staff Augmentation, is simply the use of human resources from a lower-cost geography to perform a function,

> *The Offsourcing Maturity Model is a roadmap and risk management framework for reinventing the IT-enabled service functions into a low-cost, high-quality service organization leveraging remote resources.*

probably on site in the United States or Western Europe. Typically this strategy is used to acquire targeted skills for mundane, repetitive tasks. It provides a variable component to your resource capacity.

Level 2, or Turnkey, is a projected-related exercise that is likely to involve a team working remotely with some specified input and output. Limited infrastructure is required and benefits tend to be narrow in scope. Quality standards must be developed onshore and workable communications must be established. Managing expectations is the key to success.

Level 3, or Integrated, indicates a significant commitment on the part of the domestic party to integrate (that is, to rely on) the offshore capability (or vendor) as an integral part of your organization's delivery engine. Significant process and collaboration tools must be put in place and cultural alignment accomplished in order for the on- and offshore operations to operate as one team, in one process, using one set of common objectives.

Level 4, or Managed, involves taking the integration to a level of fluidity that allows for metrics-driven control of the environment. The focus is on speed and quality of delivery, as well as ensuring that the process is visible to management and that metrics can be improved over time.

Level 5, or Optimized, assumes that an organic offshore operation has been established, with complete transparency across all environments. Functions, tasks and personnel are placed in the most effective environment without regard to organizational, cultural or geographic barriers. Process improvement is ongoing, and cost per unit and quality are balanced and managed effectively.

Applying the Offsourcing Maturity Model: If you are implementing a solution with the goal of adding a minimal number of lower-cost resources to work on site, your total cost to offsource will primarily comprise the cost of an hourly rate plus accommodations. You will require little or no additional infrastructure to operate in this Level 1 OMM mode. If, however, you are going to offsource a long-term capability within your application development group, your goal state will likely be at Level 4 of the OMM. This implies considerable up-front investment plus ongoing costs that are not required in a staff augmentation model. Think of this as a cost of resources plus an overhead cost to provide the appropriate infrastructure to ensure high levels of productivity.

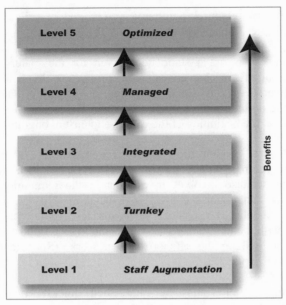

Figure 5: OMM Overview

Key Elements

As you review your goals in the context of the OMM, you will need to address the four major areas below or run the risk of achieving only marginal benefits or failing:

- **Tools and infrastructure**—Visibility, control and collaboration are all essential components of success. Which tools does your own organization use for e-mail, collaboration (e.g., instant messaging, peer-to-peer videoconferencing), change requests and content management? Depending on the level of integration between the onshore and offshore operation, these tools will be required, along with significant training to use them effectively. Some of your internal policies may also require updating to allow an offshore partner to have direct access to these tools.

  If you have limited infrastructure today, you may require additional infrastructure investment or manual procedures to manage the offshore environment effectively. These costs including redundancy, communications, power, training and productivity factors, and should be part of the overall Business Case.

- **Process**—The bad news is that you have to have an established process to be successful in an offsourcing environment. The good news is that in applying it to the offsourcing initiative you will adopt a rigor that may have positive spillover impacts on other areas of the organization.

Further, process is not a static item. Even for the mature organization, moving to an offsourcing environment requires a division of labor that changes its processes. As the organization moves greater amounts of work offshore, the process will continue to evolve. Resources and plans must be put in place at the beginning of the exercise to ensure ongoing success.

- **Personnel**—The organization must recognize that offsourcing work involves more than simply moving work from the local to the remote environment. It also involves investment in the remaining personnel to upgrade their functional, technical or managerial skills or, in cases where that isn't feasible, replacement of those resources with more senior personnel with better managerial skills and (most importantly) a vested interested in making the offshore option work. (Specific examples are discussed in Chapter 17.)

- **Time**—Initial benefits may be established quickly, particularly when pursuing smallish development efforts, but what about the 40%–65% cost savings promised in the vendor literature? How can you hope to have an impact on that order of magnitude on the entire IT services budget? These results only accrue from moving ever-greater components of the work offshore, and that can only be achieved through sustained efforts over time.

Specific cost areas that map to the OMM are highlighted in the matrix below. They are dependent on the objectives, time factors, and long-term goals of the offsourcing initiative and should be considered as part of the overall business planning process with a full understanding of scope and time to implement.

Note that not all offsourcing initiatives require high degrees of sophistication or advanced levels in the OMM, and that for them significantly less investment is required. Additionally, some initiatives may start at low levels and then evolve over time as your interest in additional savings and your comfort level in making the required investments grow.

- **Voice communications**—Cell phones are readily available in all desirable offshore venues, though the cost of service and coverage can vary significantly. You can expect to pay $0.25 to $2.00 per minute or more for international calls. However, for remote personnel that are traveling extensively at odd hours, they're a great investment.

- **Direct data communications**—The cost of a T1 direct link between India and the United States at the time of writing is approximately $7,000–$15,000 per month, or approximately the cost of one to two offsourced resources per year. The cost can vary dramatically depending on your provider and the levels of discounts you have negotiated for your networks.

- **Web access**—Web access is readily available. As the emerging markets have adopted the Internet, there has been an explosion of ISPs to accommodate the growing demand. You will require redundancy in your ISP access and will be forced to pay accordingly.

	Offsource Maturity Model (OMM) Levels				
	1	2	3	4	5
Voice communiations	Y	Y	Y	Y	Y
Web access	Y	Y	Y	Y	Y
Direct data communications	N	N	Y	Y	Y
Travel (offshore to US)	Y	Y	Y	Y	Y
Travel (US to offshore)	N	Y	Y	Y	Y
Disaster recovery plan	N	N	Y	Y	Y
Insurance	N	N	N	Y	Y
Process investment	N	N	Y	Y	Y
Offshore infrastructure investment	N	N	Y	Y	Y
Onsite personel - onshore using offshore	Y	Y	Y	Y	Y
Onsite personnel - offshore using onshore	N	N	Y	Y	Y
Training of offshore personnel	N	N	Y	Y	Y
Business case and roadmap	Y*	Y	Y	Y	Y
Time to achieve benefits	Y	Y	Y	Y	Y
One time staff reduction	N	N	Y	Y	Y

* If only level 1 is desired the business case and roadmap processes are abbreviated.

Figure 6: TCO/OMM Correlation Table

- **Travel**—Frequent travel by team members to promote cross-pollination of resources, particularly in the early stages, is important to establish group norms and expectations. This travel does not come inexpensive. Aside from lost productivity due to travel fatigue, there is the out-of-pocket cost of the travel itself. Business class fares between the United States and Asia are in the neighborhood of $5,000 to $7,000, while coach can run between $2,500 to $3,500, and this is with advance purchase. Of more minor consequence is the cost of processing visas and getting the requisite vaccinations where required.

- **Disaster recovery planning (DRP)**—Your operations are up and running and your personnel are getting the visibility they need to manage their delivery risk; however, events outside their control could impact the environment. The 21st century is no more immune to the ravages of armed conflict than was the last; however, the means are available to manage business risk more effectively. A discussion in Chapter 4 reviews this in greater depth, but DRP represents an appropriate cost of doing business remotely and must be adequately budgeted.

- **Insurance**—You may decide to insure yourself against an event that would cause a catastrophic interruption to your work as part of the DRP process. You will likely also require additional health or travel policy coverage for your personnel if yours is a domestic organization planning to operate overseas for the first time.

- **Process investment**—This cost can be the most difficult to address. Any commitment beyond staff augmentation will require some level of investment at either a project or program management level. Be aware that if you are attempting to reach higher levels of maturity from a software development perspective, process investment will become an ongoing full-time function within the organization.

- **Offshore infrastructure investment**—See Chapter 15 on Infrastructure.

- **Offshore personnel coming on-site**—To the extent that you can provide additional context to your offshore team members, you will be doing yourself an invaluable service in the long run. On-site experience translates into better understanding of your organization's business issues, challenges and ultimate goals. It also creates opportunities for networking and building relationships that can be leveraged in accomplishing the work.

- **On-site personnel going offshore**—This can be an effective way to jump-start your operation in the first few months and will be required in the event that you pursue an organic approach. Remote living for US personnel may be considered hard duty, so budget an appropriate expatriate commitment for the selected resources.

  > *The labor cost differential more than makes up for any additional overhead required.*

- **Training of offshore personnel**—Both the tools and the process that you implement in the onshore/offshore environment are likely to require some formal pedagogy. If the environment is complex or you are imposing your structure on a vendor, then you can expect to incur significant training costs.

- **Developing a Business Case and Offsourcing Roadmap**—These are high value–added activities, but they carry an associated cost. A third party can help you to accelerate the time to savings. (See Chapter 11 on Developing an Offsourcing Roadmap.)

- **Time to achieve benefits**—A ramp-up time will be required to achieve the fully operational environment that you are seeking. The higher the level of maturity you seek, the longer it will take to achieve and the more investment will be required.

- **On-site staff reduction one-time cost**—Restructuring will require a financial commitment for layoffs, severance and the like. It may also require that you run some functions in the business in parallel for a period of time while you complete pilots, testing or your infrastructure build out. Do not underestimate the ramp-up time required to attain optimal performance.

TCO plus Onshore = Hybrid

The total cost of offsourcing is usually higher than a simple comparison of labor rates would indicate. Many considerations that are moot in planning a domestic operation must be addressed prior to conducting business-as-usual in an offsourcing situation. The challenge is to identify these gaps prior to initiating your offsourcing program, so that you can set realistic expectations with respect to financial benefits and operational efficiencies.

You should look at the TCO from two perspectives:

- What is the TCO for the offshore operation?
  - o   This amount can be estimated by adding the average labor rate per hour to the infrastructure cost per hour to reach the TCO/hour cost.
  - o   Think of this as the "offshore TCO."

- What is the blended cost per hour (hybrid) that includes the domestic resources and offshore TCO?
  - o   This should include the many one-time costs described above plus additional training and possibly the cost of the higher-level skilled personnel required of your domestic staff.
  - o   Think of this amount as the "total project (or program) TCO."

The Good News

The discussion above may lead you to ask how you can possibly save money by implementing an offsourcing initiative. There are so many investments necessary: in infrastructure, communications, travel and restructuring, to name a few. The answer is that in the correct operational model, staggering savings are achievable:

- **Wage differentials**—The labor cost differential more than makes up for any additional overhead required. Imagine a 100 seat call center with a labor cost of $40,000 x 100 = $4,000,000 per year. Now assume that the same center is in an environment with a labor cost of $10,000 x 100 = $1,000,000 per year. The net savings on labor easily makes up for infrastructure, one-time or ongoing expense increases.

- **Vendors**—Vendors may or may not bundle a number of the items above within the scope of their services. The important thing is to establish what is and is not covered so that you can be in a position to ask for what you want at the negotiating table.

- **Technology parks**—As discussed in Chapter 15 on infrastructure, technology parks can mitigate many of the infrastructure availability issues, although costs may still be higher.

What is required is a full understanding of all the costs, obvious and hidden, as a prerequisite for building the appropriate offsourcing model for your organization.

Summary

Unrealistic or unclear expectations and underestimating the cost of achieving a smoothly running operation can harm professional relationships or shut down the operation before success can be achieved.

If you are working with a vendor, be sure you understand exactly what is included in their rates to adequately compare the value of their offerings versus the competition and to more accurately estimate the cost of the initiative. Do not assume that your offshore supplier can manage all aspects of the program as part of a turnkey service; they will need commitment from you to be successful.

It is easy to be blinded by the very compelling hourly rates that will be quoted, but there are real costs in addition to labor that someone will have to pay. By being an educated buyer and understanding your TCO, you can significantly enhance the scope and depth of your successes. Both you and your vendor will benefit.

Chapter 5 Summary
Total Cost of Offsourcing

Chapter Theme

The total cost to offsource will vary based on the level of maturity that you expect to achieve within the Offsourcing Maturity Model, the size of your operation and the speed with which you expect to see results. Wages are only a piece of the cost equation. Beware of the discussion where the vendor discusses rates and not the other cost elements.

- ☐ **Maturity model target**
- ☐ **Active executive support**
- ☐ **Infrastructure plan**
- ☐ **Identify training needs**
- ☐ **Communications plan**
- ☐ **Cultural integration plan**

Key Points

Don't underestimate the TCO elements if you want a highly productive, efficient and scalable offshore operation.

Expect to pay more for higher service levels.

Plan conservatively and then beat your plan. You'll be a hero and a genius to your executive team.

- ☐ **Infrastructure**
- ☐ **Process**
- ☐ **Training**
- ☐ **Travel**
- ☐ **Disaster recovery planning**

Reader Take-Away

You should see the offshore rate as only one component of the TCO while having a strong understanding of the other cost items. You should have a head start on the fundamentals that must be included in the Business Case.

Questions for Consideration

- ☐ Have you built a Business Case that reflects the total cost of offsourcing?
- ☐ Have you considered approaches that will speed delivery of benefits?
- ☐ Do you understand the cost of the commitment that will ultimately yield the most benefits?
- ☐ Do you understand the implications of process changes that may be required?
- ☐ If you are working with a vendor, do you understand which cost components are included in their pricing?

Chapter 6

Legal Structures

Overview

This chapter groups a number of issues together under the rather vague umbrella of "legal structures." A better description might be "How your production goals, your business associates and your timing determine the type of legal entity best suited to meet your offshore IT-enabled services needs." The decision to adopt one approach over another should be driven as part of the Offsourcing Roadmap process discussed in Chapter 10; however, we discuss it here in the context of the scrutiny this decision is likely to receive at the board and executive level.

Offshore entry strategy	Local entity	Advantages	Disadvantages
Direct with offshore provider	No	Lowest cost of entry Limited contractual commitment	Limited control Long term, more expensive than owning capability
Use third party	Possibly	Market knowledge Relationships Experience Strategic approach	Knowledge transfer
Local presence	Yes	Direct control Max cost savings	High entry cost Operational risk Additional overhead
Local Options			
Branch office	Yes	Limited investment Local management capability	Long term commitment
Build, operate and transfer	Yes	Low cost of entry Flexibility Max cost savings	Short term premium
Joint venture	Yes	Reduced entry cost	Management expectations IP issues
Acquisition	Yes	Reduced time to operational center Total control	Initial cost is the highest

Table 9: Legal Structures

Table 9 outlines the various relationships that we discuss in this chapter, with an indication of the requisite establishment or absence of a local presence.

The specifics described here regarding the creation of a local offshore presence are most applicable to the regulatory regime in India, because of our experience in this market. However, most of the discussion of the options is driven by variables independent of the venue.

Know Your Objectives

Available legal structures for the would-be offsourcer run the gamut from a simple US-based contract in an arm's-length vendor/buyer relationship to a wholly owned international subsidiary. Your approach will reflect the vision that you adopt in your Business Case and Offsourcing Roadmap for your future offshore business model. Types of activity reflect levels of commitment, which have much to do with what is and is not required, based on your near- and long-term objectives:

- **Pilot/project(s)**—Are your initial objectives simply to test whether offsourcing works for your business? Or are you pursuing this capability to offload projects of a particular size or complexity?

- **Capability**—Do you see the offshore capability as integral to a future state cost model for the business—or integral to the core capabilities of the organization? Or is it something that you want available to turn on and off as needed?

- **New business model**—Your objective may be to completely revamp the way that you conduct business, tearing up the old model and reinventing the way you provision internal and external services in the organization.

- **Additional capabilities**—Once your organization meets with initial success, might you require flexibility to consider other areas of the business?

As in building a house, most things are possible given enough time and money. Building your offsourcing model involves financial and temporal goals that will help to determine your selected legal structure. These goals may include:

- **Fixed versus variable cost**—Offsourcing externally creates the opportunity to turn fixed costs into variable costs that can be scaled up and down according to the business cycle. Do you operate your business in an environment of high variability?

- **Timeline to benefits**—The most rapid path to benefits will come through leverage of someone else's infrastructure; however, it may not prove to be the most efficient path in the long term, since the vendor needs to build in a premium to cover their risk of delivery. What is your optimal timeline?

- **Financial resources**—The act of creating a new offshore entity may require minimal investment; however the cost of operationalizing this investment may be significant and is certainly likely to take longer than your initial estimates. This is directly linked to the timeline to benefits. Are you looking for short-term cost relief or want to make a broader, longer-term strategic commitment in building a different cost structure?

Understand Other Influences

Beyond the future-state vision and goals, there are numerous organizational considerations:

- **Executive and board level commitment**—Is your team of executives and directors committed to Re-engineering the business? Or do you anticipate instead that your first step into the offshore space will be a pilot exercise to prove the model and generate executive interest? Remember that anything resembling the creation of a new entity, be it a joint venture or a subsidiary, will require involvement of legal counsel, the CFO and board approval. Further, should yours happen to be a public company, this will require disclosure to investors (and your competition) perhaps before you wish to alert the world to your intentions.

- **Maturity of internal processes**—The successful execution of an offshore strategy requires an added level of discipline to what may already be a complicated set of business processes. The significant geographical and cultural distances between groups in the onshore/offshore division of labor must be aggressively managed. Understanding what you currently operate provides a blueprint for the organization to build an integrated model. In cases where little process exists, selection of a strong vendor should help move the organization up the process maturity learning curve.

Your decisions will not exist in a vacuum, so you must be prepared to adapt your approach to the current constraints of the organization while leaving yourself maximum flexibility for the day when the offsourcing vision becomes reality.

Direct Contract with Offshore Firm

There are literally hundreds of vendors offering IT-enabled services in one form or another from offshore domiciles. Many of our readers have likely already been contacted by at least one of them. Most are credible and have delivered value for clients on an ongoing basis.

Executing a contract with an offshore vendor is similar to executing one with a local provider, with a few notable exceptions that are covered in the discussion on contracts in Chapter 13.

Contract Through a Third-Party Intermediary

Third-party intermediaries or niche boutiques represent an emerging model of service firm designed to accommodate organizations looking to leverage the benefits of offshore service capabilities. In the past these organizations may have been composed of an individual or individuals brokering transactions. Scant informed resources were available to educate the potential consumer on the scope of offshore services available and the merits of working with one provider over another. In many cases the service rendered by these brokers was limited to introducing those with a need to reduce costs and increase service levels to vendors that had offerings that fit the prospective client's needs. The primary value proposition consisted of:

- Understanding of the available services
- Knowledge of the vendor community
- Understanding of offshore providers' cost and pricing models
- Perspective on contractual arrangements

As offshore activity becomes more mainstream, IT executives are becoming more knowledgeable about the options available to them in this new environment. Consequently, the informational (and financial) arbitrage opportunity for individuals working in a pure brokerage capacity will be eroded. Intermediaries will continue to serve a role, but to survive and grow they will have to find new areas in which to offer value-added services.

The new breed of value-added intermediary focuses less on vendor identification (though this may still add significant value) and more on proper planning and execution. At the ISANI Group we focus on the strategic planning and implementation aspects of a client's move to adopt offshore business practices. We believe that in a world where there may be multiple organizations that can pass the bar on provision of services, the value is on strategic planning, transition and execution. Consequently, beyond vendor identification we focus on execution issues including:

- **Business model alignment assessment**—This service examines how your business model can be modified to take advantage of the full range of offshore IT-enabled services (e.g., application development and maintenance, call centers, and BPO).

- **Organizational readiness**—Have you identified champions of the new model at an execution level? Offsourcing initiatives are likely to fail unless line management is sufficiently educated on the new model and is committed to making it work as part of a long-term strategic plan.

- **Financial restructuring**—Correctly estimating and planning for the move to go offshore includes severance packages where appropriate, retraining when possible and other considerations.

- **Communications planning**—What will be the impact on your remaining workforce when you communicate that you plan to begin offsourcing? Transparency and sensitivity will be key issues in keeping your organization informed.

- **Cross-cultural integration and training**—Coaching on how to build a common level of understanding in communication patterns, particularly from the perspective of US groups understanding behavioral characteristics of their foreign colleagues, will be key to success.

- **Methodology implementation**—In the application development space, for example, consider the trade-offs between CMM and ISO9000 and the necessary modifications required to develop methodologies like the Rational Unified Process (RUP) to accommodate a widely distributed workforce.

- **Project management deployment**—Services include establishing communication patterns, implementing disciplined organization behaviors (on- and offshore), cultural integration, recruiting team members in the on- and offshore operations, establishing metrics, negotiating key contracts with offshore vendors and other vendors necessary to implement the program, and overall project control as necessary.

- **Program management**—This may be accomplished on an outsourced, interim or periodic basis. Working with an experienced partner to establish and implement your program offers the advantage of avoiding unnecessary missteps.

- **Ongoing Q&A**—This can be performed as part of a continual risk management program or with a focus on taking advantage of cross-client experiences and emerging practices. In either scenario a strong case can be made for the value to the organization of having an ongoing external review as part of an aggressive process improvement or governance initiative.

Local Presence

Overview

Should you elect to establish a local presence, a number of options are available to you. For example, the Indian legal system is amenable to the creation of foreign owned entities. Under the Indian Companies Act of 1958, two options are available for companies wishing to create a corporate presence.

- **Private Ltd. Co.**
  o   Closely held corporation, affording all the expected shielding of owners from liability
  o   Maximum of 50 shareholders

- **Public Ltd. Co.**
  o May have multiple classes of stock

Expenses related to incorporation are minimal and there is a minimal capitalization requirement of $2,500. Beyond that there is a stamp tax for all monies brought into the country that are used to capitalize the company. The current rate is approximately $100 per $2,500.

Incorporation can be completed quite rapidly, with the potential to complete most of the necessary paperwork within 30 days. Beyond that, it requires approximately 60 days to establish a software export license classification. Benefits include:

- Company tax holiday until 2009
- Option to hold profits in the US without repatriation
- Option to hold profits in dollar-denominated accounts in India

Some of the current financial rules for the sale of a company in India are

- Long-term capital gains kick in at 12 months.
- Short-term taxation is at 36%+.
- Long-term gains are taxed at 20%.

Operating Approaches

The Indian government has addressed the mechanics of creating corporate entities; but beyond the facts noted above, additional flexibility has been created for foreign entities simply wishing to lay the groundwork for operations: the entity is not required to have employees at the time of its creation or to have a citizen of India as CFO. The former allows the would-be foreign owner to conduct an orderly ramp-up, and the latter means that if the organization is small, the accounts may be maintained either remotely or by a local services firm.

Having made the decision to establish a local presence, the question of which operating approach to pursue again relates directly to the issues of risk, control and time.

Wholly Owned Subsidiary
The wholly owned subsidiary offers the advantages of full control, since it is completely subordinate to the parent corporation and will likely (at least initially) be run by a tenured employee of the parent. This is a particularly attractive alternative for large organizations that view the activity in question as strategic to their business and have the financial resources to build the necessary infrastructure. Examples include Microsoft, Oracle, IBM and Texas Instruments.

Other organizations may elect the wholly owned subsidiary option because they will have very large operations committed for the long term and/or they want to achieve much lower costs on resources. The economies of scale offered by an existing domestic service provider may not be sufficient to make up for the return on investment expected from going offshore. Dell, with its several thousand people in call centers in India, might be considered to fit into this category.

A final category includes businesses that are early to the market with a particular function that no current provider offers (or offers with sufficient sophistication). The profiles of these organizations vary by function, but there are some that went offshore originally to reduce costs and now find themselves with an asset that they can leverage as a revenue growth engine to provide services to other US-based companies.

Joint Venture
Joint ventures reflect a "meeting of the minds" of two organizations aiming to capitalize on a synergistic relationship. The grand vision is conceptually alluring: two organizations commit people, process and technology, with both enjoying some level of financial or strategic gain from the exercise. In theory one party will gain access to infrastructure, talent and possibly process in a compressed time frame, while the other will gain access to either a captive market or a distribution channel. However, we believe that a number of challenges exist in joint ventures, including the following:

- **Control**—Which entity is in charge? From an ownership perspective, building your own offshore center or managing a vendor has significant advantages. In both cases you have control (at least to the extent, in a vendor relationship, that you have written a strong contract, are dealing with a reputable firm, have managers who are experienced in international business and have the required processes and controls in place).

- **Expectations**—The onshore company will want to leverage the offshore's low cost of service delivery and sales channels, while the offshore company wants a distribution channel and some level of exclusivity. There tends to be a strong desire for guarantees on volume, which is a time-consuming challenge given that under the best of circumstances the onshore company must reorient its sales force to sell a different solution.

- **Intellectual property rights**—As the joint venture creates new intellectual property, the subject of who owns it and how it can be assigned may become complicated and contentious. This area requires care and precision in structuring your contracts to ensure that IP rights are clear and recourse is defined in the event of any IP loss.

We stop short of recommending against the joint venture as a form of local presence, as there are some very prominent success stories. Unfortunately, experience suggests that JVs are often implemented with half measures and limited understanding of internal incentives, and so are often doomed to failure from the beginning. Further, they can severely limit your options in the event that you decide to pursue alternative strategies. Many of their benefits can be realized in other legal forms.

Branch Office

A branch office allows an entity to have a minimal presence on the ground that is responsible for managing one to many vendors in the geographic market. In a typical scenario, after conducting a couple of pilots and perhaps executing a couple of contracts, the organization moves to formalize a local project management office (PMO) that works with the parent on the management and day-to-day operational tasks of managing the vendors.

Given that the branch office will be an outpost of the organization and that it will spend perhaps more of its time and resources working with vendors than with the parent, it is crucial to establish a sense of community and feeling of belonging. The branch office approach offers the parent the opportunity to continually assess the local operating climate while still building a long-term relationship with a primary vendor or vendors. It also provides some level of infrastructure for future initiatives of the parent company and a base from which visiting executives can operate. In the short term, you may decide to piggyback on the existing infrastructure of a primary vendor to operationalize this function.

Build, Operate and Transfer

The build, operate and transfer (BOT) approach offers the advantage of pushing a portion of the infrastructure build out costs onto the vendor without ruling out the long-term possibility of having your own local presence. Under this scenario, the vendor will naturally want to recoup their infrastructure investments over the life of the contract with some level of return on the working capital that they tied up. Perhaps a better way to think of this option is that the vendor is providing you with a way of financing your infrastructure investment out of the future savings that will be accrued from moving to a low-cost environment. You are also benefiting from the vendor's local market knowledge and reducing the risks associated with building out the infrastructure.

Many vendors are open to this discussion, since the focus on revenue represents an immediate need versus the far-off prospect of a client moving on to operate a capability that has been built specifically for them. You may also view this transfer as a fairly unlikely event, but your ability to negotiate it under highly favorable terms will never be stronger than at the onset of the relationship. Do not underestimate the lock-in leverage that a vendor will gain over time as it learns more about your business. The vendor's goal, and rightly so, is to create value for you by becoming increasingly indispensable.

Summary

The various options carry a good news/bad news scenario for the majority of companies. For organizations that have the balance sheet and critical mass to go it alone, the decision-making process may be fairly straightforward. Most companies, however, must recognize that flexibility and a steep organizational learning curve will be critical elements in their choice of option.

Chapter 6 Summary
Legal Structures

Chapter Theme

Various options are at your disposal in moving to establish an offsourcing capability. They range from a purely outsourced arrangement to a local organic presence. Your long-term objectives, internal capabilities and need for flexibility will all impact your decision.

- ❑ **Local presence**
- ❑ **Offshore direct**
- ❑ **Offshore intermediary**
- ❑ **Build-operate-transfer**
- ❑ **Joint venture**

Key Points

Third party intermediaries can provide a wealth of information on the best approach for you while speeding up the entire decision-making process.

- ❑ **Pilot project**
- ❑ **Process verification**
- ❑ **Integrated or not?**
- ❑ **Third-party assistance**

Build, operate and transfer (BOT) solutions offer the best marriage of of local knowledge and long-term flexibility.

Reader Take-Away

You should have an understanding of the offsourcing options from a legal structure perspective. You should be able to converse with an executive audience on the merits of the various approaches and the need to maintain flexibility early in the process as the target model is refined.

Questions for Consideration

- ❑ Does your organization have a history of international operations?
- ❑ Do the scope and volume of your operations warrant owning the infrastructure?
- ❑ Do you have an existing presence in your offshore geography of choice?
- ❑ How mature are your internal operating processes? Are they well documented?
- ❑ In what time frame do you need to be operational to meet your objectives?

Chapter 7

The Providers

Overview

The IT-enabled services space is broad and varied. The providers in each of its segments have diverse origins, sizes, capitalization, target customer bases, competencies and operating models, and run the gamut in work quality. As is the case in any sector, it is possible to find track records of smashing successes as well as painful projects that limped over the finish line while exhausted sponsors declared victory and moved on. The figure below provides a perspective on the number and size of providers in the largest markets. Navigating these environments is challenging at best for the uninitiated but is likely to become easier over time as the markets mature and consolidate.

Country	Est. number of IT Companies	Est. Avg. # of Employees per Company
India	900+	461
Philippines	1000+	290
China	5,000+	40

Figure 7: Estimated Companies in Three Offshore Markets

It is interesting to note that many groups in India and the Philippines are already international companies in their own right having subsidiaries operating and channeling business to their offshore centers in many countries. As an example, one offshore group with whom we have worked extensively has its corporate headquarters in the US and offices in India, the UK, Singapore, Australia, Hong Kong, Canada and Malaysia.

This chapter presents a segmented view of the way these markets are organized, with India representing the most mature market today. As you move down the path to offshore implementation, it is essential to examine the characteristics of the general segments from the perspective of matching your organization's needs to the capabilities and operating styles of the vendor. We segment the markets as follows:

- Application development and maintenance
  - o Offshore companies
  - o US-based multinationals
  - o Hybrids
- Customer relationship management and call centers
  - o Integrated global players
  - o IT spin-offs
  - o Market specialists
- Business Process Outsourcing
  - o IT spin-offs
  - o New pure plays

Application Development and Maintenance

Indian Tier One

The first-tier Indian players are the grandfathers of the offshore segment, with the oldest having operational capabilities dating back over 30 years. They are highly profitable and increasingly diversified across all IT-enabled services segments. A few have employee bases of close to 10,000 and the largest has 26,000, making it a large player even by global standards. They have impressive qualifications including Fortune 100 former and present customers. And they have aggressively implemented quality and standardization programs across their organizations to overcome large-buyer objections to moving services offshore.

Operationally, this group has traditionally hired graduates directly from college and placed them in large accounts where they can quickly gain exposure to real customer work. Customers benefit from very low rates, while the vendors benefit from the opportunity for what amounts to on-the-job training. After a period of months, the staff may be rotated or reassigned into different accounts where they can apply their solid hands-on knowledge and therefore carry a higher billing rate.

These groups can effectively manage their "bench" while wringing out margins that are the envy of their onshore competition due to the size and relative standardization of service offerings (by comparison US-centric consultancies often have many verticals and practice specialties that limit the ability to optimize bench time). More recently these margins have begun to see significant pressure as large customers have become more educated on their models; and more importantly, the market for services in general has come under pressure from the bursting of the tech bubble in 1999. In response to this and as a part of a long-term strategy to continue to move up the value chain, this group is also beginning to acquire small, niche providers in the US to provide a front end for their clients. Expect more of this over time, as the larger firms must find ways to increase their margins given the pressure they are feeling from both onshore and the smaller offshore providers.

Indian Tier Two ·

The second-tier players are in the 1,000- to 3,000-employee range, reflecting a variety of stages of evolution but decidedly not second string in quality. While some reflect staff augmentation models that are simply too new to have reached the size of the tier-one players, others have simply experimented with a variety of business models as they hone their go-to-market strategy.

These vendors continue to grow and prosper, even with higher unit costs than their larger competition, due to:

- **Flexibility**—These companies tend to be more flexible in their approach to handling client requests. They are smaller, hungrier and may not be burdened with some of the internal policy restrictions that are required of the big companies to operate their companies with consistency. Clients, particularly smaller or midmarket ones, appreciate the opportunity to interact with the top management team, which might be difficult to arrange or impossible to accommodate on an ongoing basis in the tier-one group.

- **Accommodation of smaller projects**—Sales cycles for any significant application development effort are lengthy, particularly in the offshore market. Tier-one companies with thousands or tens of thousands of employees would become ungovernable proposal factories if they chased every deal, so they tend to focus on the large deals or on a more regimented delivery model. The tier-two providers can and do make money on these smaller-deal, 10–100 person development programs. They may charge slightly more than the benchmark rate for very large commodity-oriented deals, but the client has more leverage in the provider's operating style over the long term, since the revenue is more significant to the provider.

- **Specialization**—Some of the second-tier players have specialized skill sets that may be particularly applicable to your needs. This is no different from the US domestic market, where different service organizations have either more experience or branded capabilities in a particular horizontal or vertical market. The level of specialization in the offshore players is less than one would find in the United States, but it exists and is undergoing a rapid evolution.

Over the long term some of these tier-two vendors can be expected to be absorbed by the tier-one players or by multinationals looking to add delivery capability in India. Nevertheless, many of these are becoming the vendor of choice for US and Western European companies looking to wet their toes in the offshore market. They provide the benefits of cost containment with the flexibility that many organizations require.

US-based Multinationals

This group has the best name recognition from the perspective of the mainstream market. It is also the group that can expect the most significant challenges and forced changes to its operating styles over the next several years. You might wonder why that is so; after all, these are dependable companies that do excellent work for their customers and have a long track record.

The challenges lie in a number of areas, including:

- **Market expectations**—Top-line revenue growth in these companies is a real concern because of expected continuing pressure on nominal rates. In other words, if the modus operandi is to have average billing rates of $150 per hour and suddenly a sizable portion of personnel are in offshore centers billing at less than $40 per hour, the provider is likely to have a significant revenue gap. Worse, even if there is a higher percentage margin on the $40 per hour work, it will be difficult to ever make up for the lost margin on the higher rates. It would be a tough transition to a hybrid onshore/offshore provider and, more important, it would be difficult to meet the client's expectations of lower costs with equivalent skills and deliverables.

- **Sales model**—Sales force incentives are tied to either nominal rates or gross margin. Therefore there is a disincentive for the sales force to offer the most affordable solutions available to clients, since this would likely reduce their compensation. The challenge, not unlike that seen in many business models during the rapid evolution of online selling models versus traditional direct selling models, is one of how to build the new business, in this case the offshore model, without cannibalizing the old. Going offshore simply has a personal, negative effect on antiquated compensation plans, so

> *The challenge, not unlike that seen in many business models during the rapid evolution of online selling models versus traditional direct selling models, is one of how to build the new business, in this case the offshore model, without cannibalizing the old.*

traditional sales forces and the companies for whom they work will not heavily push these initiatives for some time.

- **Delivery structure**—The delivery model focuses on staffing engagements with local, regional or occasionally national resources. The largest services groups have developed vertical practices that draw on national resource pools, but even in those cases there is a focus on local resources to reduce travel expenses and increase local revenue targets. Client work, when it is taken off-site, has the backup of quick access to either project teams or site visits. The work is all completed domestically. The delivery structure described here has the same characteristics whether for long-term contracts for staff augmentation, ongoing project work, or even outsourcing programs.

- **Sense of urgency**—Big companies with long-term clients, long-term revenue streams and high perceived barriers to entry rarely feel the same call to action experienced by smaller businesses. This is not necessarily hubris. Companies are like ships: the bigger they are, the harder they are to turn. It is simply a difficult task that requires time and very significant events to spur the hard changes.

Among the best known of the US-based multinationals are IBM Global Consulting, Accenture, EDS and Hewlett-Packard (HP). Interestingly, the move to split the old Andersen consulting services, renaming it Accenture and taking it public, may help it dodge more than just the Enron bullet. As a public company, Accenture has shareholders with a primary focus on maximizing their return on investment. This means that where other former competitors struggle with reductions in the numbers of partners required to support the new operating model, Accenture is apt to be a strong survivor.

Each of these companies is investing in offshore delivery capabilities; however, the size and scope of their plans (other than what they have announced) are unclear. IBM, EDS and Accenture have all announced growth in their Indian facilities that reflects compound annual rates at or above 45% for 2001–2005. Each will have approximately 5,000 employees in India by the end of that time frame. The position that they have taken would seem to reflect at least an acknowledgment that the trend is moving toward hybrid (combined on- and offshore) models while leveraging the attractive cost structure that offshore represents. It is unclear whether the scope that they seem to be pursuing will have a material effect on their cost structure. Ultimately they will be judged by their customer base, which is becoming increasingly sophisticated about offshore options and wants to see lower blended rates on consulting and outsourcing services. If they cannot perform, over time their customer base will slowly be eroded from a combination of increasing competition and diminishing barriers to offsourcing. The large offshore providers are trying to penetrate the outsourcing business and over time are sure to see success.

Hybrids

The hybrids (as we call them here) are the most interesting of the operating models. These are organizations that reflect target operating models with a blended onshore/offshore mix, including a stronger focus on project management and domain knowledge.

Traditionally, offshore providers have focused largely on the application programming or development portion of the application life cycle and paid less attention to the requirements, system testing and release management aspects of system integration projects. They have not invested in areas that required business analysts and pure functional knowledge—in other words, where they would need to compete in the US market on dimensions other than cost. This has left the door open to companies with remote geographic delivery capabilities willing to aggressively court the higher value–added aspects of the end-to-end application life cycle projects.

A number of these groups have emerged in the past couple of years, although no single company appears to have found the magic formula. Like the second-tier players, they are differentiating themselves by their flexibility, but they also possess a strong focus on project management. They are beginning to have notable success as their larger competitors continue to grow but are commoditized at the low end.

Among this group may be a future "incumbent killer." Anyone who can design and execute a delivery model that can successfully manage risk, provide analytical skills and domain knowledge on the front end while seamlessly integrating that to a low-cost back end, and bundle it all in a low-cost, high-quality package will have built the incumbent killer.

Customer Relationship Management and Call Centers

The call center market is an area of rapid growth within the spectrum of offshore IT-enabled services. The reason is simple: cost. The blended fully loaded cost of a US call center worker is between $32 and $37 per hour, whereas in Barbados it could be in the low $20s, in the Philippines slightly lower and in India in the teens. Maybe 75% of all call center employee in India earn $7,500 per year or less, so it is not hard to understand why the costs are this low.

What is surprising is the speed at which the offshore delivery capability has evolved beyond the basic help desk to more enterprising and higher value–added activities. These centers manage a combination of e-mail and inbound and outbound traffic. Basic capabilities on one end of the spectrum are rapidly being upgraded to provide head-to-head competition with high-end in-house US domestic capabilities. At the same time the domestic providers are rapidly trying to implement centers offshore as they are seeing their future markets erode through price competition. Not so long ago the offshore providers in this area were not seen as credible because of perceived language barriers, infrastructure challenges and telecommunication costs. Today, sophisticated language and dialect training, dramatically reduced telecommunication costs and the changing cost differential have many incumbents scrambling to move offshore.

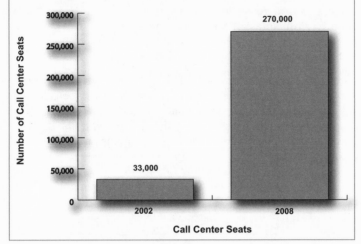

Figure 8: Projected Call Center Seat Growth in India

Source: NASSCOM

Integrated Global Players

The large integrated global call center outsourcing players have been in business for about 20 years. They have reached their current mass through a combination of organic growth and acquisitions. They tend to have a focus on the US, Western Europe and (to a lesser extent) Canada.

As the industry has matured and become more competitive, these companies have looked to nearshore geographies to provide lower-cost alternatives for clients. Canada is an option in some cases for US clients, although the savings may be limited. Other alternatives include Ireland for Western Europe (Ireland also serves as a good linguistic hub for Pan-European call center needs) and the Caribbean for some US clients.

Very recently these integrated global players have begun to look at options in the Philippines and India; however, they are new (everyone is relatively new) to these markets and they will undoubtedly move through a learning curve as they hone their offshore models.

Indian Tier-One Spin-offs

The tier-one vendors identified in the application development and maintenance space have begun to diversify their operations into other areas of the IT-enabled services value chain. As they do so they bring tremendous financial leverage, an understanding of managing services business and a terrific distribution channel through their existing customer base, sales force and partners. They are growing through a combination of acquisition of market specialists and cross-selling to existing customers in core businesses. They are likely to benefit significantly from the launch of offshore call center activity initiatives.

Market Specialists

Market specialists are providers with US-based financial backing that have staked out a specific remote geography from which to service customers. They provide a blend of US sales, marketing and operational talent connected with a remote source of low-cost, high-quality labor. As with the hybrids in the application maintenance and development space, this is an area likely to evolve rapidly in the coming quarters.

> *India and the Philippines have extremely strong players in this market, some of which are working on high value–added activities that require intensive customer interaction.*

Most of these market specialists are likely to be survivors, as they have a demonstrated early-mover advantage with facilities and people in place. Whether they are able to remain independent in the long term depends on their ability to grow sufficiently to achieve economies of scale before their more mature competitors begin to make competing investments. They will undoubtedly become either interesting acquisition targets for those looking to have a delivery capability in low-cost areas or the consolidators of diversified call center operators that are unable to make the transition to the offshore model.

India and the Philippines have extremely strong players in this segment, some of which are working on high value–added activities that require intensive customer interaction. The Philippines' close cultural affinity to the US and the generally excellent accent quality makes them formidable competitors against many Indian providers that may have slightly larger critical mass. We know of one group that is balancing loads in real time between facilities in India and the Philippines, presenting clients with an interesting blended option.

Business Process Outsourcing

BPO is a rapidly growing sector of the offshore market with many new entrants. With the exception of possibly the medical transcription market, there are no dominant industry players in the BPO market. It is too new, broad, fragmented and growing too rapidly to project a clear stratification of the market and players. The figure below represents the current areas of BPO that are currently being moved offshore. This is by no means a comprehensive list, but the more significant processes are sure to grow in scale over the next few years.

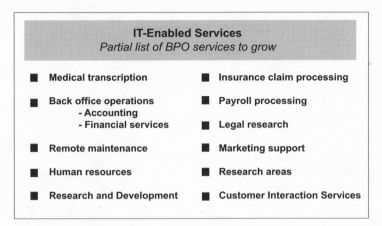

Figure 9: IT-Enabled Services Evolving as BPO Offerings

As in the case of the customer relationship management market, the first-tier players are aggressively opening up to the opportunities in this field. They are leveraging a combination of customer base and financial strength to stake out territory. Many of their larger customers have now been enjoying offshore services for some time, and so the leap to taking more strategic processes out of the domestic organization is not a large one. At the same time venture capital (VC)–backed groups are also sniffing out opportunities to take on large-scale blocks of business, a trend that is expected to increase in 2003 and 2004.

In addition, some companies that have built organic capabilities offshore for the purpose of cutting internal costs to a greater degree than possible with domestic outsourcers, a point that we will revisit at the end of the book, have the opportunity to turn cost-saving investments into revenue-generating propositions. Tens if not hundreds of manually intensive business processes have yet to be taken offshore to any significant degree, leaving room for early movers to capitalize during this window of opportunity.

Summary

The field of providers in the offshore IT-enabled services industry is as wide and varied as the industries that it supports. Many providers can provide a given service, given sufficient investment and realistic expectation management between buyer and provider. The challenge is to find a vendor that can both accomplish the work and evolve to truly become a strategic partner in your business. For this reason we recommend a process-driven approach to navigate the sea of information.

Chapter 7 Summary
The Providers

Chapter Theme

There are over 9,000 offshore providers of software and BPO services. In India and the Philippines alone, there are over 2,000 companies reflecting a complex web of options. Market knowledge and experience are key in choosing a vendor as part of your strategy.

- ❏ **Domestic presence**
- ❏ **Offshore only**
- ❏ **Global diversification**
- ❏ **Hybrid models**
- ❏ **Integrated global firms**
- ❏ **US based multinationals**
- ❏ **Market specialist**

Key Points

A good match between your firm and the offshore firm in terms of culture, process, size, geographic location and business model is a critical success factor. Do not underestimate the importance of the business model of the provider and how it fits with yours. Compatibility can mean the difference between success and failure.

- ❏ **Alignment of:**
    - **- Culture**
    - **- Processes**
    - **- Size**
    - **- Business models**
- ❏ **Process verification**
- ❏ **Know your goals**
- ❏ **Total cost of ownership**

Reader Take-Away

You should have an appreciation of the competencies and modus operandi of the various segments of the provider markets. You should be in a position to identify key characteristics of a vendor that will meet your needs and you should be able to build a case to management as to the value of a 3rd party in the selection process.

Questions for Consideration

- ❏ What volume of work do you expect to move offshore?
- ❏ Do you have a broad set of needs with a widely diverse group of skill sets?
- ❏ Do you have an existing relationship with a domestic outsourcer that is moving into the offshore venues?
- ❏ Are there any offshore providers operating in the domain in which you require service?
- ❏ If you are a service provider, have you considered the incentive structures required to drive business development efforts in your organization offshore?

Chapter 8

Critical Success Factors

Overview

Critical success factors, or CSFs as they are often called, are the bane of most business literature. Either glaringly obvious or so esoteric as to be impractical, they are often so hyped that they leave the consumer a bit jaded when they are finally revealed. Here we will deliberately set your expectations low and refrain from the obligatory Top Ten List.

Critical success factors in offsourcing are about common sense, planning and commitment. You may well ask how they differ from CSFs for onshore IT-enabled activities. The answer is one of degree. Your ability to manage issues, control the environment and respond to the expected and unexpected can be significantly challenged in the offsourcing environment without the appropriate baseline and controls. Throw in cultural, change management and international vendor issues and you begin to see a new layer of complexity. Domestic projects may succeed or be saved in spite of the way they are managed, thanks to heroic efforts on the part of a few. Offsourcing projects rarely have that luxury; the challenges are just too great.

 In this chapter we highlight some of the key items that must be considered if you are to build an offsourcing success story.

Education

It is human nature to fear what you do not know, do not understand or perceive to be a threat to your livelihood. For most professionals the offshore environment represents all three of these elements.

The education of your organization on the offshore industry is likely to address the first two of these issues while increasing the sense of foreboding about what is coming. That is both expected and healthy. Organizations, like individuals, usually must feel pain before they are moved to take medicine.

Educating yourself is likely to be the easy part; the fact that you're reading this book indicates that you are investing time in understanding the offshore markets and probably believe that there is some potential for application within your organization. (A resource section is included in Appendix C. that lists online destinations where you can continue your individual quest for knowledge.)

The challenge is how to bring the rest of the organization along through the education process, passing through successive stages of awareness, interest and a desire for action. We recommend the following:

- **Awareness**—There are a variety of studies available from the major technology analyst groups that provide reasonable introductory reading on the subject. If you do not have membership privileges you can still purchase many of the texts. Consider circulating these among your colleagues and subordinates.

- **Interest**—Consider inviting a third party into the organization to conduct a workshop or seminar on the emerging possibilities of offsourcing. Look for someone who has actually implemented solutions as opposed to simply being an analyst—ideally someone who can respond to queries on the challenges of implementation.

- **Action**—In your strategic planning process, challenge the organization to cut costs or improve service levels in a way that demands a step-function change in the way that you conduct business. Let information about others in your industry that have accomplished these benefits become a call to action.

In every paradigm shift there are those who see the possibilities of the new paradigm, those who see things in the context of the old one and those who never see or understand the new paradigm. Expect that the education process will take some time and that there are those who will never understand the new model. The education process gives you a chance to find your champions and uncover the pockets of passive (and even active) resistance to the offsourcing paradigm.

Clear Objectives

As the saying goes, it's hard to know where you're going if you don't have a destination. Unlike some of the expensive advice dispensed in the dot-com days about starting with a loose set of principles and the need to be accepting of failure, we instead support an absolute focus on preparing for success. Missteps can be expected during the course of any new endeavor, but an offshore initiative, with its many operational hurdles, will

> *Unlike some of the expensive advice dispensed in the dot-com days about starting with a loose set of principles and the need to be accepting of failure, we instead support an absolute focus on preparing for success.*

certainly fail if a culture of tolerance toward failure is promulgated. This is hard work, not rocket science.

As you begin educating yourself about the opportunities, you should crystallize a set of short- and long-term objectives. You will never have perfect information about the environment and challenges that you are approaching, so begin with a set of principles that will provide guidance to the strategic planning effort. These may relate to:

- **Timing**—Be firm about committing to specific dates to complete phases of your process. These are difficult, fundamentally strategic issues with which you are dealing. Be prepared to make assumptions where you do not have complete data. Plan the work, work the plan and be flexible if new information arises. *Do not allow "paralysis through analysis" to set in.*

- **Return on investment (ROI)**—Know the internal ROIs that you must meet. Establish an understanding with your CFO of the magnitude in savings expected if you are able to take on offsourced solutions. The size and scope of the offshore activity will determine the investment required for it to succeed, but experience suggests that only months, not years, are required.

- **Cost reduction versus increased capacity**—Determine whether your goal is savings or enhanced capacity or both. This has important implications for the solution that you will ultimately develop.

- **Incremental change versus obliteration**—Many years ago there was an article in the *Harvard Business Review* calling for radical change, "obliteration," as companies worked through their business process Re-engineering initiatives. What is your goal with offsourcing? To save a few dollars or to reinvent your business as the low-cost model in your industry?

You will revisit these objectives as you begin to develop your Business Case and Offsourcing Roadmap (see Chapters 10 and 11). You are expected to learn as you go, but it is critical to begin with a clear vision and to develop interim targets with expected results and time frames.

Planning

In the most robust scenario, your planning process must cover a wide range of issues from the strategic to the tactical, from the financial to the operational and from the business process to the technical. This is a tall order. Reinventing a business around the offshore model really involves planning a new enterprise and adding the headaches of transition on top.

The planning process that we advocate in this text (and detail in Chapters 10 and 11) begins with setting objectives, developing a Business Case and creating an Offsourcing Roadmap. Each of these activities requires different levels of strategic versus tactical versus operational input that will come from different sources within the organization. You will never be able to plan for every contingency, but with the right methodology and tools you should be able to identify, document, plan and execute your goal.

Your challenge is to manage this multivariable problem in real time while recognizing that most of the variables are in flux at any given time. This requires a **combination of task-mastering detail and executive sponsorship that can push through the log jams** that will invariably arise from imperfect information or organizational resistance. This leads to our next critical success factor: commitment.

Commitment

There is nothing insignificant about going offshore. It is a step function in business process and mind set. Offsourcing requires that you deploy often scarce resources to define and execute an organic approach to realizing a new business model or to define and work with a new vendor/partner relationship towards the same end.

We believe that the client must embrace and be prepared to sign up for the following:

- **Executive commitment**—Executives should be involved in the formation of the relationship and be accessible beyond regular status briefings to resolve and provide coaching on cross-departmental issues as they arise. Executives must also be prepared to get on a plane and spend time in the remote geography in order to understand the operating constraints, or be prepared to engage an experienced third party to do so.

- **Program management**—Beyond the executive commitment, line managers must be truly integrated into the process and made to understand the long-term nature of the new model. Succession and career-planning activities should reflect the new set of skills and experiences required to attain executive level in the organization. Your offsourcing program and project managers may not be the same ones you have today unless their behavior and commitment align with the requirements of the offsourced operation. Success will require the deployment of the best the organization has to offer.

- **Compensation alignment**—We have established that the new model carries significant financial benefits as well as a corresponding set of operational challenges. The skills required to manage a team physically located halfway around the world are different from those required to run a project down the hall. Cultural sensitivity, long periods of international travel, extended (or different) working hours and more persistent reviews of project status are all par for the course. To attract and retain individuals who can execute at this level, the organization should commit to spending a portion of the overall savings on aligning compensation to on-the-job performance.

- **Training**—Personnel identified as possessing the potential to work successfully in the new model will require training. This could range from the "hard" skills attached to technologies that support a more rigorous execution process (e.g., modeling tools in the application development space) to the "soft" skills for which cultural sensitivity and understanding along with improved communications are central. The offsourcing environment demands that you not sit in the glass house and direct. You must be hands-on involved, communicate better than you ever have and be rigorous in every step of the process.

Of course commitment costs time and money. Therefore there is a tendency to believe that by starting small the organization can wet its feet, learn a little and, as experience is gained, ratchet up the span of operations and commitment. Without a clear focus, this is a dangerous approach. If you lack one of the four items above or clarity in your objectives, you run a serious risk of failure even in a small effort. If you should fail in your first attempt to go offshore, what are the odds that you will be given a second chance, either by your organization or by your competition? The cost of failure is a hidden cost that you will never see.

Offsourcing in a small way initially is okay, with the right process and expectations; but offsourcing without commitment is a rapid path to failure.

Vendor Integrity

Assuming your offsourcing strategy includes the use of vendors, the vendors themselves will obviously become a primary critical factor in your success. There is an old saying in consulting circles that when a buyer signs a small contract he gets a new vendor, but when he signs a large contract he gets a partner. That is even truer in the offshore market, where the time and investment required to reach an optimal state of operational efficiency can be longer than with a domestic provider.

For vendors to be viewed as more than providers of a commodity service, they must also be willing to commit to building a long-term, value-based relationship. This criterion is more pressing than ever as the bulk of service delivery models become commoditized. India alone has more than 800 vendors in the IT-enabled services space, with more setting up shop every month.

We believe that the supplier must commit to the following behavioral patterns:

- **Continuity of resources**—All service organizations (domestic and offshore) benefit from building a leveraged model in which they deploy "newbies" on their largest accounts, to give them practical experience that is then leveraged into other accounts at more senior billing rates. Offshore projects that are operated with 12,000 miles between the off-site team and the client team provide ample opportunity for the temptation to abuse this structure. Manage these procedures carefully and ensure you have processes in place to review team members on an ongoing basis. Make sure that the vendor is contractually obligated to ask you if they can swap out resources. This provision has typically been in US service contracts for a long time, but we have not seen it in the standard offshore service contract.

- **Willingness to discuss skill-set needs**—As you push your vendor into more value-added roles, the client and vendor must be prepared to work together to build the resource pool and processes required to service the work. Some skill sets may be more difficult to find than are others. A couple examples from application development follow:

  o **Business analyst**—The traditional paradigm for performing the business analysis and even the design of applications onshore has meant that offshore personnel trying to focus their careers in this area were putting themselves in a risky position. There was simply no guarantee of steady work. It was better to stay close to the technology and be assured of always having work to do. This is changing slowly, but we have run into more than one developer who is afraid to allow their technology skills to erode by taking on more analytical roles.

  o **Testing manager**—Unit testing skills in general can be said to be good, even if on occasion offshore application development is not as systematic as you might find in the US. However, there are very few managers with the experience and skills to put together comprehensive testing strategies for delivery of product-based and even large-scale integrated custom applications. This comes from both a historical and a current perspective, as a majority of the revenues have been and are still in application maintenance and support.

- **Honesty about their process delivery skills**—Most offshore vendors historically have been in the "body shop" and application maintenance business. They provide highly skilled, low-cost labor that can be turned on and off on an hourly basis. Much is made of the litany of certifications that every organization has achieved, including their proficiency in ISO9000 and the Software Engineering Institute's (SEI) Capability Maturity Model (CMM). As some of the larger vendors make their pitches, they may even present esoteric metrics of the number of field bugs per line of code by year. This is excellent marketing and usually reflects a level of infrastructure; however, a CMM Level 5 certification is not worth the paper on which it's written if the assigned team doesn't have sufficient training or project management skills and experience to use the tool for purposes other than checking boxes.

- **Commitment to challenge the client**—Beyond selling work, the role that partners played in the old Big 6 model was to manage risk. In this regard they were responsible for managing the risk of both the firm and the client. Sometimes that means saying "no" to unrealistic deadlines, "no" to scope creep and certainly "no" to solutions that are *unfeasible*. There is an art to providing negative feedback to demanding clients, which is difficult in the best of circumstances. Add to this equation a relatively junior (from the perspective of US-based service models) resource who has limited authority and experience and is trying to bridge a cultural divide, and you have a recipe for trouble. Vendors must do more than they have traditionally done to equip their teams with the soft skills to say "no" diplomatically.

Further, **the buyer must understand the vendor's business model.** That doesn't necessarily mean that you should be privy to their most intimate financial figures, but an understanding of how your vendor makes money is a key element of moving from a purely vendor/client relationship to a strategic partnership. If you are trying to push project management risk off onto a vendor that is only equipped to provide individual technology contributors but is willing to accept the task because it does not want to lose all your business, who is to blame for the consequences?

> ...[A]n understanding of how your vendor makes money is a key element of moving from a purely vendor/client relationship to a strategic partnership.

Summary

The critical success factors all seem so simple, and yet in practice the number of failed, terminated and marginally beneficial projects suggests that these factors have not been adequately addressed. That is not to say that offshore projects fare any worse than domestic ones: the numbers in that sector are equally distressing.

What can be said is that onshore products that are poorly managed at a minimum have the potential for success given the cohabitation of employees and access to the guilty parties. The 12,000 mile divide negates that hope and pushes most if not all poorly managed offshore projects into the failure zone. Bear in mind that many of the onshore antagonists who have not bought in to the offsourcing model may assign blame to the offshore resources for problems during a period of transition. Management commitment and hands-on involvement are critical to overcoming these challenges. Be clear about what you want, do what you say you'll do, be honest with yourself and your partners and good things can happen. Sounds like grammar school—but the rules of offsourcing are elementary.

Chapter 8 Summary
Critical Success Factors

Chapter Theme

Critical success factors (CSFs) in offsourcing are about common sense, thorough planning and commitment. If you get these right and have executive commitment and sponsorship, offsourcing will work for your organization.

- ☐ Education
- ☐ Clarity of objectives
- ☐ Commitment
- ☐ Vendor integrity
- ☐ Offshore knowledge

Key Points

Know the critical success factors. The single most important CSF is executive commitment. Without it, your odds of success fall significantly.

- ☐ Cultural alignment
- ☐ Process alignment
- ☐ Understanding of goals
- ☐ Thorough planning
- ☐ Total cost of ownership

Reader Take-Away

You should have an appreciation that successful offsourcing of any scale requires education and commitment. Proper preparation and planning will allow you to make the right decisions while minimizing long-term arbitrary constraints and rework. Should you elect to use the services of a vendor, frank and open discussions about what they can and cannot do as part of their business model will serve you well.

Questions for Consideration

- ☐ Have you considered how your constituents can best be educated?
- ☐ Is there a consensus in your organization on the objectives of your offsourcing initiative?
- ☐ Have you completed a detailed strategy and planning exercise?
- ☐ Are the management and executive teams aligned as to offsourcing objectives?
- ☐ Are you currently dealing with an offshore vendor which you have confidence in and that you feel has strong integrity?

Part II: Planning and Preparing for Success

Chapter 9

Building Sponsorship

Overview

Moving IT-enabled services offshore is not an incremental or minor exercise. It is a step function in transforming the way that those offsourced business functions are performed. It requires education of the decision-making parties and an understanding of the context in which the current process lives. It also requires recognizing that sponsorship for offsourcing will require building support at multiple levels of the organization—the timing of which will be critical to your success.

In this chapter we begin by examining some of the signals of resistance that you can expect to encounter as you begin to build your case for going offshore. We then provide a perspective on how the organization's profile, maturity level target, international experience and market situation play into possible adoption issues. Finally we address specific actions that champions can take to address issues of sponsorship at executive and broader levels of the organization. The process of building sponsorship can be time-consuming and frustrating, but it is a necessary step in aligning the organization behind this key initiative.

Recognizing and Overcoming Internal Resistance

No matter how enlightened your company is, you can expect some level of resistance to the offshore model as a means of reducing costs and raising service levels. Typical objections and some of the responses that you might consider are included in the following table:

Comment	Possible response
It's too far away.	It's a long way, but fortunately with the right training, videoconferencing, and collaboration tools we can minimize the travel or have a third party manage the relationship for us.
We will lose control.	We may lose some control but what other areas of our business are we outsourcing? how many remote operations do we have and how do we manage them? We will need to improve our internal processes to make the initiative work efficiently.
We tried it already and failed.	Why do you think we failed? Did we have the wrong approach? Did we really commit to making the program successful? Did we have a strategic and operational plan that in place? Maybe we should conduct a post mortem on that effort and reconsider starting up again with a better managed process.
Look at the bad press.	Microsoft, Dell, Oracle, JP Morgan, Citibank, American Express, Texas Instruments, GE and many others are investing heavily and growing their operations. These are the visionaries, are they wrong? What are our competitors doing?
The geopolitical situation is too risky.	Terrorism seems to be a global problem these days. We should definately consider spreading our risk geographically over the long term and establish a disaster recovery plan. Do we have a disaster recovery plan for our US operations that we can leverage?
We're not sending our people over there.	Building an organization model before we determine the benefits is premature. The good news is that we can hire a third party that would manage the operation for us and as the center matures we won't have to have any of our people there.
Everyone who goes there get's sick.	There are over 75,000 people from the US and the UK living in India alone. How do they handle it? We will need to provide some education for our people that would travel over there.
It sounds great, but I don't have time to look into this until maybe the fourth quarter or early next year.	We can get a third party to help us establish the business case and build the Roadmap. With your executive support we can then run a small pilot to prove out the Roadmap. We should move rapidly if we want to see savings next year.

Table 10: Objections and Mollifying Responses

Internal resistance can come from many sources and may in part reflect the company's overall financial condition. We explore three different scenarios below:

- **The company is growing rapidly**—Organizations experiencing high growth rates often suffer the fatigue of having too much to do in too little time. Outsourcing provides an attractive option to achieve objectives while limiting investment of scarce resources in non-core infrastructure. Offsourcing provides the same alternative at a lower price point, albeit with a few more operational challenges. Internal resistance may arise from issues associated with:

  o **Speed**—Can the environment be set up and operationalized quickly to meet expected growth needs? As a change agent you must be able to demonstrate the speed of execution and the ability to implement without negatively impacting current operations.

  o **Flexibility**—Companies in their growth phase are often experimenting with different product and service offerings as they build the franchise. Can the service levels be adjusted or changed to reflect changes in the core operations? The change agent must be able to demonstrate how the contractual arrangement, program management, and process flexibility will support the growing company's need for rapid change in operations.

- **The company is static or growing only at the rate of the market**—Such companies are probably in the middle of their maturity cycle. The focus should be on aggressively reducing unit costs; but too often, significant infrastructure and historical organizational lines prevent the adoption of new approaches. Internal resistance can take the form of:

  o **Ostrich syndrome**—What does someone with his head in the sand sound like? The following is a real-life example: "We avoid talking about offshore solutions with our clients. They usually underestimate the political risk of going offshore." Let's face it, there is not a huge amount of literature in the market about offshore operations, and it is easy for executives and managers in "safe" companies to be complacent. And conversely, managers in companies destroyed by disruptive technologies or business models often carry a frame of reference that blinds them to the obvious.

  o **Organization displacement**—Some individuals measure their power by their number of direct reports and organizational headcount. Losing headcount or having to manage an offshore service level might just be the most unappealing job responsibility they can imagine, and when viewed in the context of an outsourcing agreement may be even more loathsome. Chapter 17 on Change Management discusses these personnel issues and how you might address them.

- **The company is in the ditch and under extreme cost pressure**—Firms that are struggling in a difficult economic climate may have an easier time taking the next steps. They are likely to have had a call to action from their shareholders, customers and even employees. However, the resistance to moving offshore, even under these circumstances, is the same as that experienced by other organizations facing radical change:

  o **Denial**—Denial stems from an inability to emotionally and rationally come to terms with the current business environment. Offsourcing is especially applicable for flagging organizations, as it can breathe new life into a losing business and, at a minimum, give additional longevity to a financially struggling enterprise. Offsourcing messaging should be packaged and directed to the CFO.

  o **Personal relationships**—This area poses particular challenges in midmarket companies, where the executive decision makers may have strong personal ties to individuals that are directly affected by the offshore changes. The change agent in this environment must focus on a couple of key points:

    ➢ **The longer you wait to act, the more pain there will be**—By acting early and aggressively, companies can utilize the savings to provide job training and comfortable severance packages for employees that are displaced.

- **There is a fiduciary duty to consider all options at the executives' disposal**—Companies in very mature or consolidating industries often run the risk of dying a "death of a thousand cuts." Drastic times call for drastic measures. Offsourcing is a potent weapon in the fight to restore profitability, protect shareholders' interests and preserve the equity value of a company.

Sponsorship Focal Points

> *Managers in companies destroyed by disruptive technologies or business models often carry a frame of reference that blinds them to the obvious.*

Building sponsorship is itself a complex strategic selling process. If you do not own the business unit in question, you must operate in a dual mode of proactive engagement and detached responsiveness or run the risk of alienating some of your peers. Areas to focus on include:

- **Education**—This is the key and can often be driven home with a few high-impact presentations. These presentations should focus on the macro environment, with clear messaging about potential impact on the bottom line, current offshore activity of the competition and clear examples of successful execution strategies. It is human nature not to like (or to be suspicious of) what we do not know. Educate your champions on the possibilities inherent in the offshore model. They will have questions, but they will also have moments of "Eureka."

- **Understanding the risks**—It is important to take the time to articulate the potential risks. Most step function changes carry potential downsides and offshore strategies are no different; but there are approaches that can significantly reduce or mitigate these risks. You will be asked the tough questions, so be ready to meet these challenges with the facts.

- **Competition**—Research and understand the financial savings that your competition is enjoying from offsourcing. You might even be able to build a case that their savings are being funneled into product development that is increasing the pressure on your own goods and services. Let the "bad guys" create a call to action for others in your organization.

- **Political landscape**—Understanding the political landscape and the disposition of business unit owners is fundamental. You are unlikely to win sponsorship from someone who has spent a lifetime building a territorial fiefdom that may soon be moved halfway around the world. On the other hand, the right owner will say, "Great; looks like a terrific challenge," or in the case of an outsourced solution, "Wow, life would be simpler only having to manage a service level."

- **Organizational biases**—Be aware of other undercurrents in the organization. Understanding the organizations' bias toward build or buy can help you bring a desirable goal state into focus for personnel who may view the opportunity through a lens of harsh skepticism.

- **Being ready with a process**—In all cases be prepared with a methodology. Once the initial questions are answered, the discussion will move on to next steps. As the saying goes, opportunity favors the prepared mind. You must be ready with a process that recognizes the constraints of the organization, the education required and a quantitatively driven approach to drive through to a target solution.

- **Being aware of exogenous events**—In the wake of press about poor governance in many large corporations, now more than ever, executives must also be sensitive to external events. These events ultimately may have a defining influence on the adopted "go-forward" solution. The newspapers are filled with political and cultural issues that will come to bear in the go/no-go decision, so be prepared.

You must also be able to speak to the above while considering an additional variable: time. Many of the questions you will be asked have multiple answers based on varying input values. Time is perhaps the greatest variable of all. How quickly does the organization expect to see costs cut? How long is it prepared to run pilot phases? What is our long-term objective? Should we insource, outsource or offsource? As you begin to respond to these questions, be prepared to answer fluently when people ask about possible outcomes. Don't put yourself in the position of saying that it depends on X, Y, or Z: you run the risk of being seen as missing the big picture. Instead the scenarios and be prepared to quickly identify how the outcomes change as you are asked about the impact of changing the variables. Create the straw man solution and get ahead of the curve. Be prepared to have experienced resources available as interest grows and you are ready to get into developing the strategy and plans for proceeding.

Executive Sponsorship

At the executive level, questions will gravitate toward the strategic and financial aspects of the proposed change. What are the savings? What are the risks? Where should we be located? What are the most advantageous structural approaches?

All these questions can be answered easily enough by conducting a Business Case and Offsourcing Roadmap, as discussed in Chapters 10 and 11. The key is to get the necessary commitment to take the initiative to that level.

The CFO or controller is always a great place to start given the enormous financial benefits available. They are free to have a more financially and strategically driven focus than others in roles that are more operationally driven.

Business unit or P&L leaders and CIOs who are under fire to produce more with less are also good candidates. The P&L leader will likely have strong incentives to improve cost efficiency, as will a CIO under pressure. CIOs with a comfortable budget may be less inclined to take the step, since offshore approaches are likely to complicate their world; however, we are unsure that there are any such CIOs left in the current business climate.

The bottom line is that offsourcing initiatives are best driven from the top down. The change management issues alone are sufficient to dictate that offshore practices require executive sponsorship, so start at the top and enlist key sponsors before working the rest of the organization.

Sponsorship from Middle Management

At the level of middle and line management, the range of possible reaction is broad enough so as to be unpredictable. It will vary from individual to individual and according to the culture and growth prospects of the company in question.

In the ideal scenario, a company is growing rapidly and, faced with the added costs of building an ever-larger IT-enabled services organization, begins to explore opportunities to move certain aspects offshore. The "brain trust" is kept onshore, while support functions and additional capacity in a number of areas are moved to a low-cost environment. The organization gains lower unit costs while the current staff is given the added responsibilities and professional challenges of building a global unit.

Even in this scenario there exists enormous potential for FUD (fear, uncertainty and doubt). Current management may not want to travel, particularly to parts relatively unknown. They may feel that they are on the block or that although they have the skills to manage a team down the hall, they are uncertain of how to begin to manage a group half a world away in an entirely different culture. (And this is the rosy scenario!)

Now imagine an organization that comes to the offshore solution out of dire financial need to cut costs to survive. You get the picture.

Successful execution requires the involvement of at least some percentage of the middle management team. The timing of their involvement may vary according to the scope of their role and the individual personalities involved; however, a careful approach to enlisting them in the formulation and execution of the strategy is paramount for success.

Beyond the areas of focus listed previously, give focus to the following as you begin to enlist specific champions:

- **Over communication**—Constant and regular communication on objectives, status and realized outcomes will help to build an environment of trust and stability during a difficult time.

- **Contribution**—Building the correct operational model for your organization will be a multidimensional, time-consuming and challenging assignment. In short, it is just the type of project on which high performers thrive. You will face a multitude of operational challenges as you implement your model, so bring the skills that your organization has to offer to the task. Challenge your management to make a contribution to the success of the effort even at the planning stages.

- **Individual goals**—Connect the organization's goals to lower unit costs and increase the level and capacity of the personal goals of the performers that you want to succeed in the new environment. International travel and exposure may be an exciting opportunity for some, while the training required to manage a distant team may be rewarding to others. The team that is left in place is likely to have higher performance expectations required of them. Plan to utilize some of the savings that will come from attaining lower unit costs in rewarding these personnel.

Summary

Tomes of literature are available on the art of strategic selling within complex organizations. When all is summarized, a few salient points stand out:

- **Understand the landscape of personal incentives**—Who will benefit most from the offsourcing initiative? Who stands to lose the most and why? Be particularly mindful of the more subtle effects, including required lifestyle changes (e.g., international travel, different working hours) and time away from home.

- **Understand the competitive environment in which the organization lives**—Is your competition moving offshore? If not, then why not? How might you use the offshore model to build a competitive advantage? Chances are that someone in your competitive space is already there and reaping the benefits. How are they using the benefits against you?

- **Identify change agents (coaches) who will support your cause**—This is as true at the manager level as it is at the executive level. Be prepared to lead from the front as you empower your colleagues with the facts. Promote an environment in which you have the opportunity to regularly and informally check the pulse of the troops. The key to building momentum is proper education and careful timing.

- **Be armed with the facts**—The stakes are high in this debate, so be sure to have done your homework. Use third-party references, point to published studies and work hard to let the literature push individuals to form their own conclusions. You will likely have formed your own opinions and conclusions, but emotional elements with the potential for dramatic change require a certain amount of time to digest. Anticipate this in your planning, but do not allow the team to become bogged down.

- **Be prepared to commit**—To paraphrase an old proverb: Be careful what you ask for; you might get it. Imagine that you are successful in winning the hearts and minds of your colleagues. At some point, someone will have to get on a plane. It may be a defining moment, so be prepared to step up and take the responsibility.

Chapter 9 Summary
Building Sponsorship

Chapter Theme

Sponsorship is the cornerstone of getting started. Without an executive mandate, it is easy to become bogged down in internal politics and turf wars, meaning that you will not get the opportunity to move ahead with a viable initiative. Understanding and overcoming internal resistance is a CSF.

- ❐ Education
- ❐ Executive sponsorship
- ❐ Organizational resistance
- ❐ Sponsorship focal points
- ❐ Resistance

Key Points

Executive sponsorship is the key. The breadth of offsourcing being considered will determine the degree of sponsorship required from business leaders during early planning and scoping exercises.

- ❐ Competitive assessment
- ❐ Ostrich syndrome
- ❐ Follow a process
- ❐ High-level benefits case

Reader Take-Away

You should be prepared with sufficient education materials, case studies and benefits to your organization before you start trying to gain sponsorship. Look around the organization for other offshore initiatives and try to piggyback on them if it makes sense. Consider a third party to deliver a high-impact visioning session as part of the education process.

Questions for Consideration

- ❐ Have you identified the points of resistance in the organization?
- ❐ Have you established a plan to educate key constituents on the market and the competition?
- ❐ Do you understand the alignment or lack of alignment in the incentives to implement offsourcing in your organization?
- ❐ Have you constructed some offsourcing straw man scenarios for consideration by your colleagues?
- ❐ Have you made a personal commitment to the success of offsourcing in your organization?

Chapter 10

Establishing the Business Case

Overview

The Business Case development is a financial modeling exercise with opportunity identification and strategy development components. It may be conducted as a precursor to the Offsourcing Roadmap, itself a rigorous planning exercise, or jointly as a subset of the Offsourcing Roadmap activities. In any event, the Business Case is critical to the Offsourcing Roadmap development and ultimately to the successful deployment of an offsourced solution.

Taken together the Business Case and Offsourcing Roadmap provide a scripted set of activities to move the organization from concept to point of execution. The delineation between where one component ends and the other begins reflects the organization's need to establish early return-on-investment projections prior to building a solution model and implementation plan. Many organizations require a preliminary estimate of benefits and associated costs even before the exact details are known. For this reason we segment the activities here and pull the Business Case into a separate discussion. As you move into the Offsourcing Roadmap, your Business Case will continue to be refined as the solution model and implementation approach become clear.

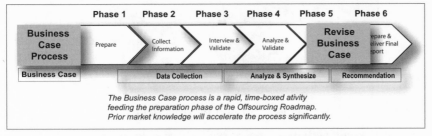

Figure 10: Business Case and Offsourcing Roadmap

Who Should Build a Business Case?

Just about every organization should consider developing a Business Case for its offshore work. If you elect to separate it from the Offsourcing Roadmap, simply recognize that you will need to revisit the numbers as you finalize the solution model and implementation approach. Even those organizations with work currently under way can stand to gain from the exercise. Your group will fall into one of four categories:

- **Minimal size of or reliance on IT-related services**—How big is big enough to take advantage of offshore services? What is the point at which it makes economic sense to move activity offshore? The answer varies according to the service, contract length, and specialized processes or requirements that are necessary. For the largest companies, it can be a simple decision if the scope is large enough; but if you run a small operation should you consider a Business Case? The answer is a definitive maybe. Availability, infrastructure and sophistication of the services continue to improve, so understanding the thresholds that your organization must meet will allow you to move rapidly as the inflection points change.

- **Sufficient scale and no current activity**—The Business Case should be considered a corporate imperative as part of your strategic planning process or year-end budgeting cycle. Even if you are not yet prepared to move toward your own offsourcing initiative, you can bet that at least one if not several of your competitors are considering or already performing functions offshore. At a minimum you should understand the impact this could have on their cost model and ability to deliver new or lower-cost services, or to pour additional investment into R&D, marketing and sales.

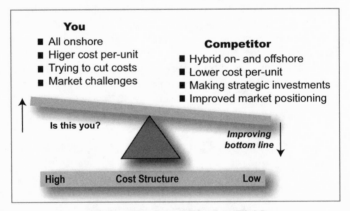

Figure 11: Level Playing Field

- **Some current activity**—You probably have a lot to gain as well. You might have some initial successes or at least activity, but are you thinking and acting strategically? Are you leveraging a vendor when you should be going it alone or working toward a build, operate and transfer model? Have you developed a plan to build and expand your initiatives or are they stovepiped efforts by individual visionaries in the organization? The Business Case is the first step in pulling ahead of your competitors as you prepare to increase your savings.

- **Significant current activity**—You probably have a strategic plan in place, but an update of the old financial model gives you the opportunity to benchmark yourself (and your vendors). As the infrastructure costs continue to fall, the hurdles for marginally beneficial projects drop.

Getting the go-ahead to build a Business Case for your area can be a project in and of itself, one that may be more difficult than the actual creation of the Case. The good news is that by grinding through this data collection and synthesis effort you will most assuredly find a compelling financial story. The challenging aspect is that the numbers are only one small component of the broader sale that you must achieve.

Identifying a Portfolio of Opportunities

You have received approval to move forward with the Business Case and must now take the next step. The fact that you have come this far suggests that there is some level of sponsorship within your organization. Build immediately on that support by first understanding any activity that has occurred, is occurring or is slated to occur, so that you can quickly identify leverage points or dead ends. Some basic questions that you should address at the outset related to past, present and future work include:

Past
- Has your organization completed any offshore or nearshore projects? Were they successful?
- If you terminated a relationship, or discontinued moving any additional work offshore, what were the reasons? Did you follow processes similar to those described in this text and still fail?

Present
- Do you currently have any offshore initiatives under way? Are those initiatives what you would consider to be strategic to your business?
- Do you currently outsource any of your IT-enabled services? Are any of those service providers operating offshore? Have they offered you the use of their offshore capabilities?
- Do you have any nearshore activities? Are you seeing process requirements and challenges similar to those described in this book?
- Does anyone in your organization have responsibility for looking at these options? For managing strategic planning?
- Are you realizing the benefits anticipated?
- Do any of your competitors currently utilize offshore services?
- Do you have unions in your company?

Future
- Has the leadership team discussed the possibility of moving parts of your operations offshore?

- How do you anticipate beginning the process of opportunity identification and prioritization in your organization?

Based upon the findings above, you should have a reasonable picture of the offshore landscape in your organization. Now you must begin to identify the areas that hold potential for your go-forward strategy. The spectrum of IT-enabled services includes application maintenance, application development, customer relationship management (inbound, outbound, e-mail) and a host of business process outsourcing opportunities. It is an enormous pool from which to draw.

Categorize the opportunities according to the general service capability. Any activity that requires labor-intensive or repetitive tasks that need not be done in proximity to the customer has potential for offsourcing. If you have well-documented processes, you can start from these to examine all areas that might be good candidates for offsourcing. Define those top two or three critical success factors for each area and establish a high-level value proposition for each, along with the anticipated complexity of offsourcing. We use a process we call the Process Prioritization Model that helps categorize and prioritize potential initiatives.

Consider building a matrix like the following to identify possible areas for consideration.

Function/ applications	Complexity	Onshore resources	# of Facilities	Potential issues
Outbound call center	Low	70	2	Nothing insurmoutable
ERP maitenance	Low	26	1	ERP customization knowledge
Inbound call center	Medium	27	1	Nothing insurmountable
New billing system	High	75	1	Requirements and scale of system
New application development	High	115	1	Time to market

Example Scenarios - the objective is to capture the right level of information for each potential application and understand it's process and technical complexity in it's current operating environment. Then, look at what it would take to move the function/application offshore. What investments would need to be made? What skills and training would have to be developed? What impact does it have on customers? revenues? Keep the analysis at this stage to a very high level and timeboxed.

Table 11: Offsourcing Portfolio Identification

As you gather information in these areas, also document the following for later use in your Offsourcing Roadmap:

- **Champions/key resources**—These are go-to individuals that can provide guidance or actually participate in the Business Case development.

- **Success stories**—Find concrete examples of prior offshore successes and specific knowledge of payback periods.

- **Failures**—It is critical to determine the reasons—personnel, process, vendor, etc.—for the activity's lack of success. This will allow you to highlight the investment required for success going forward.

- **Metrics**—These are key indicators that must be collected, measured and monitored on an ongoing basis to support an implementation and track your progress.

- **Competitive environment**—Monitor the offshore activities, investments and plans of your competition or potential competition.

- **Vendor relationships**—Examine any parent company, subsidiary or business partner affiliations that may be leveraged in the vendor selection process.

- **Governance models**—How does your organization effectively manage change, vendor relationships and large programs? Does it have a successful track record or will you need to implement new methodologies to support the migration?

This will be your first procedural opportunity to begin enlisting support within the organization for your initiative. The CFO or controller is a natural ally, but you must enlist others if you are going to build the requisite momentum. The higher you aim in the organization, the broader will be your mandate and the more savings you will be able to demonstrate.

In some cases you will be able to compile the requisite material without discussing the objectives of your process. However, the sensitivity of the information dictates that in some cases you may elect to document certain assumptions rather than involve additional subject matter experts. For those individuals and groups with whom you are disclosing your objectives, you should be prepared for your discussions with a list of frequently asked questions (FAQs) on offshore concerns. You are engaged in an education process and you must be poised to respond to queries or risk slowing the process—or, worse, appearing inconsistent, which will weaken your case.

Creating a Set of Ranking Criteria

Once you have established an exhaustive set of offsourcing possibilities, the next step is to build a set of ranking criteria that allows you to begin prioritizing your initiatives with some level of empirical foundation. Table 12 lists a few criteria that may affect your selection.

Function/ application	Complexity	Annual cost	Estimated savings	Risk
Outbound call Center	Low	$5M	$2M	Low
ERP maitenance	Low	$4M	$2M	Low
Inbound call center	Medium	$2M	$900k	Medium
New billing system	High	$10M	$5M	Medium
New application development	High	$15M	$5M	High

Table 12: Offsourcing Initiative Ranking

It is important to note that most unfavorable characteristics (with the exception of headcount and lackluster sponsorship) can be overcome with additional time and investment. The criteria simply help you begin to prioritize and focus on where you want to invest your time. Consider putting together a series of "magic quadrants" with size versus complexity or cost versus complexity comparisons that can provide powerful illustrations of the potential to act decisively in certain areas.

Building a Financial Model

With a realistic set of priorities in place, you can now begin to build a financial model. This model should encapsulate information about the current environment, future environment and the transition costs required to move your organization from one to the other. Your organization probably has a preferred approach to building project ROI models; however, it is unlikely to contain a packaged list of all the items to consider.

At a minimum your model should incorporate:

- Productivity rates
    o Productivity rates below your domestic source in early stages
        ➢ First few months in application development
        ➢ First few weeks in call center outsourcing

> ➢ Variable in the BPO environment
- o Important to distinguish between cost and productivity in your model and to be consistent
- Training costs
  - o Internal
  - o Vendor
- Telecommunications costs
  - o Line charges (dedicated circuit if required)
  - o Redundancy (if required)
  - o Phone and/or video charges
  - o Equipment: e.g., for videoconferencing
- Restructuring costs
  - o Facility closures
  - o Equipment disposal
  - o Severance packages
- Change management
  - o Process definition
  - o Coaching
- Administrative
  - o Travel to and from the offshore location
  - o Travel related (visas, vaccination shots and passports)
  - o Incremental insurance
  - o Legal

As you are building the scorecard, there are a few items that will require your special attention:

- **Overhead allocation**—The larger the organization, the more Byzantine the accounting is likely to be regarding how fixed costs are allocated across the business units. As you consider moving certain components of the business offshore, you may find that you are unable to attack some fixed costs— meaning that as you move capacity offshore, the unit cost of your onshore work goes up. This can be a problem or a blessing. On the negative side, it may mean that the numbers do not look as attractive as they otherwise might. On the positive side, this may give you the ammunition to take more aggressive action against cost centers under the banner of an all-or-nothing campaign.

- **Training costs**—The technology or process you are moving offshore and the competency/experience of the vendor will determine the overall training requirements. There will be two types of training required: for hard and soft skills. Hard skills are those applied in being productive and efficient in performing the required tasks. Soft skills training is in company, culture and communications to ensure that the teams integrate and can communicate effectively. Make sure you factor in time for both the onshore and offshore teams. Review whether the training requirements can be done via vendors or has to be custom developed. Note that in India, for example, many of the same technical training classes are offered as in the US. One difference is the price, which is much lower in India for the same training class.

- **Taxation**—Be aware that significant government incentives are available to organizations placing foreign direct investment into an offshore development zone. For example, India allows the retention of all earnings for software-related industry activity to remain tax free until 2009.

- **Infrastructure assumptions**—These are useful for examining the way that you currently operate your business (see overhead allocation, above) and the way in which you will be required to operate in your go-forward model. A comprehensive discussion of infrastructure is included in Chapter 15.

Development of the Business Case is also the point at which you will begin to influence the sequence and approach to moving the work offshore. Therefore the return on investment expected must be tied to individual opportunities' having a sufficient level of granularity to break out into individual initiatives. It should also demonstrate the return on investment expected from a comprehensive approach, with the many start-up and ongoing management costs distributed over a range of initiatives.

Build versus Contract versus Buy

For smaller organizations, the decision to contract given the overhead of setting up shop in a remote geography will likely be clear; however, for large companies and even some midsize ones, the savings available from building or buying your own capability will be significant. At a macro level, the decision to outsource usually centers on one of three areas.

- **Focus**—The outsourcing company has decided that some repetitive activity is not core to the business and that it only wants to manage a service level.

- **Skill**—The outsourcing company will be able to take advantage of the skills that the outsourcer maintains at a depth that is difficult to find or retain internally.

- **Scale**—Scale translates into cost. The vendor should have much more scale in its operation that should drive the unit costs of providing the service down for the client.

Interestingly, offsourcing for some will delay or eliminate the need to seek an outsourcer to find scarce skills and to achieve the scale required for lower unit costs. Offsourcing venues are packed with many of the skills required, and the cost differential often negates the need for greater scale. Offsourcing allows you to look at cost reductions and benefits much differently than in the past and gives you previously unexplored options.

Although many offshore providers do offer low costs, the margins that the most successful vendors are earning are impressive. The first-tier incumbents mentioned above in application development on average enjoy a gross margin of 50+%. Over time this will reflect margins similar to those onshore, but not until the education of clients dramatically improves. As the margins go down, offshore companies will seek revenue growth opportunities in higher value–added services and differentiated offerings.

For firms large enough to consider going it alone, there are a number of considerations:

- **Management bandwidth—** Implementing and integrating an offshore facility to the onshore

> *Interestingly, offsourcing for some will delay or eliminate the need to seek an outsourcer to find scarce skills and to achieve the scale required for lower unit costs.*

 operations will require significant focus. Do you have the senior management talent to execute the plan, and is that talent committed to its success? Do they have the experience to be successful in the offshore world?

- **Build versus buy**—You can build the facility you desire, staff it and then bring it online or you can seek to purchase an existing capability. For example, a number of the international investment banks have a presence in Mumbai and therefore have access to local market data on which entities are for sale and at what price. Acquisition multiples vary based on the size, revenue, expertise and onshore sales models. If you are simply looking for a facility, some infrastructure and personnel we would highly suggest building versus buying. The real factor here is your time horizon. If you need it very fast, buy or contract. If you have more time and expect significant size, building may present a more attractive option.

- **Time to savings**—Contracting provides a path to the earliest but possibly not the greatest savings. You must define how long your organization intends to be in the market, the risks of withdrawal and the potential total cost and implications of earlier withdrawal.

Understanding which of the above are critical drivers from a management perspective is fundamental to building your sponsorship.

If you are thinking of setting up your own facility, naturally you will have to consider significant additional activities in order to build a picture of the costs, including:

- Land acquisition
- Permitting
- Construction
- Maintenance
- Brokerage fees
- Infrastructure upgrades
- Security personnel
- Food service for employees[14]
- Transportation for employees[15]
- Taxation

Presenting the Findings

This is the most important step in the Business Case. After all, you can have terrific data, but if your presentation is weak, you could be seen as lacking credibility—or in an environment with only minimal interest in your goals, the data could be viewed as not having sufficient impact to justify further investigation.

The Business Case is a strategic and financial exercise, but it is also a selling exercise. You are selling a vision and a new way of doing business to the organization, so you must be prepared for some level of skepticism and resistance. You must recognize that individuals process information differently and that your job is to make this information available to your audience in a way that is easiest for them to assimilate and in turn communicate to their constituents.

Your findings should be communicated in:

- **Executive slide presentation**—It should comprise no more than 15 to 20 slides of high-impact, summarized material. Articulate the vision, demonstrate the numbers, identify the risks and communicate the process.

  o **Target**—Executive audience.

- **Detailed slide presentation(s)**—This slide deck may run to 50+ slides and should contain well-developed sections on risks, portfolio opportunities, value proposition, savings, infrastructure requirements, change

---

[14] It is customary for large employers to provide both food service and transportation facilities for their workers, many of whom will not have access to timely or reasonably priced transportation.
[15] Ibid.

management, cultural integration and the long-term benefits and impact on the company. It can be used to educate the same executive audience but will also form the foundation for working sessions with line management as you move on to the planning phase. Additional sections will develop perspectives on technology, skills and implementation timelines.

o **Target**—Executive audience; line management.

- **Narrative**—The Business Case should have a detailed narrative that includes vision, objectives, process, risks, and financials. You can build this narrative as you are collecting the data and use it as the basis for your slide presentations.

o **Target**—Possible use by anyone, but of particular interest to those that are very detail oriented.

- **Financial model(s)**—Just as you are communicating the qualitative aspects of the Business Case at multiple levels through narratives and slides, you must be prepared to do the same with the quantitative information. Your model must be detailed enough to survive the scrutiny of a controller's audit but have information that is accessible enough for the executive team to rapidly understand the impact and opportunities that you are presenting.

o **Target**—Executive audience; controller.

Summary

The Business Case articulates a strategic offsourcing vision for the organization with a supporting high-level financial case. It creates a North Star reference point for the work that will follow, while building a formidable quantitative snapshot capable of overcoming most objections to the offshore model.
Data collection activities must focus on:

- Understanding current and prior activity
- Organizational readiness
- Range of opportunities, categorized by process
- Value proposition for taking each process offshore
- Build versus buy versus contract disposition
- Current costs for areas under consideration
- Infrastructure required to perform the associated processes under consideration

In many cases you should be able to work from departmental budgets and industry benchmarks to construct a picture of the costs. The ROI will be there, so don't overcomplicate by trying to analyze everything to death. The Business

Case will be finalized and detailed during the Offsourcing Roadmap, which is the subject of the next chapter.

Chapter 10 Summary
Establishing the Business Case

Chapter Theme

The Business Case is a rapid, time-boxed process intended to establish a financial perspective on the costs and merits of offsourcing. It rapidly takes the organization through an opportunity prioritization and provides key sponsors with the data they need to set realistic expectations and seek budgetary commitments.

- ☐ **Opportunity identification**
- ☐ **Strategy development**
- ☐ **Savings opportunities**
- ☐ **Investment assumptions**
- ☐ **Estimated return on investment (ROI)**

Key Points

The Business Case is the first formal step in a process to deliver an executing model; get the facts, but be prepared to come back later and refine the numbers once a target operating model has been established. Nail the presentation of the benefits and challenge the organization to think big.

- ☐ **Benefits**
- ☐ **Internal restructuring**
- ☐ **Time horizon**
- ☐ **Competition**

Reader Take-Away

You should have a framework for building the Business Case, with a realistic impression of the total costs of doing business in the new paradigm. Be prepared to make reasonable assumptions about facts that are not easily available and be cognizant of the needs of your various constituents to process information in different formats: presentation versus narrative versus financial model.

Questions for Consideration

- ☐ What is the organization's history of outsourcing or offsourcing?
- ☐ At what level was the Business Case development process endorsed?
- ☐ Do the Business Case results have executive endorsement?
- ☐ Do you have confidence in the total costs factored into the Business Case?
- ☐ Does offsourcing give you the room to avoid an outsourcing decision?
- ☐ Have you adequately prepared and summarized your findings? And do you understand the organizational sales process that wil be required to gain endorsement of any offsourcing initiative?

Chapter 11

Developing an Offsourcing Roadmap

Overview

The Offsourcing Roadmap picks up where the Business Case leaves off to begin detailing the solutions and the possible approaches to their implementation. It assumes that a set of financials is in place to justify the approach, although some time is allocated to close gaps or firm up numbers in several of the option scenarios. The Roadmap delivers comprehensive perspectives and deliverables on the financial, process, organizational, contractual, change management and implementation issues associated with moving some part of your operation into an offshore environment

Like many analytical exercises, the Roadmap is fairly generic at a high level; however, there is great deal of complexity in its application. Technological, organizational and cultural analyses must be integrated with project and financial planning, with sensitivity to the company's political landscape:

- Are you "bringing the rest of the organization along" and educating them as you proceed with interviews and data collection?
- Are you working to leverage the time and distance divides in the final work or are you simply transposing your work process into a remote environment? Have you phased your implementation in a way that demonstrates early results—with reasonable up-front investment?
- Is your objective purely cost reduction? Or are you aiming for additional capacity at the same cost?
- How developed is the change management plan for your strategy, in the event that downsizing is significant?
- Do you need to build an operation that will expand over time?
- Do you need board approval to move forward with the initiative?

As you consider the questions below, consider the political context of this activity within your organization.

- Which groups need to be involved?
- Who will the executive champion be?
- Where do I need sponsorship along the way?
- Who is going to actually develop the Offsourcing Roadmap? Do they have enough offshore experience to make it real?
- Do I need some outside expertise to support or implement the Roadmap?

Process

The following is an overview and brief description of each phase of the Roadmap process:

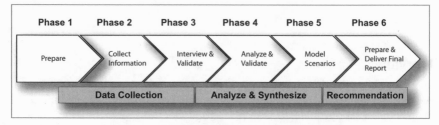

Figure 12: Offsourcing Roadmap Process

- **Preparation**—In this step you will gather the findings and source documents from the Business Case and document feedback from the reviews of this material. This step should also include the creation of a work plan with milestones, interview schedules and descriptions of deliverables. You must ensure that you have all the appropriate people involved from the disciplines required to establish a comprehensive plan. You will begin collecting the raw information required from various sources around the company.

- **Collect Information**—Your Business Case probably stopped short of the work process documentation, an area germane to this activity. The Roadmap requires sufficient data collection for you to fully understand the process landscape, financials, and organizational structure (pre– and post–offshore solution). In addition, governance models for new corporate initiatives should be clearly developed.

- **Interview & Validate**—You will be required to reach out to many of the process owners in this step to understand the current operating model in detail. These interviews should be highly structured. Notes should be taken, returned to interviewees for confirmation and additional follow-up sessions scheduled if necessary. Ensure that you get the perspectives from key owners of processes that are being considered and the executive team as to expectations of areas such as transition time, capital costs, process equivalence, internal ROI hurdles and risk perspectives.

- **Analyze & Validate**—The analysis activity involves reviewing information collected from interviews and source documents to piece together a detailed picture of the current environment along with a set of new requirements for the target environment. Expect to do some of this in parallel with your initial interviews. As gaps are identified you must reach out quickly to collect relevant information or schedule necessary interviews, or otherwise risk delaying the modeling exercise. In this step you should also document a set of baseline constraints and assumptions for the offsourcing scenarios. These may be personnel, processor even production volume related.

▪ **Model Scenarios**—With the requirements in hand and an understanding of the constraints of the offshore model, you can now begin modeling the go-forward scenario. This involves the construction of the process model, organizational model, governance model, technology platform requirements, infrastructure plan and baselines metrics in the target environment. More than one approach exists, so your modeling may include a variety of scenarios with the associated financials and organizational structures. As you model each, you will also assess the options for the offshore capability that are discussed in Chapter 6 on Legal Structures.

▪ **Prepare & Deliver Recommendation**—As in the Business Case, information delivery is a key success factor. Be prepared to have previewed your findings repeatedly with key stakeholders as you move through the Roadmap process. Your mantra should be "No surprises." The final set of recommendations should be delivered with a financial model, a narrative description and PowerPoint presentations that you should assume will be reviewed by your executive team, and possibly a summary by the board of directors.

Executed well, the Offsourcing Roadmap delivers to the organization a seamless plan and transitional approach to gaining the benefits of offshore IT-enabled services. Executed poorly or in an incomplete manner, it may later cost you valuable recovery time, switching costs and key resources. To illustrate, assume that a contingency planning exercise is missed during the Roadmap development when data could have been gathered in a controlled, proactive fashion. Assume further that as you move into implementation, there is a hiccup that requires you to react in real time to recover the process. You might now have to respond by going on-

> *Executed well, the Offsourcing Roadmap delivers a seamless plan and transitional approach to gaining the benefits of offshore IT-enabled services.*

site, an exercise that could take you an additional two or three weeks, wreak havoc with your schedule and possibly delay the project. The Roadmap development process is the time and place to prepare for as many "what if" scenarios as possible.

Information Collection

The information collection exercise must be detailed enough to instill confidence in the executive management team. It must cover the "who, what, when, where and how" with more rigor than other initiatives due to the additional perceived risk of offsourcing. You must be prepared to "dig in" to get the data and to budget the time required to interview key personnel and solicit relevant source documentation.

The summary list of both categories of information and a few specific information elements is shown in the table below.

■ Offshore / Nearshore
   - What functions
   - Who is performing
■
  Product/Service
   - Collateral/functional
   - Technical specs
   - System documentation
   - Training materials
■
  Organizational
   - Charts by division
   - Location information
■
  Infrastructure
   - Network providers
   - Development environment
   - Maintenance systems
   - CRM system
   - e-mail system
   - Content management system
   - Release management system
   - Licensing arrangements

■ Process/Methodologies
   - Development process
   - Project management methodology
   - Build process
   - Maintenance/emergency fix process
   - Q/A process

■ Financial
   - Offshore/outsourcing objectives
   - Base case financials for each area
    > both direct and indirect costs

■ Maintenance
   - Calls per month
   - Average duration of calls
   - Bug fixes per month
   - Number of customers

■ Set up brainstorming session
   - Service levels
   - Governance model
   - Benefits timing

Figure 13: Information Collection Categories

Opportunity Prioritization

The Roadmap adds further scrutiny to prioritization of opportunities identified in the Business Case. You will have received significant executive feedback from the presentation of the Business Case and will now begin to possess the gritty details that will ultimately make the difference between inclusion and exclusion.

Consider taking the initial ranking criteria and building a formal prioritization model. It should look at each potential area in terms of financial benefit, investment requirements, process complexity, infrastructure requirements, change management complexity and estimated time to results. Assign a numerical scale to each of the criteria, weighting the areas based upon the bias of your organization. You can then run the model to examine and compare different opportunities.

Expect to go through several iterations of this process toward the end of the Roadmap and in the final stages of gaining approval to implement the first couple of processes. Depending on your team, this can be an emotional exercise that requires much discussion regarding not only the values assigned for each opportunity, but also the relative weighting of criteria in the model. Once the model is agreed upon and the first initiative has been reviewed, adding additional processes should become easier.

Interview, Analyze & Validate

From the Business Case and understanding of the structural options you probably have a strong direction in mind, but you have not necessarily utilized all areas of expertise within the organization. The Business Case team made numerous assumptions regarding technical, transition, human resource, legal and other areas to build the cost versus benefit analysis. The Roadmap team will draw a wider circle of experts into the fold. They will work to confirm these assumptions and expand the analysis of prioritization goals, critical success factors, transition issues and change management activities, which will in turn feed the definition of initial entry strategy and subsequent phases. Other constituents that must be considered include:

- **Business unit leaders**—The business unit leaders will be intimately involved in the Roadmap to define the most attractive portfolio prospects, evaluate detailed costs/benefits of those processes, review improvements required to achieve success and determine infrastructure needs. Ultimately they must support the recommendations or the Roadmap will hit a brick wall. They must believe that the operational efficiencies can be achieved with the appropriate ROI.

- **Process owners**—A process owner is an individual or group that consumes the output of your organization. They may be located internally or externally. As you move into the Offsourcing Roadmap phase, they are key constituents that need to be informed and apprised of the process. They may raise serious objections if they feel that the quality of your end product or service is at risk of being impaired, so come prepared to share your data. Begin with a discussion of market trends, competitive actions and the positive financial and service level impacts that going offshore might have on your ability to provision them.

- **Legal**—At a minimum your legal team will be required to review vendor contracts, and at a maximum they will be responsible for setting up an international subsidiary. They must understand the risks and will develop their own legal/litigation risk assessment. Their involvement will dramatically increase once you get into larger-scale outsourcing scenarios where the risks and contract complexity increase. The team's input and understanding of the offshore legal structure and how recourse can be achieved is a must. Once you get beyond the Roadmap and actually look at potential providers it will be beneficial to have your in-house legal team work with the offshore legal team to ensure a mutual understanding of the structure of both entities

- **Financial/accounting**—These groups will likely be involved to review numbers and assumptions, so if the opportunity presents itself, recruiting them into the process to "own the numbers" will be beneficial. They can rapidly validate key financial metrics and assumptions such as overhead rates and severance costs (if applicable) and can field questions that could arise over billing practices if a vendor is involved. Consider having them deliver a part of your executive presentation, extolling the virtues of the cost/benefit analysis.

- **Human resources**—Terminations, furloughs, new hires in existing positions, travel policies, training: there is much for the HR team to do. If yours happens to be a union shop, HR's involvement should start as early as the initial Business Case to understand possible ramifications of the plan and how best to deal with any additional HR-related issues.

- **Customer support**—If you are looking to offsource any function related to customer support, get the customer support team involved early in the process. The initiative will impact them in potentially all areas. Key statistics that are required to size up the offshore versus onshore capability, particularly regarding communications, problem resolution, trouble ticketing, CRM application access and many other facets that ultimately touch your customer, must be defined, reviewed and agreed to by the customer support organization. This is also a focal area to consider as the Roadmap is progressing: What is the potential impact on our customers? How can we maintain or improve customer support with an offshore-based solution?

- **Application development**—Your application development group will probably be involved in this effort from the beginning if the offshore initiative has anything to do with either application development or application maintenance. The application development group will need to help develop the process enhancements and governance model for managing the initiative. They will also have to define the software development tools and support infrastructure required for either the application development or maintenance function. This will be a significant area in initiatives that involve application development processes. You will have licenses that need to be reviewed, purchased or transferred, and human resource impacts will be inevitably felt in this area. The buy-in and confidence in the solution must be supported, and defined, by this group.

- **IT/infrastructure**—The communications, facilities, systems and related issues are likely to require the most lead time of any area. A review of internal policies and procedures might be necessary before permitting vendors to use some of your systems.

The IT group, which most likely owns all software-related contracts, will have to research and verify costs for all software license issues. This group will need to arrange for the pooling of buying power with your vendors to set up voice and data communications. It may also be necessary for the IT group to put someone on the ground in the offshore country for a period of time. Consider hiring someone from the offshore firm to report directly to the IT group in order to maintain certain service levels of communications and system uptime. If you are looking to use offshore resources for a call center or maintenance group, both communications and CRM system access must be addressed, or at a minimum integration to those systems will be required. The IT group will be involved heavily during the Roadmap phase, so get them involved early in the process.

Developing the Appropriate Entry Strategy

The entry strategy or scenario modeling is at the crux of the Roadmap. How, when and on what scale should the organization go offshore?

At this juncture you should have all the requisite information to begin building your scenarios. Your summary level options will resemble some variation of the following diagram:

	Option 1 Direct	Option 2 Intermediary	Option 3 Onshore Provider	Option 4 Subsidiary	Option 5 Acquisition	Option 6 BOT*
Offshore country knowledge	H	L	L	H	H	L
Initial capital investment	H	L	L	H	H	M
Time to deploy solution	M	L	L	H	M	M
Regulatory hurdles	M	L	L	H	H	M
Due diligence required	H	M	M	M	H	M
Training	H	M	M	M	M	M
Near-term cost savings	L	M	L	L	L	M
Long-term cost saving	M	H	M	H	H	H

* Build, operation and transfer.

Figure 14: Offshore Entry Strategies

Each scenario has relative merits that must be considered in financial, time-to-market, long-term flexibility and operation complexity dimensions. Be open to conducting a ranking exercise of the different approaches or even to beginning a parallel planning activity if one approach is not an obvious standout above the others for your organization.

You will likely gather much of the information about the organizational readiness and even some of the opportunities from discussions with a limited group of people. As you broaden the range of potential candidates and dig deeper into the operational and financial concerns, you will necessarily rub elbows with more personalities. Expect that many will have strong opinions as to the appropriate entry strategy.

Phased Planning

Once you have established an appropriate entry strategy, you will embark on an intensive planning exercise.

From an operational perspective, the Big Bang approach to implementation may be exciting and even give the team a shot at terrific visibility, but it is also a high-risk strategy. As you develop your Offsourcing Roadmap, we highly recommend building a phased approach for your offshore implementation. One approach might be to elect a three-step process:[16]

- **Pilot**—The goal of the pilot phase is to confirm the efficiency of the business model and its reliability within a broader set of business initiatives. The pilot should have its own set of metrics and performance objectives (probably pulled directly from the Business Case). It will likely take the form of a small project or processing of a limited number of transactions over a 30- to 60-day time frame. You must assume that some investment will be required on your part to bring the pilot team members to a maturity level from which you can compare performance between your domestic and offshore operations.

  Give strong consideration to using a vendor in this first phase even if you plan to have your own capability at some point. This will limit your financial exposure and greatly simplify your ability to pull back should your pilot not achieve the expected success. Consider pushing your vendor to provide the pilot services at cost-recovery mode; remember that the pilot is still part of their sales process. The pilot is intended to verify your business model assumptions and not to teach you how to implement your model. Using an intermediary—someone with experience—in the pilot phase will

---

[16] Chapter 21 provides a detailed discussion of phasing your offshore commitments and building a mature services delivery model for application development: the Offshore Maturity Model.

ultimately pay for itself in saved time and the ability to focus on the objectives of the pilot, and not on learning the environment.

You may want to consider running multiple pilots that can examine different processes, providers or even locations. If so, you should have sufficient personnel to perform them, as each will take some capacity of dedicated resources, depending on the process complexity.

- **Implementation**—Your pilot plan should include a target date when you expect to have the data to show successful execution, and your implementation schedule should be triggered from that date. You can accomplish lots of preparation work in parallel with the pilot phase and in expectation of positive results, thereby narrowing the gap between completion of your pilot and the beginning of your full implementation. You will have to weigh the costs versus benefits of making investments in the full implementation prior to completion of the pilot. The high-level plan shown in Figure 9 below is just an example, but the key time frames that impact full implementation are the process enhancements and infrastructure deployment. These two end dates will have the largest impact on the overall schedule. Many of the other tasks can be performed in parallel but these two cannot, and they typically have the longest lead times.

- **Optimization**—The optimization phase is really an ongoing process of improvement guided by your performance metrics. There is an overhead cost associated with each process improvement in terms of training, documentation, downtime and launch activities. Consider scheduling fixed rollouts of these updates on a quarterly or semiannual basis and then backing into the cutoff times for new additions.

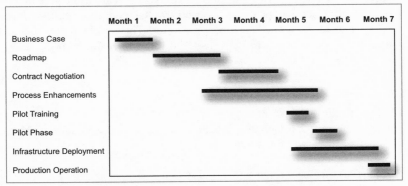

Figure 15: Phased Implementation Plan

A phased approach has a variety of advantages, including:

- **Lower operational risk**—A pilot phase or smaller volume/size initiative will likely have significantly less complexity.

- **Validation of operational assumptions**—Validation of financial expectations is probably the most critical aspect of the pilot. Make sure as you select a pilot type that it depicts a sufficiently complex process that can help you verify key assumptions in your business plan.

- **Lower financial risk**—Because the pilot phase doesn't require long-term commitments, you have less exposure to investing in something that has not yet been proven in your environment. If you are working in a call center of a business process servicing environment, be open to using a modified process during the pilot phase to reduce the technology investment required. If there are some activities that are automated in your current environment but that would require investment to accommodate them in the long-term offshore model, perhaps they could be performed manually with minimal cost during the pilot phase.

- **Organizational learning**—Key managers can be given the opportunity to hone their skills and get any additional training they need prior to the actual launch.

- **Refinement of the model**—The pilot phase allows the organization to learn in a mode of rational experimentation without the fear of destroying a full production run.

- **Rapid vendor analysis**—The pilot gives you a real-world perspective of the potential service provider as well as the country's culture through working in an integrated fashion on a pilot. This is always a very sound investment and one that must be factored into the business model and plan from day one.

Other Considerations

In addition to the entry strategy and operational planning, you should deliver complete plans in a number of other areas as part of the Roadmap. Many of these items are covered in depth in later chapters:

- **Infrastructure and tools**—Developed in collaboration with your IT group, this plan will document the hardware, software and physical infrastructure required to support the organization. In a build scenario, this will require significant time and resources to accomplish.

- **Process**—The current state plan was documented as part of the information collection exercise. The future state will be created as part of the implementation plan. If you plan to use a vendor, they should be able to provide you with a model of their current process.

- **Administration and governance**—This plan presents the approach to chain of command, conflict resolution and ongoing documentation requirements. It will contain the approval process and sign-offs required to inform both the internal and external communities.

- **Personnel**—The onshore/offshore division of work will be drawn up as part of the process plan. The personnel plan may also include the training approach, or this may be documented separately as part of the change management plan. The personnel plan should be developed with your human resources department to identify the criteria and timing for any potential reductions in force.

- **Change management/communications**—This should include a timetable for the form and timing of announcements to the organization as well as specific programs that will be made available to affected resources. The actual messaging may be developed at the time of implementation, but the plan should be developed as part of the Roadmap. (See Chapter 17.)

- **Contingency and disaster recovery planning**—Contingency planning in the context of the Roadmap should also include process contingency issues such as pilots. What will you do if your pilot is only marginally successful? Will you do another pilot with a different vendor? What if you elect to build your own center only to find that the implementation time frame is prohibitively long? These issues should be captured and documented as part of the Offsourcing Roadmap. (See Chapter 15 for a discussion on DRP.)

- **Vendor selection**—You will likely be working with a vendor or vendors throughout the Offsourcing Roadmap phase. A thorough planning process will allow you to expedite your selection process and offload some of the Offsourcing Roadmap work into the hands of your potential vendor. (See Chapter 12.)

Presenting the Findings

As in the Business Case, the presentation of the Offsourcing Roadmap findings is a key deliverable of the process. It must be baked into the work plan, previewed with various parties and honed for maximum input. Unlike in the Business Case, however, the Offsourcing Roadmap findings are likely to be communicated to a diverse audience, spanning the company profile from line worker to executive management.

The Offsourcing Roadmap data should be assimilated and communicated on a variety of levels. Consider structuring the information in a combination of spreadsheets, narrative formats and PowerPoint presentations to accommodate the various ways in which your audience will feel must comfortable assimilating the information. You know your audience better than anyone.

Resources and Roadblocks

> *Leveraging a third-party offshore intermediary that knows the players and understands the challenges of offsourcing implementations can reduce risk and accelerate the development of your Business Case and Offsourcing Roadmap.*

Depending on the approach, buy versus build, you may essentially be looking at building a new business. If you decide to build, the Offsourcing Roadmap must be expanded to include resources from additional disciplines. If not, you may take a more virtual approach, in which case a dedicated project manager and a couple of support analysts may be sufficient.

There is a third and possibly best option: Leveraging a third-party offshore intermediary that knows the players and understands the challenges of offsourcing implementations can reduce risk and accelerate the development of your Business Case and Offsourcing Roadmap. They can bring market knowledge and experience in deploying these types of solutions. This translates into lower long-term costs and faster return on investment for you. However, beware of possible conflict of interest: in the event that you select one of the offshore providers to execute the Roadmap be sure to understand their strategy capabilities and don't be surprised if the entry option includes their own organization.

The Roadmap will also require some level of change management, which is why a key critical success factor is having executive sponsorship from the beginning. As you construct the model demonstrating a goal state of reduced costs, there are likely to be reduced domestic outlays for key functions within the organization. The implication is one of staff reduction.

Expect that the Roadmap team will encounter roadblocks, and that those who are skeptical or fear cutbacks will find numerous reasons to slow down or stop this initiative. The naysayers will want to inject new information into your process, thereby delaying your schedule in an attempt to kill or sidetrack the initiative. Of this you can be absolutely certain. Remain vigilant and focus on the facts. It is easy to get bogged down in a form of "paralysis through analysis," and if this occurs for an extended period the initiative will be at risk.

Third-party involvement should allow you to defer some of the potential change management issues until a later date. The bottom line is that if you allow barriers to get in your way, they will.

Summary

The Offsourcing Roadmap is a detailed planning process designed to get you from the Business Case to the "go live" event. This is the most critical stage in your journey to offsourcing. If the Roadmap is performed to the appropriate level of detail and the executive level of your organization agrees with the approach and findings, you should have a smooth transition to a fully operational offsourced operation. During creation of the Roadmap you will confirm assumptions; document objectives; identify possible vendors, resources and activities that you must engage; and finally rework the Business Case as per the final solution model.

The Offsourcing Roadmap will broaden the number of people "in the know" about the initiative. This can have both positive and negative implications, since you will now begin working with people who are likely to be directly impacted by the changes. Be prepared to proactively answer questions as they arise and begin working on an internal communications plan. Chapter 17 provides additional guidance on the subjects of communication and change management.

Chapter 11 Summary
Developing an Offsourcing Roadmap

Chapter Theme

The Offsourcing Roadmap is a detailed planning exercise taking the organization from financial case to transition offshore. In addition to data collection activities, it includes rigorous analysis and the synthesis of the right target operating model for your organization. As the model gels, the Business Case is updated to reflect final assumptions.

- ☐ **Opportunity prioritization**
- ☐ **Finalize strategy**
- ☐ **Detailed assumptions**
- ☐ **Investment requirements**
- ☐ **ROI plan**
- ☐ **Cultural integration plan**

Key Points

The Roadmap can take as few as 4 weeks and as long as 6 weeks depending on the size of the organization and the scope of offsourcing that is envisioned. Experience will accelerate the ability to identify options, address transition plans and deal with the many contractual, change management, and cultural integration issues.

- ☐ **Six-Phase process**
- ☐ **4 to 6 Weeks**
- ☐ **Experience is invaluable**
- ☐ **Involve key parts of your organization**
- ☐ **Communications plan**

Reader Take-Away

You should have a clear understanding of the planning activities and areas that must be addressed in preparing for a successful offsourcing initiative. The Offsourcing Roadmap addresses all of the key areas required to ensure a smooth transition. You will also gain an appreciation for the importance of phasing activities to reduce risk and maximize the probability of success.

Questions for Consideration

- ☐ Have you established a prioritization model for your offsourcing initiatives?
- ☐ Has the organization established an offsourcing entry strategy?
- ☐ Have you established a phased implementation schedule for your approach?
- ☐ Have you adequately researched, prepared and involved the required parties in your Roadmap development?
- ☐ Would the organization benefit from the experience of a third party in the planning process?

Chapter 12

Selecting a Vendor

Overview

You have your Business Case, your Offsourcing Roadmap and a mandate to move forward with the solution from a third party. Now you are faced with the question, Which one? Fortunately, the market for many of these services is well developed and you can find multiple service providers. Certainly in the call center and software development and maintenance arenas, competition is not only established, but cutthroat. BPO services will vary largely in the level of complexity offered, with items like medical transcription being well developed and stock portfolio management services less so.

Broadly speaking you will have two options to approaching the vendor selection process: Go it alone or work with a third-party intermediary that knows the market. Each has its merits, but (at the risk of sounding self-serving) the speed, experience and market knowledge that a third party can bring to the table has the potential to pay for itself many times over in the form of lower risk, better pricing and faster, more thorough implementations.

As you consider the following selection process, consider the cost and time required to truly validate data you gather without prior experience in the field.

Establishing Your Criteria

The first priority is to determine what it is that you think you want. In your Business Case you have devoted considerable time to establishing your objective and possibly what you need in a service provider.

Based on the processes and magnitude of your deployment for a Phase 1 solution and beyond, you will want to consider many of the following criteria:

- **Clients**—For whom have they worked before and with whom are they currently doing business? If yours is a multibillion-dollar company you can afford to invest millions in the selection process. For everyone else, the names of those who have gone before is important.

- **Infrastructure**—A world-class facility will have a combination of redundant data and voice connectivity; redundant power supply including power grids, batteries and diesel generation; physical security and space capacity.

▪ **Technology**—What type of technology does the organization offer? Does it rely on custom built or client server systems solutions or has it invested in package-based, supported solutions? In an application development or maintenance environment, this naturally is related to the skill sets of the individual team members. Experience suggests that it is not so important where they performed the work, but whether they performed it.

▪ **Pricing**—Time and material rates give the provider little incentive to improve performance; and yet without a baseline, the rational provider will be unwilling to make contractual commitments. Low cost does not mean low quality, but it is reasonable to expect some trade-off. You will enjoy tremendous savings by going offshore, so **don't become overly focused on price, especially the hourly cost.** Consider the discussion in Chapter 5 regarding the Total Cost to Offsource and the blend of onshore and offshore expenses. Your objective must be to establish the quality goal and then negotiate the best price based on the TCO for the level of quality that you desire.

▪ **Quality control**—Does the vendor have a quality control process? How long has it been in place? Are they affiliated with external certification boards? And what is their record of continuous improvement? Most importantly, what incentives are being offered to individuals in the organization to deliver improvements?

▪ **Organization**—What is the experience level and track record of the management team? How long has the organization been in business and how well financed is it? Who are its backers and what is the corporate vision? How much does it expect to grow and what investments has it made to manage that growth?

▪ **Political risk**—What is the internal and external political risk in the country where the facility you plan to use is located? How might political or economic calamities impact the vendor organization and ultimately your program?

▪ **Lifestyle considerations**—Do you plan to spend long periods in the location in question? If so, what is that experience likely to be? How accessible is the location? How are the working conditions? How are the living conditions and the weather? All of these have an impact on the likelihood that individuals will get on a plane and deal with issues that are best handled in person rather than letting them go untended until they become serious problems.

- **Location**—What country or even area of a country has the most desirable operating environment, and how will that impact the vendor's ability to service you? What if you have transnational needs? Can this vendor grow beyond the borders of its current geography?

Certainly this is not an exhaustive list, and your organization will be particularly sensitive to some areas and not so sensitive to others. One recommended approach is to break the items above into multiple specific areas whose value can be measured. The larger groupings can then be given a weighting relative to one another, possibly adding up to around 100%. You can thereby fashion an empirical model out of a combination of numerical and qualitatively assumptions and data. (Note: The difference between two equally competent vendors can be nothing more than an arbitrary assumption on the weightings, so it is often instructive to run the numbers with more than one weighting scenario.)

In addition to the above issues, questions first raised in the Business Case about focus, skill and scale should be reexamined at a more detailed level. These provide great insight into the weighting of different areas of the model we have discussed. A focus on obtaining skill means that quality control and possibly technology may be important, whereas a focus on gaining scale (lowest unit cost) may mean that you should be dealing with the largest vendors (without the greatest economies of scale) and the best potential pricing.

You will likely trade some cost for enhanced skill and enjoy some level of benefit in more than one dimension.

Doing the Research

When it comes to identifying which companies have the capabilities and the track records to meet your goals, there are many different sources of information:

> *Fair play and openness will ensure that you get the best effort from those who are courting your business.*

- **Trade or industry organizations**—These groups can offer you the broadest set of information on the participants in the areas in which you seek services.

- **Regional marketing groups**—Numerous regional marketing/trade promotion groups are actively promoting their own territories even within countries. These can be excellent sources of information about the players operating in the geographies that interest you.

- **Colleagues**—As the offshore phenomenon becomes more mainstream, there are necessarily more professionals who have had a hand in either vendor selection or the implementation process.

- **Competing vendors**—You might feel uncomfortable asking the question, but most companies have a good idea as to who their competition is. There is nothing unethical or unseemly about asking who a company's competitors are so long as you are candid about your reasons for asking.

- **Third-party specialists**—The large technology analyst groups are all gearing up practices and perspectives to accommodate the emergence of the offshore space. They can provide guidance on many of the market information statistics and the providers, but beware: There is no substitute for practical, hands-on implementation experience in this market. Be sure that you understand the frame of reference from which your specialist is working. Is it academic or real life?

Managing the Process

Vendor selection processes can be time-consuming and painful. It requires enormous amounts of time to research, contact, coordinate, test, validate and otherwise probe, compare and vet the group with which you ultimately decide to do business. One recent anecdote concerns a company that involved 40 people full time in conducting an inquiry that solicited information from over 50 organizations, conducted 40 site visits and ultimately approved 3 vendors for business.[17]

Worse, unless you have preexisting knowledge, you can expect to begin with one set of criteria and, based on your learning curve, potentially end up with another one. This may frustrate your superiors, delay your timeline and raise issues with the vendors, since there is a cost associated with their sales process and a limit to what they are willing to spend.

That said, a clear, transparent process should allow you to absorb any learning while limiting the investment that your potential vendors are required to make and ultimately getting the best information.

Vendor Selection Process

The first step is to recognize that the vendor selection process should be recognized as just that: a process. To work well, it requires a project plan, specific deliverables, commitment to dates and clear objectives. This plan should be communicated openly to the vendor community. Fair play and openness will ensure that you get the best effort from those who are courting your business. While the ultimate goal of a vendor is to win your business, a

---

[17] The company in question is a large multinational for which this process may have made sense, but it raises the question of whether the company could have built a new facility for the cost of this exercise.

professional process will give you the option of going back to a vendor that you have not selected for previous pieces of business.

Request for Information

After doing your research and establishing a set of base criteria, you will want to write and send a request for information (RFI). The RFI is intended to gather demographic information on companies with which you believe that you have an interest in doing business. It will solicit standard information about history, size, clients, service capabilities and other criteria.

Request for Proposal and Preliminary Pricing

Step two is to solicit more project-specific information, as by a request for proposal (RFP). By necessity this will involve sharing information with the potential vendor about your offsourcing goals.

Items that you will want to consider and have in place are:

- **Overview of objectives**—This may include a project description, environment overview or proposed operation. This will allow the vendors to target their solution description to your needs. Be sure to include information about size, phasing, commitments, variability and unique operating requirements.

- **Rigid and flexible response format**—Be firm in your demands for specific information regarding capabilities, but if at all possible allow the vendors flexibility in how they operationally approach the problem. Their model will likely be the most cost efficient one for them—and therefore, in the long run, for you.

- **Nondisclosure agreement**—Vendors may ask that you sign mutual nondisclosure agreements, since they will be sharing proprietary information with you. You should not be concerned by this except to the extent that it may apply to pricing and you want to share the target price in the context of a final pricing negotiation.

- **Sample contract**—It is often a good idea to request a sample contract at this stage, since this may also give you an early indication of the ease with which you can work with the vendor. There are two reasons:

- **Context**—You will benefit from seeing a variety of approaches to contractually frame what are probably very similar services. This may be useful to you when you negotiate the final agreement. In addition, you may learn something about the flexibility or inflexibility with which the vendor approaches business relationships.

▪ **Timing**—Once you have decided on a vendor, you will likely be very anxious to move on to implementation. After all, you have gone through a Business Case and Offsourcing Roadmap planning process and are now ready to move into execution. By previewing the Master Services Agreements early, you won't have to waste time with vendors with whom you are unlikely to reach agreement or to cajole your overworked legal staff into doing a rush job on a very important document.

Presentations

Once you have identified a short list of vendors to present their solutions, be prepared to invest some time and effort into maximizing your opportunity to understand their capabilities. Consider the following:

▪ **Off-site meeting place**—You have a business to run and you may from time to time be called out to address real-time issues, but an offsite meeting place provides focus away from distractions. If you are working under a veil of silence, it will also help to ensure that you do not inadvertently advertise the process that you are conducting.

▪ **Confirmed agenda**—Be sure to provide a scripted agenda that guarantees that you will have an opportunity to understand the issues important to you.

▪ **Overview of your operation**—After introductions, be sure to spend time reviewing your needs and possibly giving an overview of your operations. This may be the first time that you have met with the vendor representatives. A review of your operations and needs will allow them to do a better job of informing you of their capabilities and applicability to your environment. The goal is to get the best information with the least investment of time on everyone's part.

▪ **Videoconferencing capability**—Plan to use a facility with videoconferencing capability if one is available to you. Most offshore operations are equipped with this type of facility, so consider including introductions to the operations group, the people who will actually be providing you with service, as part of the presentation.

Client References

Vendors guard these interactions jealously since they are asking their customers to spend scarce time on something with no discernable payback. Consider holding back on seeking client references until you are sure that the vendor meets all known requirements and you are moving into final decision-making mode. Your vendors will appreciate this consideration.

When you do speak with references, you will undoubtedly make calls to clients that have had smashing successes. They are references because they are happy; but what of the clients that were not so happy? An organization's ability to engage in constructive self-criticism says a lot about its ability to continue to improve. Have the vendor talk you through projects that have not been a success and understand what action was taken internally in response.

When it comes to the logistics of the calls themselves, keep a few simple rules in mind:

- Honor the time frame that you have allotted.
- Be on time.
- Come prepared with your questions. If you can get them a copy of the more technical questions in advance, you may be able to gather more information on the call.

Finally, follow up with your contact information and a thank you. The reference may later recall a point that he or she wants to share with you or you may want to swap best practices at some point. Remember, you will be a customer one day, too.

Site Visits

Site visits are always an option, but by the time you have moved through the RFP, presentations and client references, you have to ask yourself whether a visit is worth it. A site visit requires a significant investment in time and expense to spend very little time on the ground.

The answer is "yes" if one of the following is true:

- **Complex strategic initiative**—Is offsourcing part of a complex strategic initiative and not simply a more straightforward cost-saving exercise? Time on the ground will allow you to assess the operational capabilities and personnel that will ultimately influence your success.

- **High switching costs**—Will your initiative involve a long learning curve on the part of the vendor? Will you be building intellectual capital in the vendor organization that makes it very difficult to change providers?

Many buyers have experienced successful implementations having never visited the offshore location; however, a graphic understanding of the operational environment never hurts. Third parties assisting you in your selection process that have spent time on the ground can also provide valuable insights that may render this activity needless.

Final Pricing and Reaching Closure

At this point in the process your head is probably swimming with a deluge of information. In the worst-case scenario you have seen RFIs, RFPs, preliminary pricing, call monitoring (for call center outsourcing), site visits and have sat in on countless conference calls. Perhaps there is a clear winner or perhaps there is simply too much undifferentiated information to make a decision.

If there is minimal differentiation between finalists, final pricing may prove an easy way to get to a decision, but beware of simply going for the low bidder. You began this process with a set of criteria that the team agreed provided a basis for evaluating the prospective service providers. Do not lose sight of these criteria as you enter the home stretch and are wined and dined by very capable and charming business development executives.

Summary

The vendor selection process can be daunting, especially if it's your first time out. If you're equipped with a sound Business Case and Offsourcing Roadmap, your goals should already be clear; the rest is just determining the vendors' ability to help you meet those goals optimally. Your objectives, experience and comfort level should all play a role in the approach that you take to this exercise. If you have no prior experience but have a huge budget to spend and unlimited time, a 50-vendor RFI and world tour may be an appealing way to spend a year. For the rest of us, though, time and money are apt to be more precious. Third-party advisors can help you navigate through the seemingly limitless morass of information, helping you to avoid the paralysis-through-analysis trap.

The offshore vendor selection process is similar to that of hiring a domestic provider, but there are notable differences:

- Variability of quality is greater.
- Cost of selection is higher.
- Visibility within your organization may be greater.
- Price of failure can be more significant.
- Upside from success can be staggering.

Nevertheless, there are many outstanding offshore vendors doing great work. Our experience suggests that many implementation failures result from poor governance, inadequate client involvement and a hands-off approach that is independent of the vendor origination process.

Chapter 12 Summary
Selecting Vendor(s)

Chapter Theme

Vendor selection can be a time-consuming and expensive exercise. The process can be accelerated significantly by establishing your criteria early and then investing in building a selection process that is rigorous, open and fair.

- ❑ **Know the vendor**
- ❑ **Understand onshore vs offshore resources**
- ❑ **Review contracts**
- ❑ **Investment requirements**
- ❑ **ROI plan**

Key Points

Establish a detailed process that requires vendors to answer specific requests in a way that allows you to correlate data. Provide sufficient flexibility for them to elaborate value-added or differentiated components of their service offerings. Site visits can be beneficial, but are probably more important for internal selling purposes than truly understanding vendor capabilities.

- ❑ **Desired geography**
- ❑ **Cultural fit**
- ❑ **Appropriate talent**
- ❑ **Flexible pricing**
- ❑ **Process maturity**
- ❑ **Governance adherence**
- ❑ **Understanding switching costs**

Reader Take-Away

Vendor selection in an offshore environment involves gathering far more data than is customary in a domestic environment, since the variability of quality is likely to be higher and the personal relationships that can be leveraged to validate information fewer. A third party can take time and risk out of the process while allowing you to focus on your implementation objectives and avoid the paralysis-through-analysis trap.

Questions for Consideration

- ❑ Which vendor selection criteria will be important for your organization?
- ❑ Have you adequately educated key internal stakeholders on; offsourcing; the roadblocks; pitfalls; and benefits?
- ❑ Have you sought the assistance of a third-party intermediary to give you advice on offsourcing or development of the Roadmap?
- ❑ Have you thoroughly researched the options?
- ❑ Have you planned a selection process that will speed information gathering and allow you to negotiation a win-win contract while protecting you?
- ❑ Have you determined what your switching costs might be if the initial selection does not meet your expectations?

Part III: Executing the Plan

Chapter 13

Negotiating Offsourcing Contracts

Overview

You have found your vendor or vendors, agreed on scope of services, defined the process for meeting the service requirements and deliverables, established an acceptable pricing scenario and now must try to conclude a contract. This is where the fun begins.

One of the critical mistakes companies often make is to go straight to contract negotiation without first establishing a sufficiently detailed statement of work or requirements document that both parties understand and agree to. The process can break down as assumptions take over.

Contracts provide an interesting study into how companies manage expectations, how they view measurements and metrics and, most important, what they think they are actually acquiring. As the lead business executive for offsourcing, your objective will be to drive a business arrangement while others take on the responsibility of adequately protecting the assets and rights of your organization through the appropriate legal language. Working with an attorney who possesses strong business acumen will ease the process, but even so you should commit to writing a set of principles that you want the contract to reflect. Clear objectives, expectations, requirements, risks and mitigation strategies, as well as a critical success factor (noted above), should ring through the contract.

Your negotiation is likely to be some blend of the following approaches:

- **Self-negotiated**—In this arrangement you may be on your own to negotiate the deal along with your legal department, which will have numerous other responsibilities and probably only limited experience in the geography selected. If your legal team has limited to no experience in developing contracts in international locations or in general with international company structures, solicit the support of an experienced international legal firm.

- **Joint negotiated**—In this approach the contract is negotiated with an external specialist, the business executive and your legal team. Quite often, the third party will do most of the negotiating until the end, when the business executive will come in to finalize and sign.

For large-scale outsourcing deals the organization will likely seek outside counsel with specific experience in outsourcing and international law, possibly in conjunction with a third party that has valuable market knowledge and metrics knowledge.

Whether you are working alone or as part of a team, understanding some of the offsourcing-specific risks and challenges will help you to build a high-quality contract. In this chapter we provide an overview of issues that you should address with your provider.

One Size Does Not Fit All

The scope of IT-enabled services is enormous, though you may purchase more than one type from a single vendor. Each activity—pilot project, staff augmentation, project consulting, maintenance, operations outsourcing, development outsourcing or business process outsourcing—has its own objectives, risks and metrics, so be wary of trying to morph one type of contract into something that it is not. It will usually end up being sloppy and potentially ambiguous. This can result in contractual disputes and significant strain on business relationships, with the potential of forcing you to seek additional vendors.

Also, do not assume that the vendor has a particularly good baseline from which to work. Your RFP process should have provided you with a good understanding of the legal issues involved with the provisioning of the service in question. Be mindful of your obligations under the nondisclosure agreements that you have signed, but put the knowledge that you have gained during the selection process to good use.

Outsourcing versus Offsourcing

Consider the maturity and scale of the offshore industry. If you are looking to achieve a full outsourcing pact involving acquisition of personnel and assets, you may find that the market is not yet ready to absorb the type of deal you seek. Contracts like these are what the large-scale domestic outsourcers use in the more traditional outsourcing arrangements. The offshore vendors are simply not large enough to take on this type of risk or make the cash outlay required to structure arrangements of this scale while simultaneously absorbing US or Western European people and assets. There are call center and BPO contracts being written today that somewhat resemble those for outsourcing, only in the sense that the parties are transferring control of a particular process; but it is not a model in which they are taking on your people or transferring assets which are the traditional outsourcing arrangements..

To put it in perspective, the revenues of the largest IT company in India are approximately $700 million—small when compared to the largest US outsourcers. As the Indian and Philippine firms grow in size and financial strength, they will doubtless become players in the outsourcing space, but this will take some time.

Redundancy in Providers

Simultaneous negotiation with short-listed providers is an option in getting the best contract. Simultaneous contracting of the parties can also add value to your organization if you have sufficient size to support it. In the short term it offers a rapid approach to negotiating the "best price" while in the medium term it allows you to assess the capabilities of organizations dealing with similar environmental constraints. If you are able to establish long-term value-added relationships with multiple providers, you will benefit from a built-in low-cost competitive bidding environment.

As with other aspects of the process, recognize the overhead that you will incur by taking on an additional vendor and determine if it makes sense versus the potential savings you expect in your offsourcing endeavor.

Negotiation Points

As you review the contract, keep in mind that there are a number of ways to insulate your company from vendor-related risk:

- **Jurisdiction**—It is advisable to deal with a vendor that has a legal presence in the United States. This permits you to have recourse within the US courts in the event of a dispute. Further, you should seek to have the US jurisdiction within the state of your choosing.

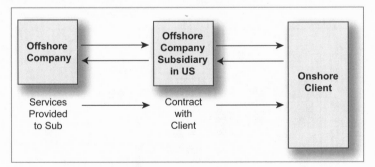

Figure 16: Typical Offshore Company Structure

- **Service level agreements**—These are highly subject to the environment and bear many similarities to those seen in domestic environments; however, there may be some differences. Your vendor selection in any offshore IT-enabled service area is in part based upon backup connectivity, power and other capabilities demonstrated during the courting process. If the service level guarantees are not met as a result of vendor business continuity planning failures, then they should be reflected in the contract.

- **Currency of payments**—Unless you have some type of offsetting foreign currency accounts receivable function, it is advisable to write your contract in US dollars. This releases you from the risk of exchange rate swings.

- **Exit clauses**—Consider pushing for a pilot phase at some reduced cost that allows you and the vendor to establish quality, volume and performance metrics. This pilot phase may be done at a reduced rate (cost recovery) with a prenegotiated move to full pricing beyond the trial period. If you have identified high potential switching costs in your analysis, be sure to construct exit clauses that will minimize them in the event that change is required.

- **Intellectual property**—You own it. In the United States the ownership and IP rights are clearly specified in the contract as "work made for hire." Specific clauses or attachments articulate the intellectual property owned, sometimes in great detail. This can still be done when dealing with the offshore company that has a US-incorporated entity. The challenge is that the IP issues will probably not arise in the US; they will arise in the offshore country. There is no fail-safe way to approach this other than to ensure that contracts stipulate termination, cause and litigation options if there are issues with either IP or confidentiality.

- **Rates**—Offshore rates are highly competitive, and the increasingly competitive environment is exerting downward pressure on costs. The diagram below shows the ranges of costs in several locations around the world.

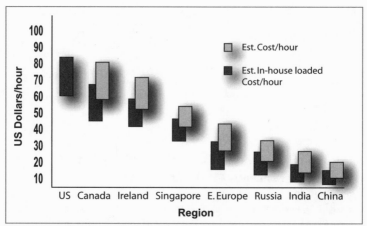

Figure 17: Typical Offshore Rates and Costs by Country

There is a range of costs by country that breaks down further by skill or specific offering within the venue. A quarterly competitive review of rate structures with the option to renegotiate based on the market conditions is recommended in some cases. The risk to be weighed is that market pressures may also drive some rates up over time as the demand for specific skill sets increases. However, we do not see this happening anytime soon.

- **Exclusivity**—*We strongly recommend against exclusivity clauses under any scenario short of significant equity investment.* Even then, expect a rocky road and be doubly sure to build in strict SLAs and termination clauses. The

> *Once you sign up for exclusivity, you lose significant negotiating power.*

  problem is one of expectations and incentives: once you sign up for exclusivity, you lose significant negotiating power. Let levels of exclusivity be based on performance over time and not rosy financial based on long-term/exclusive relationships.

- **Travel**—Travel falls under three categories: 1) travel requested by the client, 2) travel that is part of a fixed price/scope arrangement or 3) travel by management.

  If the client requests to have key people on site for short or extended periods of time, the client should pay the travel expenses. However, both parties should share training and initial service establishment costs. There are costs associated with getting a relationship moving and into production, and these costs should be bundled into a project initiation budget.

- **Communications**—Communications may account for a significant portion of the infrastructure costs for your offsourced solution. Many of the larger firms have dedicated network facilities that extend to the US that may or may not come bundled in with your pricing. If it is not bundled, remember that you must factor in the direct line/service cost plus usage and installation, and be specific about understanding the difference between the data and voice communications setups and costs.

  In order to expedite or in some cases even get new service, you may need to pay additional "agency" or service tips. This amounts to an expediting fee and is usually nominal. Understand what is typical and push as much of this as possible onto your vendor. Be wary of terms that force you to assume liability for communication breakdowns in the United States, but do not give the same liability to your provider. An opening position of mutuality of performance should be considered reasonable.

- **Hardware**—Most of the vendor firms have their own desktop computers; but if key people have to travel back and forth to the US they should have laptops. During the contract development process make sure you understand specifically what the vendor has and does not have. If more hardware is necessary, get this information in writing.

- **Software**—Software is a slightly more complex issue in terms of both providing it to the partner and dealing with the maintenance. Beware when the offshore provider wants you to provide all software licenses. Some software companies will increase their maintenance fees significantly for use offshore and add a license kicker to accommodate your moving a software license that you own to an offshore location. We have seen companies put a 100% offshore premium on a per-user basis plus adding significant maintenance percentages on top. This is potentially one of those hidden costs that must be thoroughly researched and understood.

  During the Roadmap phase make sure that you have assessed the software needs in detail. This will entail reviewing all of the software license agreements and talking to those vendors. Once you understand the costs of transferring or adding licenses, have the vendor assess the best deal they can get in country. Once you have done the detailed comparison you can make the decision. Also, include limits or stipulations in the contract in the event that government regulatory agencies change their software policies. Make sure this is a shared risk situation, so that you do not find yourself with significant exposure down the road.

- **Governance model**—Develop a governance model that fits into your company and culture as part of your Offsourcing Roadmap and then build specifications of the process, checks and balances into the contract. Work with your vendor to help them understand the importance of the approach and the positive impact it should have on the initiative's success. Some vendors may push back in an effort to retain a model that is more comfortable and traditional for them, but beware: Traditional approaches have demonstrated limitations. For more information refer to Chapter 14 on the Governance Model.

- **Training**—Base training of personnel should be done on the vendor's nickel. Program-specific training is a negotiation point, but a good place to start is at rate commensurate with cost recovery. If you require personnel to be trained on commercial products specific to your environment, then we recommend that you offer to pay for training, but not for the personnel's time while they are in training. It should be enough that you are helping the vendor build more valuable assets.

Best Alternative to Negotiated Agreement

As you are preparing to enter into the negotiation, remember that you may require more than just the knowledge of what you want in order to get it. You should have a Best Alternative to Negotiated Agreement (BATNA) in line to assist in giving you the leverage you want.

Fans of negotiating theory will be familiar to this term. Your BATNA is your fallback position in the event that you are unable to come to terms with a specific vendor. To the extent that you have a strong second candidate, you or your proxy will be in the best position to negotiate a high-quality contract for your organization. There are even accounts of some companies forcing offshore vendors to face off against one another in final three-way negotiations.

Summary

Which elements of your offshore engagement are most critical to your success? Consider this question carefully and, where appropriate, seek advice from legal counsel that has international experience. Document your business arrangement and needs before moving to the legalese, visit with people who have undertaken these types of initiative before and make sure you know whether and how the critical success factors can be measured. Where appropriate ensure you have metrics, expectations and the governance model documented and referenced in the contract

Chapter 13 Summary
Negotiating Offsourcing Contracts

Chapter Theme

Negotiating offsourcing contracts is an extension of the Roadmap process. Remember, your key negotiation points that you should consider as you are working toward a legal understanding with your prospective provider. The negotation phase is the best time to establish a governance model that must be reflected in the agreement.

❏ **Offsourcing is not necessarily outsourcing.**
❏ **Establish a BATNA**
❏ **Roadmap TCO contains costs elements**

Key Points

Understand which costs are covered as part of the contract and which costs you should expect to bear. Be wary of committing to long-term agreements prior to some type of operational success. The deal will still be waiting for you after you have been through the pilot and some operational time has passed. Competition is high and is not likely to slow down any time soon.

❏ **Cultural fit**
❏ **Required talent**
❏ **Flexible pricing**
❏ **Process maturity**
❏ **Governance model**
❏ **Proven results**

Reader Take-Away

You should have a clear sense of many of the terms and negotiation points that you should be seeking as part of the contract negotiation. You should also have a sense that time is on your side during the actual negotiation, as there are many providers apt to be seeking your business. Do not be rushed into exclusive relationships that do not give you the long-term flexibility you require.

Questions for Consideration

❏ What are your objectives and requirements? Have you developed a model for operating roles and accountability?
❏ Is your pilot program defined and have the parties agreed to the operating terms and time frames?
❏ Are you seeking a tactical solution or a long-term strategy?
❏ Have you established your BATNA and are you negotiating with more than one provider?

Chapter 14

Restructuring to Build the Franchise

Overview

In your Business Case and Offsourcing Roadmap you identified a set of financially attractive opportunities with a detailed understanding of the steps required to execute them. The potential benefits from delivering on one or more of the elements of your offshore portfolio are tremendous, but they do not come easily. Depending on the service area, your work may require no small amount of dislocation or "restructuring" of the organization. "Restructuring" is most often equated with job cuts, and in the case of offshore operations that is often (although not always) the case from the perspective of the domestic workforce.

But restructuring for offshore leverage is about much more than simply cutting W-2s. It is about structurally, organizationally and financially positioning the company to take advantage of current and future offshore advantages. Your new work process may require a fundamental rebuilding to split work between on- and offshore locations as you optimize efficiencies—taking advantage of enabling technologies that were simply not available only a few years ago. As you achieve this new model you will have created an offshore "franchise" including governance model, metrics, technology, communications infrastructure, project management tools and quality assurance methods.

The elements of this new franchise, including tools, templates, approaches, personnel and resources, are the building blocks required to launch a new enterprise. As the sponsor you are the master franchise owner and will have the opportunity to replicate the process in other areas of the organization if you are successful. Plan well, lay a strong foundation and your journey will be made easier.

Building the Execution Team

The assistance and input of many people were required to build the Business Case and Offsourcing Roadmap. You might have had members of the executive team, the CFO or controller and individual business unit owners or domain experts as planning partners. In addition you may have had a couple of analysts modeling the numbers, documenting the findings and spending countless hours honing the message. But what about the implementation? What is required of the individuals working on the implementation teams to achieve success?

Clearly, strong leadership is required. For the leader, experience counts; but attitude and good operational and project management skills are paramount—which is fortunate, since individuals with true, deep, offshore change management experience are few and far between. The leader must also be able to span the strategic and the tactical, focusing on resolving specific issues while never taking his or her eye off the long-term goals.

For the leader in particular, a number of qualities are necessary:

- **Communications skills**—Expectations, process, and issues must all be overcommunicated to ensure a harmonious working environment. The leader must be equally comfortable addressing an executive audience and a project team. Further he or she must be able to present information at various levels of abstraction to maintain the attention of these various groups and be a strong motivator.

- **Absence of intimidation**—The leader and the offshore mandate are likely to be viewed within the organization with mixed emotions. It is critical to be able to deal with potential negative reactions by peers and superiors in a constructive fashion and be comfortable working through the internal politics that may arise.

- **Access to key executives/willingness to make decisions**—The project leader must have sponsorship and the complete trust that key executive sponsors are willing to ride the negatives with an absolute belief in the positives of going offshore. The leader must be able to assume the responsibility derived from this executive access to drive decisions quickly and decisively. If an offshore team detects a lack of support or an unwillingness to deal with the tough issues, morale can plummet, attrition can begin and success becomes far more difficult.

For both the leadership and the team members, certain attributes are essential:

- **Commitment to the model**—Commitment was earlier identified as a critical success factor for the organization. It should come as no surprise that we reiterate this CSF at an individual level. The obstacles can be daunting and the challenges significant. Successful execution will require team members that can push on through any difficulties they encounter. Without commitment, team members can grow weary of the process, focus on the easier, onshore solutions and come up with excuses as to why offshore success is not possible.

- **Appreciation for different working styles**—International experience does not necessarily equate to international effectiveness, just as the lack of experience does not preclude excellent performance. Respect, curiosity, professionalism and a willingness to walk a mile in another person's shoes are far more important than the number of stamps in someone's passport. Failure to internalize an appreciation for cultural differences will result in a rapid escalation of frustration. Even with a strong interest in different ways of approaching problems, communications and expectations can get out of sync.

- **Rational experimentation**—Failure is not an option, but nor can you foresee all the tiny variations on your future state model at the outset of the initiative. If you are hitting roadblocks in raising the metrics in your environment, you must be prepared to explore variations on your current approach to break through the logjam. Successful personalities in this environment are those prepared to challenge the status quo, observe and learn, and respond nimbly and creatively to changing circumstances.

- **Flexibility regarding travel**—It is difficult to play a significant role in the development of offshore capabilities without spending at least some time on the ground. Many offshore locations do not rate highly on Western living standard indices and they often require difficult travel to reach. Team members must be prepared to invest the time away from home in sometimes challenging environments to make a contribution to the process. Failure to exhibit this flexibility can lead to trips never taken, diminishing communications over time and a slow unraveling of focus on the optimization of the model.

The process of building a strong execution team is never-ending as people cycle in and out. However, experience suggests that it can take up to nine months, with several changes along the way, in order to create a fully synchronized and motivated team.

Your organization should prepare an indoctrination program for new members and consider periodic refresher exercises where team members have an opportunity to share their frustrations as well as knowledge gained.

Governance Model

The model in Figure 14 below represents two governance models that have worked very well. The traditional modus operandi for the offshore firms has been to provide at least one person on-site as the program manager and coordinator/liaison. Experience suggests that the historical approach may limit the ability of the organization to optimize benefits. On-site managers may have cultural hurdles to overcome that limit their ability to extract the domain expertise, risk management activities and guidance required from the client to optimize the offshore output. This model is described as the vendor model and will work for low-complexity, smaller situations.

In our experience, for more complex, larger and longer-term situations, the partner approach works much more effectively. In this scenario the client will put a program manager on site at the partner location offshore. This program manager works hand-in-hand with the offshore team and in many cases has the final say on key issues. Vendors with whom we have worked are enthusiastic about client presence in the offshore location as a means to minimize communication problems and risks. Make sure that you have your model defined and the appropriate terms and expectations in the agreement.

Defining your terms and expectations and ensuring you have the right people with the right skills and experiences are key elements of success. If you do not have the right model in place and checks and balances are based on your weekly status report, the initiative will not meet your expectations.

Tie the desired operating model into the contract. Make sure that there is a process in place that measures effectiveness and quality. Don't let inexperienced managers run rampant and operate by the seat of their pants.

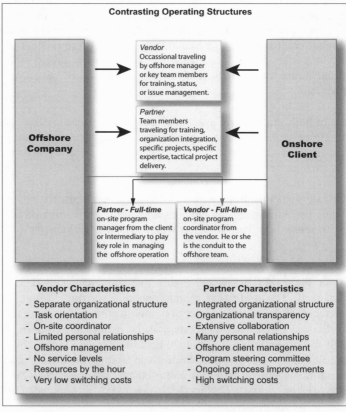

Figure 18: Contrasting Operating Structures

Resource Optimization

As you work through the appropriate placement of resources for your organization in the new environment, you will face tough decisions about how and when to meet the ongoing manpower target in your current facilities. The Roadmap will have determined the target headcount by month that will be key to determine the anticipated ROI; fortunately, there is more than one option available in achieving this goal:

- **Attrition to target size**—Many call center and service bureau facilities have high turnover rates or dramatically fluctuating resources to accommodate seasonal work. With some domestic call centers running at 300% turnover (less in a down economy), the workforce may completely turn over in a 120-day period. This gives you the option of allowing many workers to leave through normal business attrition rather than a large layoff. This approach can be advantageous to the company since it allows you to avoid some severance costs, particularly if local labor laws require longer-term packages in the case of large employee headcount adjustments.

- **Staff reductions**—There will probably come a time when in order to adopt the offshore model you are required to make cuts to the current workforce to meet the ROI and needs of the company. This is an emotional and difficult task, particularly where it involves relationships that have been built over time. It is not easy for any manager. We offer some guidance here:

  o **Low performers**—The most obvious and logical area to address at the outset of the implementation process is the low performers. This is a typical strategy in many industries; for example, most of the best consulting firms have an ongoing policy to reduce the bottom 10% of the performers every 6 to 12 months. This helps the firms maintain a higher level of competencies and performance.

  o **Duplicate functions**—Second, reduce the duplicate functions. Unless your plan called for duplicate functions, the higher-cost area must go. If possible, the top performers in specific areas should be leveraged and moved to other areas.

The following are some key points to consider:

  o **Avoid the "bleed"**—The most economically efficient approach to making cuts is not the recommended one. Be wary of making repeated reductions in force (RIFs) over a sustained period. Some of this may be unavoidable as you move through new phases of your implementation plan, but repeated cuts are bad for morale and erode management's credibility.

o   **Group and individual communication**—It is advisable to convene a group session to inform individuals that they are on the list for cutbacks and to communicate the exit process to them. Once this has been accomplished, defer further questions to one-on-one exit interviews in which you provide detailed information on benefits, counseling and severance.

o   **Survivors' meeting**—Hold a survivors' meeting for those who were not cut but are part of a group that is directly affected. They will have questions and will undoubtedly be frustrated, angry and potentially concerned about their own employment. Your job is to help them through this difficult time.

▪ **New capacity**—Companies in the enviable position of having a growing business may explore the offshore model as a lower-cost approach to gaining new capacity. There is good business sense behind this:

o   **Risk mitigation**—The continued presence of domestic facilities allows the organization to scale rapidly in the event that there is an impediment with the offshore capacity. It may also provide system redundancy in the event of a hardware or software problem.

o   **"Brain trust"**—For companies that have dynamic operations with ongoing changes in needs or programs, the new capacity offshore may be dedicated to the "static" or lower value–added activities. The local capacity may also continue to be used in a role of thought leadership, with new or particularly difficult tasks being part of its long-term responsibilities. Examples of ongoing local activities might include system architecture in software development or new campaign testing in outbound call center environments. The point is that you have a local, easily reachable and verifiable source to which you can apply changes with complete visibility.

o   **Speed to product**—Through offsourcing you can add additional capacity faster, given the lower costs, and get to product faster. The benefits can be astounding. In a call center environment, adding capacity offshore can help you work the time zones and potentially improve customer service.

The regulatory issues associated with restructuring should be primarily confined to human resources; however, your particular situation will determine the extent to which this is the case.

Protected Classes

Be aware that the diversity of your workforce may shrink as you move to reduce headcount. You must clearly document the reasons for the reduction and establish the criteria by which individuals are released. This is a job for the professionals in your human resources department. Do not make communications, commitments or plans without their involvement.

Unions

Unions have not historically had any traction in the area of IT-enabled services. The coming wave of offshore activity may change that dynamic, but for now expect little impact in this area. If you do find that you are going to restructure an area that affects unionized employees, involve the human resources department from the outset. There may be specific obligations that you need to accommodate.

Re-engineering the Workload

A company's history often has as much to do with the way that it performs certain functions as does the current industry best practice. This is particularly acute in the case of organizations that have grown through roll-ups or in industries that have come under limited pressure to invest in technology. The status quo has considerable inertia.

Your migration to offshore IT-enabled services provides you with an opportunity to revisit the status quo.

- **Application development and maintenance**—Success will require that you adopt rigorous management and development techniques that will benefit your organization, if it does not already have them.

- **Call centers and repetitive business processes**—These areas may be ripe for process improvement and can benefit tremendously from a reexamination of their current processes in light of recent changes to the business or in technology.

> *Your migration to offshore IT-enabled services provides you with an opportunity to revisit the status quo.*

- **Process understanding—** You will be required to document your as-is processes in order to establish the new "reengineered" processes. The term Re-engineering relates to a process optimization approach deployed frequently in the late 1980s and early 1990s. It was primarily tied to developing automated systems to eliminate manual steps. This same process can work well to optimize the processes and design the checks and balances required to split a process geographically. Determine accountability by process step and design the new "offsourced process."

- **Re-engineering**—The investment you make in documentation is a portion of the same investment required to reengineer any process. Why not spend a little more to improve it rather than simply replicate it elsewhere? After all, you will have significant accrued savings that can be applied to support this transition cost. You have to ask yourself which is an easier sell: Re-engineering as a stand-alone project or process improvement within a guaranteed savings from an offshore initiative?

- **High value–added tasks**—Consider examining large, repetitive jobs currently conducted by highly trained personnel for possibly packaging and moving offshore. One financial services institution is currently directing its private clients to offshore agents that provide a human interaction to all their transaction-related needs. The transactions are then pushed back to the US for execution. The organization gains because it can offload part of an expensive broker's task load to a well-educated, certified lower-cost resource that can spend significant face time with the customer. The broker is then free to focus on customer acquisition and offering advice on investment strategies. The customer gains from having a personalized interface rather than a voice prompt.

- **Technology investment**—You may already recognize opportunities to significantly improve the productivity of your organization by applying automating or enabling technologies but are simply unable to make the investment required to get to "best in class." The offshore move gives you that opportunity.

You have the option of applying some of the savings in early years to improving the technology foundation of your organization. This will ultimately be staffed by lower-cost and fewer personnel.

Summary

This chapter details further steps toward implementation. When combined with a heavy dose of process and methodology, these actions will allow you to build out the offshore model. This model is a blueprint, or franchise, that once adjusted to reflect your organizational needs can be replicated in many areas of the business.

Chapter 14 Summary
Restructuring to Build the Franchise

Chapter Theme

Restructuring is about more than cutting onshore headcount. It is the often difficult exercise of ensuring that you are positioned with the optimal team, processes, governance model and resourcing plans for success in the new paradigm. You are not doing business as usual, so don't expect a walk in the park.

- ❏ Governance model
- ❏ Resource optimization
- ❏ Capacity planning
- ❏ Technology planning
- ❏ Metrics definition
- ❏ Process optimization

Key Points

Establish the executive sponsorship.

Build a committed team to support the new model. Key players must be able to span the strategic and the tactical; hands-on attitude is crucial.

Take the opportunity to revisit existing processes as you build the replacement model.

- ❏ Best communicators
- ❏ Executive access
- ❏ Commitment to model
- ❏ Cultural appreciation
- ❏ Broad and deep knowledge

Reader Take-Away

You should recognize that this activity as part of the overall implementation process is where the rubber meets the road. During the Roadmap, concepts and processes are detailed. When restructuring, you are making the final decisions. Staff optimizations will get difficult but are necessary to achieve the benefits and gain the anticipated efficiencies.

Questions for Consideration

- ❏ Is the executive sponsor leading the effort and setting the strategy?
- ❏ Has the team been seeded with the right leadership from key operational areas?
- ❏ Have you laid out a program that will avoid prolonged restructuring?
- ❏ Where will the offsourcing initiative go in your organization after you have established and proven the model?

Chapter 15

Infrastructure Requirements

Overview

Infrastructure here is broadly defined as the public goods over which individual companies outside the Fortune 100 have little influence, such as transportation networks and energy distribution, as well as more specific, solution-related structures (physical, technological and virtual) that a company can achieve through time and investment. It includes power, communications, roads, technology and even education.

In a US or Western European frame of reference, the availability of at least basic infrastructure is usually assumed. In an offshore environment, the first rule of thumb is to assume nothing and to leave no question unasked; assumptions in this context can be costly later on.

Beyond pure availability, there are also temporal considerations. A domestic frame of reference carries an assumption that business users can rapidly purchase most utilities in incremental amounts. In many developing countries this is simply not the case. Significant delays and a scarcity of resources may require an elongated setup time frame. Further, setup may also require the assistance of an agent to get the last mile of fiber-optics or get that critical server through customs. The point is that from a planning perspective, you must look far ahead and prepare well in advance.

In this chapter we review a few infrastructure-related items that you should consider in your offshore initiatives. Conditions vary by country, but for purposes of illustration we will use India as a model. Your infrastructure planning will begin during the Offsourcing Roadmap process and become part of the vendor or partner selection criteria should you seek external assistance.

Communications

Communications are perhaps the most obvious uncertainty since they are the lifeblood of IT-enabled services and the single item that allows remote geographies to provide real-time or near real-time services.

Each country has different levels of redundancy, capacity and tariff regimes. In general it can be said that the cost is dropping dramatically while capacity continues to rise. However, there are still gaps. Individual countries may still have limited options.

You will want to consider the following:

- **Physical versus virtual**—As part of your due diligence you need to understand not only the redundancy in carriers, but in the physical lines that the carriers are using. Two carriers on the same line do not offer redundancy if the line is cut.

- **International versus domestic**—If you are working in a call center or BPO environment and plan to use a vendor, you should review the pricing for the telecommunications component. Some vendors will quote an all-in cost that takes you from point to point as part of a blended rate, whereas others will cover the international component and leave you to pick up the tab on the domestic portion.

> *Two carriers on the same line do not offer redundancy if the line is cut.*

- **IP-based voice and video**—Plan to take advantage of your investment in bandwidth for internal communications. IP voice requires point-to-point connectivity. Although it does not have the requisite quality yet for a call center operation, it has more than sufficient quality to conduct conference calls and meetings.

- **Dedicated versus burstable bandwidth**—Once you have determined approximately what bandwidth you require, obtain quotes from your carrier for both dedicated and burstable frame relay circuits. You will be able to get much lower costs on the burstable circuits, so depending on the level, volume, and duration of data flow of your needs, this approach may offer the best solution. .

- **Satellite**—Satellite may form part of your infrastructure, but probably more as a backup than for day-to-day use. The challenge is one of distance. A signal that has to go up 36,000 miles and bounce around a few times before making at the 36,000 mile return trip to earth, even at the speed of light, will suffer delays.

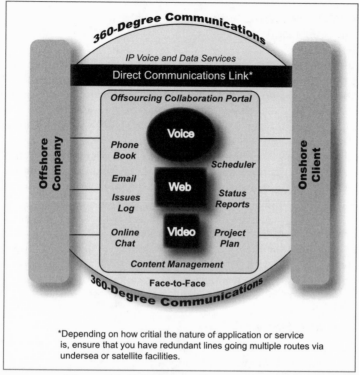

Figure 19: 360-Degree Communications

As you work through the above, keep in mind that using the Web to access applications from the offshore venue can be challenging. You may experience slow response time and timeouts and ultimately take a hit on productivity. Understand if your provider is using shared lines or has dedicated capacity free of competition for bandwidth.

Power

Power and connectivity go somewhat hand in hand. Lose one or the other and your operation is likely to be severely impacted if not completely shut down.

India, like most developing countries, is experiencing a demand for power that outstrips its supply.[18] Operations can expect to experience brownouts and fluctuating power supplies if not adequately resourced. The good news is that these challenges are manageable with appropriate forethought and planning. Be sure you understand your providers' capabilities in this area or run the risk of taking productivity hits.

---

[18] According to the India Development Report 2002, published by the Indira Gandhi Institute of Development Research, 2001 demand was calculated to have exceeded supply by 13%.

As you build your Offsourcing Roadmap, consider that power redundancy will come from a combination of the following:

- **Local grid**—Most buildings in the US have access to only one power grid, so it should come as no surprise that same will be true in most developing economies where power tends to be a treasured state monopoly. There are exceptions, and you should be prepared to pay a premium if you are selecting a site for this particular aspect if you build your own center.

- **Battery**—Battery life being what it is, this component of the power redundancy plan is more about smoothing over sudden dips and giving the data center the breathing room to power down in an orderly fashion than providing anything but minimal backup.

- **Generation capabilities**—Diesel generators are still the preferred way to bring significant amounts of power online in a short time frame. Your planning/due diligence should include the tank capacity and expected longevity of output under normal loads. In addition you will want to ensure that contracts are in place with guaranteed delivery for refills.

Hardware and Software

The complexity of the hardware/software infrastructure primarily arises from the diversity of options and the availability of local support. Particularly with software you are apt to run into export license issues that must be addressed on a vendor-by-vendor basis. You have four basic options:

- **Purchase domestically and ship**—This approach offers the advantage of purchasing exactly what you want and being able to install, test and generally prepare to be production ready in a highly controlled environment.

  o Disadvantage: Lack of support, import/export regulations, time lag, shipping costs.

- **Purchase in offshore location**—This approach has the advantage of guaranteed local support.

  o Disadvantage: Loss of setup control, potentially higher list prices and the question of what to do with the equipment in the event that your offshore program does not proceed.

- **Lease in offshore location**—This option can potentially solve support issues while giving you the choice to pay as you go. If you do pursue this path and are working with a vendor or partner, try to negotiate the option of assigning this lease to the vendor in the event that your initiative does not proceed.

o   Disadvantage: Loss of setup control, potentially higher prices.

- **Your vendor can purchase**—This is the easiest route with respect to financing and disposal costs. For vendors that are experiencing strong growth, however, this is a costly use of working capital, so they are likely to want to pursue other alternatives.

o   Disadvantage: Loss of setup control.

The hardware and software issues are manageable, but you will want to stay on top of them. Identify the policies and global service capabilities of your hardware and software vendors, understand the process to ship equipment and then build the appropriate lead time and costs into your Offsourcing Roadmap.

Security

In our discussion of risks we noted that some geographies carried credible political risk of both internal and external varieties. External risks cannot be managed beyond simple avoidance of the geography during the selection process.

Internal risks manifest themselves with great variety and thus offer the potential for mitigation in some form. It is hard to imagine defending a call center against the onslaught of an armed guerilla movement; however, it is reasonable to expect that basic security would prevent a lone gunman from walking into the data center. Typical security infrastructure items to plan for are:

- **Security force**—Expect to have security personnel manning the front desk and possibly even on the grounds if you are in a compound. The same cost savings present in offshore geographies for technology professionals are also true of security personnel—perhaps more so, since there are far more people in need of work. This means that the increased security in your offshore location will not materially impact the financials of your Business Case.

- **Secure building access**—This refers to the controlled access to the front door and to individual floors and, if you are working with a vendor, to various project-related spaces in the edifice. Here you may not be looking to have anything beyond your current domestic setup, but it is recommended that you avoid free entry and circulation.

- **Secure data center access**—This is standard practice at both domestic and offshore locations.

- **Video monitoring**—You may decide to be more aggressive about video monitoring in your offshore environment. George Orwell aside, people are more inclined to the right thing if they feel that they are creating an audit trail that may be reviewed at a future date if circumstances warrant. Further, by linking the monitors to an IP connection you will be able to monitor (or show off) your or your vendor's facility from the comfort of home.

Technology Parks

The creation of technology parks in many developing countries has had an enabling affect, since they can go a long way toward isolating workers from the paltry infrastructure surrounding them. They are most often government sponsored, often at a state or regional level, and beyond the infrastructure may come with some level of tax incentives or abatement. In addition, there is the advantage of having other technology providers from whom you may require services in close proximity.

India currently promotes two types of technology parks: Software Technology Parks (STP) and Electronics Hardware Technology Parks (EHTP) that focus on providing the appropriate infrastructure for each of the respective business models. They are sponsored by the Ministry of Information Technology and must meet specific requirements in order to achieve their designated status. The parks typically maintain power and communication redundancy, but you will still need to validate how adequate they are as part of your Offsourcing Roadmap.

For those considering building out their own offshore facility, these are excellent locations from which to begin. Beyond infrastructure these parks can offer benefits such as:

- 90% income tax benefit per section 10A of the IT Act.
- 100% customs duty exemption on import of capital equipment.
- Equipment can also be imported on a loan or lease program.
- 100% foreign equity investment in the companies is permissible in some circumstances.

Some of these same benefits are also available in other offshore countries such as the Philippines.

Educational System

Educated resources are a part of your infrastructure, and although you cannot turn a switch on and expect job-specific trained employees overnight, you do have the opportunity to significantly influence curriculum over time. Many service vendors and companies operating in local domiciles have established long-term relationships with the best institutions, so that they can guarantee a trained set of resources. Need technical students that can also manage financial spreadsheets? Then work with the local university to have it added to the curriculum.

For countries with developing IT service sectors, a close relationship between business and education is not simply a way of driving down employer training costs. It is good public policy. The IT sector is a source of high-paying jobs, contributes little in the way of pollution and adds to the country's infrastructure. To the extent that the educational system best prepares students for their careers, they make the geography a more attractive target for foreign investment.

Disaster Recovery Planning

DRP, or business continuity planning as it is sometimes more fashionably called, is a key element of your offshore infrastructure planning. There are tough choices to be made about what is reasonable to expect and what warrants investment. The options are rarely inexpensive.

Various scenarios that must be considered include:

- **Travel restrictions**—Constraints placed on individuals entering or leaving the country.

- **Data loss**—Loss of application-related data.

- **Loss of data communication**—Disruption of data lines between the US and the remote geography.

- **Loss of voice communication**—Disruption of telephone lines between the US and the remote geography.

- **Loss of equipment**—No availability of critical servers, network equipment or electrical equipment.

- **Loss of facilities**—No availability of development facility, including equipment.

- **"Doomsday"**—Loss of all of the above.

DRP is not a destination exercise, once checked off and forgotten from future plans. It is an ongoing part of your management processes. Business needs change over time, key resources come and go and particular infrastructure components look more or less vulnerable based on exogenous events or real-life experiences. The environment changes and your DRP must change to reflect the new realities.

There are myriad mitigation approaches, escalation procedures and the like to address each of the contingencies above. Each requires some level of redundancy, which in turn translates into an overhead cost that takes away from the potential savings. As you are putting your DRP in place, you must deal with what you know to be true today and what you believe is a reasonable approach to managing through a spectrum of crippling events.

Beyond detailing the plan, you must also test it with varying levels of vigor. You should regularly exercise your backup generator or redundant telecom provider to ensure that you have the capacity that your backup plan assumes. You may also want to have contractual options with equipment suppliers or commercial real estate firms in the event that you are required to get hardware and space quickly.

There is something alternately disturbing and heroic about the notion of investing to prepare for possibilities that you hope will never come. Events of the recent past have demonstrated that even the United States is not immune to the most tragic of disaster scenarios. So as you move offshore you must understand and make preparations for business-interrupting events. In the end it is impossible to hedge completely against catastrophic failures, particularly as they relate to your most precious resource: human beings. The board or steering committee to which you report will understand this but will still want a copy of the plan and the latest DRP test results. Be prepared.

Summary

Your infrastructure needs will depend greatly on the objectives of your offshore initiative. Every initiative, however, will require infrastructure for:

- Communications
- Power
- Hardware and software
- Security
- Education
- Disaster recovery planning

Organizations large and small are having tremendous success in spite of issues concerning lagging infrastructure. That in itself is not the issue. The challenge is to understand how your requirements will qualify the target geography for your operation or how you must invest in that geography to support your needs. Early and careful research and planning in this area can mean fewer surprises in costs or productivity later in the game.

Chapter 15 Summary
Infrastructure Requirements

Chapter Theme

Always assume that you can make no assumptions about the infrastructure in your offshore venue. Redundancy and business continuity planning are required to adequately insulate your operation from the vagaries of infrastructure deficits.

- ❒ **Communications**
  - **- redundancy**
  - **- physical versus virtual**
- ❒ **Power generation**
- ❒ **Capacity planning**

Key Points

Infrastructure setup costs may be a significant portion of your total cost of offsourcing if you decide to establish your own presence in an offshore venue.
Understand the requirements before you make the commitment or negotiate a contract with a prospective vendor. Exit clauses should take into account the shutdown costs.

- ❒ **Hardware**
- ❒ **Software**
- ❒ **Security - physical and electronic**
- ❒ **Disaster recovery planning**
- ❒ **Technology parks**

Reader Take-Away

Your infrastructure needs are directly correlated to the complexity, size and long-term strategy you have for your initiatives. Make sure you factor the infrastructure into your TCO and ensure that you plan 3 to 6 months in advance for operational infrastructure. Remember, the offshore environment may require significant lead times to put some pieces of the puzzle in place.

Questions for Consideration

- ❒ Have you built an infrastructure plan and defined your timelines?
- ❒ Have you identified any domestic hardware or software licensing restrictions?
- ❒ Have you adequately prepared a disaster recovery plan?
- ❒ How do your infrastructure requirements factor into any SLA?
- ❒ Have you factored some or all of the infrastructure components into the legal agreement?

Chapter 16

Methodology and Process Management

Methodology is applied ideology.

Mason Cooley

Overview

Watching discussions about methodology can be a little like watching a political debate. Candidates often have similar goals but disagree on the nuances of how to reach the target. Extremists in either camp are regarded by the mainstream as dangerous, while most people lead lives in the middle. The majority believe in the need for dialogue and the flexibility required for progress in the real world. Successful offsourcing requires defined repeatability of process; methodology is a roadmap for just that.

The following discussion is intended as a primer on the subject and to give you some context for what you can expect in the offshore environment. No doubt your organization already has a number of methodologies hard at work with varying degrees of success, but the right approach can make a dramatic difference in managing your offshore risk and ultimately the success of the project.

Identifying Your Needs

In their most comprehensive forms, methodologies will include volumes of process descriptions, guides, deliverable templates, metrics and automated tools. A few basic program management documents and tools are included in Table 13.

With limitless options to choose from, the better question to ask is, "What is required?" rather than "What is available?" Recognize the difference between program management tools and development, process Re-engineering or domain-specific certification criteria. Some solutions range across both elements of managing and performing, while others are very specific.

The high-level requirements coming from your Business Case development will give you a picture early on as to what your eventual needs will be. Regardless of size, your current organization will have some level of methodology, albeit potentially informal, for getting the job done. Begin by getting an inventory of

Deliverable	Description
Project definition and charter	Detailed overview of the offsourcing program. The vision, objectives, tactical goals, and benefits among other items must be articulated to ensure alignment of expectations.
Project work plan	Detailed set of tasks with estimated time to complete, key dependencies and whom is accountable for each task including key deliverables. Interim milestones are good to incorporate to ensure rapid feedback.
Organization strategy	Concise, articulate depiction of the organization strategy to be implemented including roles, responsibilities, benfits, span of control, onshore changes and offshore integration must be taken into account.
Issue management plan	Develop a detailed approach for addressing issues, documentation, routing, escalation and resolution of each issue.
Quality assurance plan	Guide to monitor and confirm quality of the end product, gate review process, resources, both on and offshore, and an ongoing collaboration system to ensure consistency and excellence of the process to ensure a high quality end product.
Risk management plan	Detailed accounting of potential on and offshore risks that would assess organization, technical, process, disaster recovery, and any other risk that has potential to impact delivery. Ensure that a solid risk mitigation strategy is articulated for each potential risk.
Operational process plan	Detailed accounting of potential on and off shore risks that would assess organization, technical, process, disaster recovery, and any other possible scenario that has real potential to impact ultimate delivery. Ensure that a solid risk mitigation strategy is articulated for each potential risk.
Testing plan	Detailed approach to testing all levels of activity including compliance, volume and accuracy.
Communication plan	Multi-channel guide to capturing, organizing and disseminating initiative information to the right parties. Plan on overcommunicating early until the on and offshore teams are functioning at maximum efficiency.
Change management	Multi-channel guide to identifying and responding to individual and organizational stresses as a result of program initiatives. Establish a buddy system and a program to make both teams culturally aware of the other.

Tools	Description
Issue management	Web-based repository for capturing, tracking and resolving project related issues. Must assign accountability and date to resolve.
Change management	Web-based repository for capturing, tracking and reaching sign-off and completion on any scope related changes.
Content management	Web-based content management (storage and retrieval) tool for managers and all team members to store and access all project/program documentation. Ideally accessible via the program portal.
Collaboration tools	Web-based collaboration tools such as email, chat, pc-based video conferencing, conference room video conferencing, and message boards for exchange of questions, answers and ideas.
Process management	Automated tool for modeling the business process and information flow. Ideally, this drives a requirements process and set of deliverables to ensure high quality, thorough, and clear requirements definition.

Table 13: Methodology Deliverables and Tools

the methodologies in place and map them to the needs that you have identified. This will leave you with a gap analysis of what you need to purchase or develop to effectively manage risk. If you are working with an offshore vendor or a third-party intermediary, define these tools or approaches for them. Each case is a little different and required definite customization for your specific environment.

The following table summarizes the generic types of methodologies required to meet your objectives in managing different initiatives:

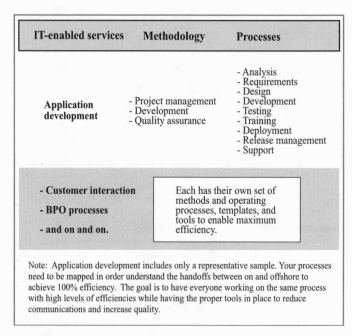

Table 14: Methodology / Process Requirements

As you move outside the organization to consider alternative approaches, remember the following: Many methodologies provide an exhaustive set of templates, issue management logs, design documents and other items but rely on the users to selectively cull the elements that are not essential for implementation. *It is important to consider that more methodology is not necessarily better methodology.* Project management and development methodologies abound in various forms, and yet the number of projects that fail or are poorly managed due to the lack of good process remains significant.

- **Practicality test**—Failure to implement the methodology in an efficient and economical fashion can result in enormous overhead with limited benefits. In fact it can increase your risk by stealing time from value-added activities and applying it to mind-numbing box checking. Does the action contribute to the end objective of a successful project or are you simply checking boxes? What is the total cost to the organization of what you are implementing (template development and use, revisions, tracking, IT support, etc.) versus the anticipated benefits of a structured approach?

> *Failure to implement the methodology in an efficient and economical fashion can result in enormous overhead with limited benefits.*

The Offshore Factor

The highly distributed nature plus the cultural nuances of the work in an offshore environment complicate process management in a number of ways:

- **Timing**—Good methodologies impose rigor while minimizing the impact on work throughput. The time zone differences in your newly distributed working environment can be advantageous if carefully worked. The potential exists in some areas for activities to be worked on an almost 24-hour basis simply by leveraging the differences in time zones; however, this can also add complexity. The implementation of the methodology must account for repeatable hand-offs with minimal time spent on handshakes if it is to be successful.

- **Division of labor**—The division of labor goes beyond the repeated handshakes to the realization that, over time, different competencies will be created in dispersed localities. Methodologies in an offshore environment must therefore evolve to recognize the organizational learning component to adequately mitigate the risk of creating blind spots in the organization.

- **Context**—Another reflection of the division of labor issue is the risk that work is performed with insufficient context about the overall market or business objective. The methodology deployed must allow for investment in artifacts that provide a working understanding of the business objectives. Some will be used to support training, but others will be reference guides and real-time support.

We know of no current popular packaged methodology that has been updated to provide reference guides, additional templates and other helpful aids for organizations building an integrated onshore/offshore environment. Undoubtedly this will change over time; however, in the meantime the organization should plan to budget additional time beyond that recommended by the methodology vendors to modify, implement and perform required training in the target environment. Depending on the complexity of the process, the multiplier may be from 20% to 200%. Assess this need during the Offsourcing Roadmap process and have a plan in place by the time you go operational.

A few options to address areas such as project management, software development and software process quality are discussed next.

The Options

Among the most widely recognized program and development methodologies are:

- **PMI**—The Project Management Institute headquartered in Philadelphia is a nonprofit group that promotes sound project management practices. It offers a comprehensive suite of management practice standards and certifications and can claim some 100,000+ adherents globally. For more information, go to www.pmi.org.

- **ISO9000**—The International Standards Organization based in Geneva promotes global standardization of practices. ISO9000 is the most rigorous of its three standards and is intended for companies and organizations that design and develop their products or services as well as the produce and deliver them. For more information, go to www.iso.ch.

- **Rational Unified Process (RUP)**—The Rational Unified Process, or RUP, is the only privately owned methodology to which we refer in this text. It is developed and owned by the Rational Corporation (recently acquired by IBM) and is an enterprise software development process managing everything from requirements gathering to system testing. Given the scope of its charter, RUP components have on occasion been modified to serve as project management tools outside of the field of software development. For more information, go to www.rational.com.

- **Capability Maturity Model**—"The Capability Maturity Model for Software (CMM or SW-CMM) is a model for judging the maturity of the software processes of an organization and for identifying the key practices that are required to increase the maturity of these processes."[19] CMM is an excellent roadmap for developers engaged in large-scale system development. It has tremendous rigor when applied appropriately, but beware of the overhead in applying it to smaller engagements or in going too far in its application. One limitation of the CMM is that it assumes that you already have a fixed set of requirements, so you will likely want to combine it with some of the elements of RUP or another development methodology in requirements gathering. For more information, go to www.sei.cmu.edu/cmm/cmm.html.

Vendor Environments

Should your offshore solution involve the use of an external service provider, the question of methodology will likely be a factor in your selection. You should consider a number of elements:

- **Certification type**—Is the vendor methodology consistent, or at least compatible, with your own? What will be required to interface the two?

---

[19] http://www.sei.cmu.edu/cmm/cmm.html

- **Certification quality**—Is the vendor certified in the methodology it is using? How was the certification obtained? Experience suggests that not all certifications are the same and that many vendors and their certifiers are optimistic in their assessments. This is after all a critical criterion for many buyers, so there is significant market pressure to have the certifications or risk early dismissal from many selection processes. You may consider having your own expert review the vendor capability to validate the formal certification.

- **Flexibility**—Is the vendor prepared to adopt your methodology to accommodate the way that you conduct your business? Are you prepared to pay for this learning curve? If you push this on the vendor without recognizing their cost, you are likely to meet with disappointing results such as low productivity along with lower quality output and much rework. If a vendor does agree to step up to this task, understand how they plan to do so and be prepared to work with them.

Another interesting question to ask the vendor is what the cost would be of working without the methodology or perhaps with a scaled-down version. As an example, companies are certified on CMM at various levels of competency (1–5). Each level requires successive discipline and also indicates a rigor and set of developer/management activities. It was, after all, developed in response to the needs of NASA for building systems on which lives depended. Therefore Level 5 might be moot for most commercial purposes, so you may try to get a break on your pricing (in a fixed-fee contract) by operating at Level 3 or 4. At a minimum, you will find out if the salesperson and project management team understands anything about CMM and its applicability to various levels of complexity.

Training

Perhaps the most important thing to know about any methodology is that it is only as good as the individuals who apply it. You would not give a set of flight instructions to a man on the street and expect him to fly a plane, for obvious reasons. Individuals require a combination of formal pedagogy, practical experience and study to be successful. And whatever is said of methodology in an onshore environment could be shown to be doubly so in a highly distributed one, where there are opportunities for communication and expectation lapses. Training is critical if the methodology is to be truly adopted and deployed correctly.

Training should not just be for internal resources but also for the vendor, if there is one involved in your activity. Training costs can be significant, should be considered as a part of the contractual relationship and may be handled in different ways:

- **Application development**—The buyer may pay for training that is directly required for use on the project, but not for the time personnel spend in training. This needs to be in your contract with an agreed upon approach for monitoring.

- **Call center and BPO**—In the call center and BPO business the offshore firms may be scaling so fast that they do not have a bench on which to draw. They may be hiring to accommodate your needs. Understand who is paying for the training and how the quality assurance or training testing is conducted as resources complete their induction periods.

Summary

As you select your methodology, understand your needs as well as the complexity that the distributed nature of offshore operations can add to your operating environment. Should you decide to work with a vendor, do not assume that a certification guarantees good process or that its absence indicates a lack of it. Get the facts.

Then, as you build your program, recognize that while the absence of methodology in your program management, development, call center or horizontal business processes would result in chaos, too much of a good thing can be dangerous as well. A methodology is not worth the paper that it is printed on if it is embraced blindly. Put another way, there is no substitute for common sense.

Chapter 16 Summary
Methodology and Process Management

Chapter Theme

The processes that you move offshore will play a large role in the selection of your methodology, though there are always choices. You will likely require a combination of program management and domain-specific methodologies that will require customization to adequately serve your needs in a blended onshore/offshore environment.

- ☐ **Project management**
- ☐ **Application development**
- ☐ **Quality assurance**
- ☐ **Operational process**
- ☐ **Escalation process**
- ☐ **Defined metrics**

Key Points

Ensure that the implementation of your methodology passes the practicality test: deliverables and forms are not being created simply as checklists; they must add value to the goal of risk management.

Understand how your vendors have worked with different methodologies and have them explain and highlight the differences and advantages.

- ☐ **ISO**
- ☐ **CMM**
- ☐ **RUP**
- ☐ **PMI**
- ☐ **Custom**
- ☐ **Defined metrics must be documented**

Reader Take-Away

As part of the TCO you will have to make an investment in process development or, optimistically, enhancements to accommodate the elements of offshore usage. Don't be fooled by the marketing hype of CMM and ISO certifications; they are not necessarily what they appear to be. Ensure that your needs are in line with reality, and take nothing for granted.

Questions for Consideration

- ☐ Are your current operational methodologies documented and "trainable"?
- ☐ Are metrics defined to measure quality, time and overall effectiveness?
- ☐ Where should you segment your current process for offshore?
- ☐ Have quality assurance processes been established for the offsourcing activity?
- ☐ What time and budget have been allocated to development and training of the process?

Chapter 17

Change Management

"**Human beings must contend with the behavior of something beyond the pattern of nature: themselves. Indeed, as civilization has pushed forward, nature's vagaries have mattered less and the decisions of people have mattered more.**"[20]

Peter L. Bernstein

Overview

Change management as discussed in this chapter is the combination of management activities, training, coaching, communication, cultural integration and counseling required to ease the organization through the turbulence of a significant event such as offsourcing. In its best form it is a proactive set of positive activities intended to manage organizational risk and minimize the professional and emotional impact on personnel of moving various functions offshore. Its absence creates the potential for fear, uncertainty and doubt (FUD) and lays the foundation for failed projects and traumatized, unproductive employees.

> "*Successful change is rooted in commitment.*"
> – *Daryl R. Connor*

Assessing the Impact of Going Offshore

The effect of a stone dropped in a pond is felt and observed as the impact ripples across the entire surface. A similar effect is created by moving work offshore. As a project is initiated, those close to the epicenter of activity are most affected, positively or negatively. The farther away from the displaced activity, the less likely that someone will be affected by the ripple; but if they are close it is likely to catch their attention and possibly even upset their boat. The following table provides direction in assessing the timing of potential change management issues.

---

[20] Peter L. Bernstein, *Against the Gods* (John Wiley & Sons, Inc.1996), page 8.

Environment	Action		
	Communication	Coaching & training	Employee assistance
Planning			
Business case	Executives	No	No
Roadmap	Executives and selected managers	Yes	No
Pilot	Across the organization	Yes	No
Full implementation			
No reduction in onshore workforce	Across the organization	Yes	Yes
Expected reduction in onshore workforce	Across the organization	Yes	Yes

Table 15: Change Management Needs Assessment

The entry strategy that you choose will determine the size and place of the near-term impact. Moving offshore has the potential to create FUD in areas well outside the scope of the intended target, since questions of who will be affected (and how) are likely to run rampant. You must be proactive in identifying these areas of vulnerability as you build your change management plan. For the majority of organizations, the decision will be driven by the consideration of cost reduction, which will result in the displacement of personnel. For some, the decision to take this step and move offshore will be a difficult one, but necessary for reasons of economic survival.

In his 1992 book *Managing at the Speed of Change,* Daryl R. Connor noted, "Successful change is rooted in commitment. Unless key participants in a transition are committed to both attaining the goals of the change and paying the price those goals entail, the project will ultimately fail." This quote hits the nail squarely on the head as it relates to offsourcing. The following figure portrays the emotional toll that may be expected, with both positive and negative frames of reference.

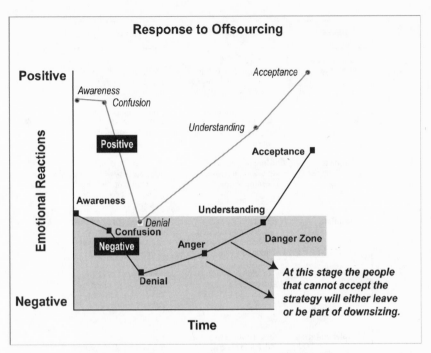

Figure 20: Employee Response to Offsourcing

The organization must internalize (and the employees understand on a visceral level) that a new set of business practices is to be added to its portfolio, or the potential exists for halfhearted measures that will lead to failure. Management has the opportunity to significantly manage the frame of reference and thereby keep key personnel out of the critical Danger Zone.

Developing a Communications Plan

Navigating an organization through the uncharted waters of the new offsourcing paradigm is a challenging task. It involves a tremendous number of disciplines including strategic and financial planning, operational and delivery excellence, and flawless communication. These communications will be targeted to strategic selling, anxiety management and simple information dissemination, among other functions.

There is a yin/yang debate that customarily occurs regarding disseminating versus holding information. The answer is specific to the situation, but there are some things to watch for. The following table highlights what can happen if communication comes too late and is not clear.

Phase	Activity	Symptoms
Information gathering	An offshore group was seen meeting with the CIO or other sr. manager.	Rumors of going offshore are beginning to circulate. People are doing their research on the affects.
Business plan	More meetings. Lots of activities with the sr. managers and some consultants.	Rumor mill escalates to the point of misinformation. Some ask what is going on.
Roadmap	More people involved at this stage. Rumors become reality.	Productivity is now affected. The potential scope is being discussed. Fear of job loss now sets in.
Pre-pilot	Limited scope of plans communicated in abbreviated formal announcement.	Naysayers get organized, and find the points of resistance to chip away at the offshore plan.
Pilot	No additional info is disseminated other than the future scope is dependent on the pilot's success.	Top performers begin to put their resumes on the street or leave the company.
Implementation	In attempting to get the company back to normal, key executives annouce that all offshore activities are limited to the current initiative. All is well and it's back to business as usual.	Offsourcing strategy has limited effectiveness given the lack of organizational alignment. Trust in management is dramatically reduced.
Offsourcing Benefits NOT Realized		

Table 16: Communications Deficits

The scenarios above can be avoided with factual and truthful discussion as the timing becomes appropriate. At the same time, have a plan to ensure that your best people are given the comfort level they require to remain focused on the road ahead.

Executive

Executive communications will be done with a focus on:

- **Educating the audience**—What is possible? What are the savings? What are the risks and the risk mitigation strategies? Who has done this before?

- **Communicating the approach**—Communicate the process by which you expect to create value in the organization, including the building of a financial case, target business model, planning process, key implementation dependencies, deliverables and timelines.

- **Establishing a common vernacular**—Language is a powerful tool that can be powerfully confusing when not applied consistently. Terms like onshore, offshore, nearshore, CMM, etc. should be defined and used consistently. The executive audience must internalize and understand these concepts at some level of mutual agreement or coordinated efforts to move forward may be challenging.

- **Sowing the seeds of change**—Many if not most executives have risen through the ranks because they recognize opportunities early and have the drive to capitalize on them. Executives have the most to win in adopting offshore strategies since their compensation is apt to be most closely tied to the business (a good thing). Communications should be made to them in a way that most directly ties them to success or allows them to see the offshore model being described as positively impacting their own operation.[21]

Everyone

The best employees tend to have the best skills and therefore the

> *The best employees tend to have the best skills and therefore the most potential mobility should they find themselves in a situation with high ambiguity and perceived low job security.*

most potential mobility should they find themselves in a situation with high ambiguity and perceived low job security. It is somewhat ironic that these personnel, whom you most want to retain, are apt to be the first to ask

---

[21] Many executives will be concerned about the perception of external stakeholders. Offshore activity has passed into the mainstream of corporate business practices, so the act of moving some part of the operation offshore is unlikely to be met with consternation by the analyst community. Quite the contrary; the notion of restructuring for cost savings is likely to meet with a favorable reception, particularly if it is accomplished through some type of outsourcing scenario. Your announcement should demonstrate:

Caution—Be wary of overcommitting on the benefits until you have seen the metrics. You will be required to invest to get to the steady-state operation, so don't box yourself in. Give yourself a generous time frame for organizational learning.

Value—Communicate the benefits and how you plan on leveraging those benefits into new markets, new revenue programs, new product development or simply increased margins and earnings.

Process—Communicate an abbreviated and conservative version of your Business Case. Make reference to the planning process that you have executed and the organization that you have seconded to add focus to this initiative.

Risk management—You are less likely to discuss this issue in an announcement, but you should be ready to speak about it if it comes up in the analyst call or during investor presentations.

themselves if their role might be serviced by someone sitting at a desk on the other side of the world.

Internal communications are a clear area of risk and they can be a source of angst among management as you grapple with: When to tell? Who to tell? How much to tell? After all, you have invested much personal stock in building an environment of openness and collaboration only to be forced to withhold sensitive information about the livelihoods of those around you.

The following are a few points for consideration:

- **Assessment**—As you work on the Business Case and even to some degree the Roadmap, limit the involvement of internal and external collaborators to as few as possible. Most if not all of the Business Case can be compiled by external resources. Consider outsourcing the Business Case or authorizing a select few employees with the external horsepower they need to get their arms around the opportunity.

- **Planning**—As you move into the Roadmap phase, you will be required to pull in project or functional owners to get specific expertise. You should have a sense of your target model before this point or you run the risk of including someone that could become a casualty of the new model. **At this point you should have identified and laid out retention plans for long-term key resources and those resources that you must retain during a transition phase.** You should also assume that you will have some attrition in your overall headcount. Taking a proactive approach to resource management will limit the organization's risk and provide material incentive for the affected parties.

- **Execution**—There can be no way to hide the move of a project team, call center or processing facility. The affected individuals must be treated with the dignity and respect that they deserve. That concept begins with communications. Further, the rest of the organization will have questions about the direction of the company, the impact on their own livelihoods and the potential for their own positions to evolve or be displaced at some point. Consider putting together a list of FAQs for those employees untouched by the execution considerations. This is no silver bullet for morale, but unambiguous messages will at least work against unfounded rumors and promote a uniform message.

- **Human resources**—One of the mandates of the human resources function is to help manage liability as it relates to employees. They are a key resource in the communications process.

Remember that, probably sooner rather than later, the word is going to get out. Your communications should be both factual and satisfy, at least on a basic level, the thirst of the questioner to be in the loop. A little preparation for this moment will go a long way toward maintaining your credibility in the long term and relieving at least some of the awkwardness of the moment.

Coaching and Training

The new model requires new skills and techniques. In the discussion of restructuring, some of the attributes required of the new team were discussed, including a commitment to the model, an appreciation for different working styles, comfort with rational experimentation and flexibility regarding travel. However, that is not enough. The right attitude will only get you so far.

Hard skills and experience are also critical success factors. Consider the following types of issues and the training to address them:

- **Example**—The strong leader that was successful in managing a team in the bullpen down the hall is struggling with resources located in Calcutta (Kolkata, as it is now called).

  o **Management skills training**—With more work being performed offshore, management challenges and complexity will increase. There are new relationships, travel time, team dynamics and business processes. Even good managers in the old paradigm may require training and encouragement to be successful. Make a commitment to the go-forward team that you will invest in their success.

- **Example**—A daily conference call is needed to check status on overnight events and progress.

  o **Communication training**—A homogenous, centralized environment might support an informal meeting schedule. It's easy to round up folks to work through issues, and if data is missing, the group can always reconvene after lunch. Not so in a geographically distributed environment where you may have a limited time window every day to communicate with your remote team. Better preparation and more rigid processes may be required to effectively push messages through the organization with speed and clarity.

Your change management program should budget for and address these areas as part of the master project plan for going offshore. Some indication of the new skills required should have been developed formally or informally as part of the Offsourcing Roadmap; however, an early step of the implementation should be to develop a detailed approach to closing skill gaps that exist between the team and target model. Training and coaching will also benefit directly from the adoption of closed-loop techniques that seek feedback from participants as to what was most helpful.

Cultural Integration and Management

"The core task of cross-cultural management is to facilitate and direct synergistic interaction and learning at interfaces, where knowledge, values and experience are transferred into multicultural domain of implementation."
                                                    Holden, 2001

Cultural understanding is a requirement to achieve level 1 or level 2 in the OMM and to take even the first or second step in the offsourcing process. Cultural integration is required to achieve the full benefits of offsourcing and to achieve level 3 or above in the OMM. The rigor of the approach that you adopt regarding interpersonal communications as a result of formal training discussed in the previous section is unlikely to address the specific nuances of culturally heterogeneous environments.

- **Example**—An individual with an aggressive US Northeastern style of interaction is giving negative feedback to a manager who is culturally uncomfortable with direct conflict.

- **Example**—Client personnel are questioning a vendor manager's judgment, in an environment where chain of command is deemed inviolate.

The scope of real and observed cultural miscues that derail offshore initiatives (or more likely condemn them to be perennially sub optimized) is vast. They range from misalignment over the perception of risk to the definition of hard requirements and an appreciation for the timing of commitments. Different cultures simply solve problems in different ways; the challenge is to effectively manage away the risk of misinterpretation by providing both parties with a baseline set of understandings that can then be used as a vehicle for common understanding and progress. This does not happen overnight and is as much about building personal relationships as about building professional ones.

A cultural integration management program should include a baseline session with follow-ups that allow individuals to discuss and reflect on exchanges they have experienced that were either puzzling or unsatisfactory. It should also identify points of exposure in the business process as a result of cultural misunderstanding that may need bolstering or change to mitigate risk.

If you are working with a vendor, encourage them to craft some type of US-centric training for their personnel. This will give you a very telling perspective on the way they perceive and manage their customer base. In the call center arena, this is usually a part of the base "onboarding" process for new customer service agents, but this is rarely so in the application development environment. Small things can make a big difference.[22]

Employee Assistance

Employees who are impacted by the changes are likely to require a number of services to adjust to the change in their employment status. The human resources department is a key partner in your change management process. It should have a defined employee exit program, but you are encouraged to considering the following as you undergo the restructuring:

- **Outplacement services**—A number of firms specialize in assisting organizations to provide job search services for employees that have are not part of the go-forward structure. This can involve everything from helping to write resumes to coordinating calendars to identifying and scheduling interviews for alternative opportunities.

- **Equipment**—Consider letting the departing employees retain their equipment. You will have to write down the book value (probably minimal), but it is not a drain on cash. You may have to wipe the hard drives to be in compliance with your software licensing agreements, but the machines themselves are unlikely to be supported overseas, so the likelihood of their finding use there is remote.

- **Counseling**—This may or may not be available as part of the medical plan. The loss of a job is a difficult emotional and financial experience. For many in the IT world the job is a part of our identity and its loss can be traumatic.

---

[22] A challenge in many areas of change management, but particularly in cultural management, is the essentially anecdotal base of data from which you are normally forced to work.

One tool that we have found very insightful, and capable of delivering good empirical data in this area when applied appropriately, is the Birkman Method. The Birkman Method (TBM) is a noncritical assessment tool designed to help an individual identify his or her own likes, needs and reactions to stress.

TBM consists of a questionnaire filled out online by individuals, scored electronically by the Birkman organization against thousands of previous compiled profiles and then interpreted by a certified Birkman consultant.

By applying TBM to a pool of critical resources from both onshore and offshore and then analyzing the data in pools, you will be able to identify the needs and operating styles across groups. Experience has shown that there are significant differences in the level of challenge desired, structure required and pressure willing to be endured. The results may surprise you, but they will give you an empirical basis from which to craft a targeted cultural/management communications training program.

The market for IT professionals is unlikely to change dramatically or for the better for some time, particularly in light of the macro changes in the way that these services can be delivered globally. Consider making a commitment to set aside some portion of the year-one savings to address the needs of departing employees.

Summary

Change management is a broad topic. Ask ten professionals for a definition and you will likely get ten different answers. We have kept the scope of our discussion here narrow, limiting ourselves to a few value-added areas that will likely require some level of scrutiny, whatever the depth of your offsourcing program.

For some organizations, those that are growing rapidly or are already outsourcing a number of initiatives to third parties, the change management issues may be narrower in scope than for static organizations that have a history of doing everything themselves. However, the subject of offsourcing can be an emotional one and the training required to manage a complex process in an integrated environment is significant. Early focus within your Offsourcing Roadmap will give the organization the preparation and time required to effectively manage issues before they become problematic.

To be successful you must:

- Identify key talent that cannot be lost.

- Rigorously plan and execute focused and factual communications.

- Demonstrate commitment from the top down.

- Provide employees with the hard and soft skills they need to both work the plan and overcome existing cultural gaps.

Chapter 17 Summary
Change Management

Chapter Theme

Change management is a crucial item at this stage of the offsourcing initiative. If this process gets off to the wrong start, recovery can be difficult, if not impossible. A plan is required to address communications, training, cultural integration and management and, last but not least, employee assistance.

- ❑ **Executive commitment**
- ❑ **Communications**
- ❑ **Onshore change**
- ❑ **Offshore integration**
- ❑ **Cultural integration**
- ❑ **Employee assistance**

Key Points

Executive commitment is the pillar sustaining the entire effort until the initiative gains sufficient support and momentum to stand alone.

Key communications during the transition phase may impact the long-term success. A clear and concise communications plan developed as a part of the Offsourcing Roadmap is a requirement.

- ❑ **Communications**
- ❑ **Identify key resources**
- ❑ **Retention plan**
- ❑ **Quantitiative cultural metrics**
- ❑ **Integrated team**

Reader Take-Away

You face a number of subtle and not so subtle issues when taking the step to migrate operations offshore. You should have an understanding of the stages of migration, during which you will need to address specific communications, coaching and training, and employee assistance issues. You should also appreciate the need to be ahead of the communications curve to adequately respond to questions as they arise.

Questions for Consideration

- ❑ Has the firm assessed the impact of going offshore on staff, organization change, governance structure changes and support mechanisms?
- ❑ Has an organized communication plan been developed to address the move?
- ❑ Has an employee assistance plan been factored into the Business Case for those affected by any staff reduction?
- ❑ Is the executive sponsor delivering the key communications?

Chapter 18

Process Implementation and Metrics Development

Overview

Chapter 16 discusses options and considerations in the methodology selection for your offshore effort. In this chapter we assume that your project is well under way and you are now into the hard part: making the project and the methodology work.

Process implementation should help you to make firm and reasonable commitments and increase your odds of meeting them. Metrics gathered during the exercise of the process will allow you to manage that same process. They should be a primary source of the data you need to identify bottlenecks, performance issues and opportunities for improvement.

Metrics essentially allow early visibility of potential problems, often prior to their being fully understood. For that reason they are enormously valuable not only to operations people, but also to the management team and other interrelated groups that may have dependencies or reporting needs of their own.

Developing Gates

Your methodology will likely join various activities together to create arbitrarily discrete units of work. In an application development environment, these units may be as broad as a design stage or as narrow as a single unit test plan, but they will have a logical grouping. A gate is simply a pass-through point: a handshake, passage of control or quality assurance check that you should place in your work plan to provide additional visibility and control. The example below illustrates a generic application development process with gates incorporated. For those using a true objective-oriented development methodology that is iterative in nature, this will look like more of a waterfall approach—and they would be right. For offshore development you simply cannot get the proper level of interaction to use iterative development unless you push the entire process offshore, which is not recommended until you have strong remote domain knowledge and unfettered access to the user community.

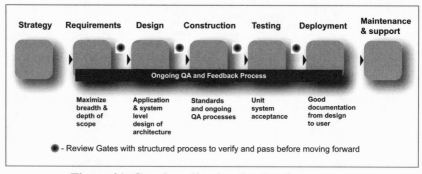

Figure 21: Gated application development process

Typically, a gate will involve a formal review by parties on both sides of it. A check sheet may be signed by one party certifying that the work has been completed according to standards and by a counter party that has reviewed the material as fit to be received. The goal of this exercise is to communicate early and often. It brings together parties in a contiguous process to share perspectives and baseline common understandings. The audit trail created is intended to assist in determining exactly where a problem began so that it can be corrected or prevented in the future, not so that it becomes the "smoking gun" for future blame.

As you reengineer you business process to leverage the new offshore environment, identify handshakes that require formal passage of control. The ultimate division of labor in your offshore or onshore/offshore model will play a significant role in the placement of gates.[23]

The Drive for Metrics

> *There are many old saws about metrics, but perhaps the best is W. Edwards Demming's admonition that you cannot control something if you cannot first measure it.*

There are many old saws about metrics, but perhaps the best is W. Edwards Deming's admonition that you cannot control something if you cannot first measure it. Metrics are the key to your ability to control the process and, over time, its outcome.

The gates you develop create a logical timeline for when you should formalize the presentation of your metrics, but in general the metric collection should be a constant and ongoing, if not real-time, exercise. Metrics can be focused on every area of the business, including:

---

[23] There is a misconception that deploying the Rational Unified Process (RUP) and a gating strategy such as may be found in the Capability Maturity Model or other project management methodologies is somehow unfeasible, the inference being that RUP encourages you to blindly iterate your way to a solution. This is unfounded and more likely indicates an undisciplined approach to the deployment of RUP.

- **Program/project management**—Number of deliverables completed, number completed on time, variances, personnel turnover, compliance, absenteeism, etc.

- **Financial**—Loaded cost per hour, cost per deliverable, revenue-producing hours versus actual hours, margin, bug fix cost, cost per lead, cost per sale, cost per call, etc.

- **Activity**—Call volume, wait times, yield rates, field error rates, design errors, missing requirements, key errors, rework rates, drop rates, etc.

In the case of metrics, as in most areas, too much of a good thing can be a very bad thing. Data collection and analysis require time and money, so you must be careful of simply collecting for collection's sake. Understand and even interview your stakeholders as you construct the target set of metrics that you wish to capture. Then consider the following data characteristics as you proceed:[24]

- **Sufficiency**—Will the pool of data likely to be collected be in sufficiently large quantities to have statistical validity? Small data pools are given to high variability.

- **Relevance**—Is the data truly relevant to your objectives? Are you tracking things that you can control and that materially impact your business?

- **Representative**—Will the data be representative of underlying trends? Do you have the correct metric defined that will uncover potential concerns in a given area?

- **Context**—Is the data likely to confuse or create misleading impressions?

Seek where possible to automate your data collection. This has the benefit of reducing the cost of collection, collapsing the time frame of collection (thus tying your ability to take action more closely to the problem) and reducing inaccuracies from manual compilation. Recognize that you will not have all the metrics that you desire on day one, but you probably need only a few to manage your exposure.

From an executive's perspective metrics are all about the micro events that when added up provide a better picture of what is going on at the macro level. It is easy to find yourself caught out when presenting metrics in a historical perspective, given the maturity curve that you are likely to go through. Keep a few simple rules in mind:

---

[24] Roth & Strong, *Six Sigma Pocket Guide* (Rath & Strong 2000), page 22.

- **Formal process**—Metrics collection is a serious and time-consuming business. You are apt to make mistakes if you are rushed to produce them on the spot. Develop an implementation plan and ongoing process for their collection and publishing. Construct and communicate a timeline around the availability of those metrics and then stick to the schedule. Constituents will need to either wait for the new numbers or accept the most recent ones.

- **Apples to apples**—If your metrics change then note that. Do not allow yourself to be cornered into comparing historical trends that are statistically invalid.

- **Metrics czar**—Hold someone accountable for the collection and communication of this information.

Correctly defined, metrics can go a long way toward telling you more about your business and how to manage it. Be sure to consider carefully not just how to collect and analyze metrics, but also how to present them. You will build credibility with your stakeholders and help yourself in the process.

Six Sigma

Six Sigma is a management discipline (largely popularized by GE, although not originally implemented there) that combines a focus on the customer with rigorous process and analytics in a closed-loop cycle to create ongoing performance enhancements. Because Six Sigma is an ongoing area of focus for many corporations, any discussion of metrics development would be incomplete without at least mentioning it.

At its core Six Sigma delivers improvement by recognizing that variability in a process is a dangerous thing. It purposely ignores averages since they tell little about the "quality" of behavior.

Consider the following:

The average downtime on a network is 1%. That might be all right if you think of it as being one minute out of every hour and a half. But what if there is a high degree of variability and that 1% is really once a week for half an hour, or once every couple of months for a few hours.

The Six Sigma approach is to Define, Measure, Analyze, Improve and Control the process in the pursuit of ongoing performance enhancements. It achieves those performance enhancements by setting reduced variability as a target. If you have a Six Sigma program in place, consider using it to help develop your project and program management metrics.

Collaborative Management Portal

You now have lots of process, lots of data and even metrics. Now what? How do you capture, synthesize and distribute information that crosses multiple competencies, possibly multiple systems and even multiple organizations? Further, how do you manage the need to give more or less information depending upon the user's position in the organization or project responsibilities?

We recommend the creation of a collaborative management portal to serve as the hub of the on- and offshore communications activity. In general having a portal is a good value proposition because of the following:

- **Customization**—The capability to customize the user experience from an administrator level to recognize your different constituencies: onshore, offshore, manager, executive, analyst.

- **Personalization**—The capability for an individual to modify his or her own experience according to need, possibly even for only a given day: add modules, change colors and resize the real estate.

- **Collaboration**—Common workspaces that allow users to collaborate and share information in a secure environment.

- **Community**—Building of messaging capabilities and bulletin boards that promote interaction, cross-pollination and a shared vision.

The offshore environment heightens that value proposition through the following:

- **Visibility**—By moving certain processes to the portal you will have greater visibility of activity and progress, a critical success factor in a highly distributed environment.

- **Aggregation**—Portals are powerful tools for front-ending numerous underlying data systems in a secure fashion that minimizes learning time and training. You can construct cross-system processes in your portal that allow people to work as the business function dictates rather than by logging in and out of legacy applications.

- **Infrastructure**—If you are working with a vendor, they may not have a workspace that is open for customers to access. The portal is a key infrastructure element in which they may wish to coinvest.

- **Modularity**—Once you have built the base infrastructure, portals allow you to bite off initiatives in small chunks. You can start small and add capabilities as your commitment and experience grow. Add a module that provides access to your application development document management repository today. Add an interface to the predictive dialer to track call volume and performance tomorrow.

Portal Development and Technology

As of the writing of this book, the concept of business portals is well ingrained in most IT organizations, though the execution may or may not be. Consider running a Portal Vision Workshop as an add-on to the Offsourcing Roadmap or as a subsequent activity to gather your portal requirements.

Your Portal Vision Workshop (PVW) should contain a functional stream that allows you to drive out a component prioritization model that identifies key modules that you will build. It should also contain two other streams of activity:

- **Technical**—The technical work will focus on identifying the enabling technologies: build versus buy versus shareware. There are strong vendors in the space, but the cost/value ratio is questionable and much is available for little or no cost. The technology work will also contain a look at your single-sign-on (SSO/LDAP) needs and the approach to integration with the systems whose underlying data you are seeking.

- **Visual**—Portals are collaborative exercises with a key benefit being accessibility and usability of the interface. Your PVW should at a minimum deliver a set of user "comps" (mocked-up screens) and better a working prototype for key stakeholders to touch and feel. This is a valuable step in delivering a system that is warmly accepted by the user community and is a great tool in your internal sales process.

Project Management Scorecards

Consider delivering project management scorecards as a capability in the offshore portal. These scorecards should provide a graphical metaphor for the current health of the operations based on underlying thresholds set by management.

Your scorecard might contain some information from a combination of legacy applications, other modules built exclusively for the portal and manual entry. The level of detail reflected and the ability to drill down should be representative of the individual users' span of control and level of responsibility.

If you developed a taxonomy or hierarchy for information grouped into the portal as part of your PVW, take advantage of this to represent some of the information in a graphical manner that will direct management's focus to areas in need of attention. A simple traffic light metaphor with green, yellow and red lights may be sufficient.

Component	Description	Value
Offshore dashboard	Web based key performance indicators (KPI's) displayed in both real time and weekly formats.	**Very High**. Critial to maximize productivity and increase overall quality.
Time and expense tracking	Web basede project time and expense tracking system.	**High**. Automates manual processes while providing visibility into what team members are focused on.
Content management	Repository of all project documents and importatnt data. This aligns the on and offshore teams on the program.	**High**. Ensures that all team members are working based on the right and latest info.
Issue tracking	Problem tracking and resolution for any issue.	**High**. Allows for both visibility and efficient resolution of issues. Provides an audit trail to verify completion.
e-mail Chat PC based video	Collaboration tools for real time and delayed communications.	**Very high**. Allows team members to collaborate with ease.
Integrated team directory	Integrated on and offshore team directory listing all info about team members and how to reach them.	**High**. Provides the team an integrated view of on and off shore teams as one. Provides easy access to contact info.

Table 17: Sample Portal Components

Accountability and Compliance

Methodology execution requires commitment and, above all, accountability. You must approach the metrics gathering and methodology while recognizing that there will be mistakes and exceptions, but that only through sustained effort at many levels of project management and implementation will you reap benefits. You must build a collaborative environment in which individuals are held accountable for their participation. Specific areas that may be addressed include:

- **Dedicated personnel**—Designate an individual as the methodology czar for the project and make sure that he or she has the support of senior management.

- **Project management office (PMO)**—Consider the creation of a PMO for large programs that are managing multiple projects. PMOs offer several advantages:

- **Scale**—The organization benefits from leveraging the investment across multiple projects.

- **Expertise**—A depth of skill can be developed in niche as well as mainstream competencies.

- **Certification**—Require personnel to achieve certain certification levels prior to taking on certain roles or moving on to new assignments.

- **Evaluation and compensation**—Build adherence to process into the personnel evaluation process and thereby link it to a powerful employee incentive: compensation.

Accountability has been discussed within the context of your own organization, but in a vendor relationship the same rules apply. Methodology with accompanying certification and performance are all subject to contractual terms.

Summary

There are rarely black-and-white guidelines to process implementation and metrics development. You must engage your end customer and your partners in the broader process of implementation, since they will ultimately judge your success or be the reason for your failure. Your methodology must reflect the logical and physical constraints of your new distributed environment while your metrics pinpoint performance challenges, opportunities and successes.

Chapter 18 Summary
Process Implementation and Metrics Development

Chapter Theme

Process implementation and metrics development allow you to make firm and reasonable commitments and improve your efficiency over time. This chapter establishes the connection between gating processes that account for logical groups of work and underlying metrics that hint at trends and actionable root cause analysis.

- ❏ **Executive commitment**
- ❏ **Sufficiency and relevancy**
- ❏ **Accountability**
- ❏ **Ongoing measurement**

Key Points

By establishing process gates, you introduce the notion of "accountability by gate". Collect only metrics that are sufficient, relevant, representative and offer appropriate context. Tools like project portals can add tremendous value by reducing the collection costs of critical data.

- ❏ **Gated process**
- ❏ **Metrics driven**
- ❏ **Portal integration**
- ❏ **Project management scorecard**
- ❏ **Integrated team**

Reader Take-Away

You should have a framework for considering the establishment of a gating process for critical activities that involve handoffs between the on- and offshore teams within your own environment. You should also appreciate the impact that accountability can have on validating the investment in metrics development.

Questions for Consideration

- ❏ Is your process/methodology gated and ready for onshore/offshore integration?
- ❏ Have your business goals been directly linked to the metrics you will measure?
- ❏ Have you developed your project management scorecard?
- ❏ Are you using a portal or other integrated tool set for ongoing communications and collaboration between the on- offshore teams?

Part IV: Maintaining and Renewing your Offshore Initiatives

Chapter 19

Managing Vendors, Building Partnerships

Overview

Defining the contract is only the beginning of your vendor relationship. All relationships, whether long or short term, require work on many levels if they are to mature into something valuable. This chapter focuses on a few areas that you can proactively manage to ensure a mutually beneficial experience.

Vendor or Partner

In managing an external relationship, first you must establish whether you view the other party as a vendor or a partner. This distinction has important implications. You will be investing time, management focus and possibly money into the venture. If you view the other party as only a vendor that could be easily replaced in the next bidding cycle, you should be careful to limit your investment to the bare minimum required to get the job done. If on the other hand the vendor is not so easily displaced, is likely to build up knowledge about your proprietary work product or process and is an entity whose long-term financial health is important to your success, then you likely have yourself a partner.

The lens through which you view such relationships will mean the difference between success and failure, collaborative improvement or positional bargaining, met expectations and lost opportunities.

Table 18 offers guidelines as to the type of relationship that you might require.

Switching Costs

Most of the items Table 18 indicate a level of switching cost (the cost to make a change in this case from one vendor to another) that is usually significant. Consider the time and money invested in getting to a signed contract and later to an implemented capability.

- What would be the cost of reaching the same stage with another vendor?
- Would you need to write off capital expenditures in the current environment, or to retrain your own or add new vendor personnel?
- Would you even have the opportunity to take another run at the offshore paradigm if you had a failure with a service provider?

Switching costs are likely to be high in many cases. A relationship that only calls for arm's-length dealings in a domestic environment may nevertheless call for your close attention in an offshore one, given the high switching costs and the price of failure when you are removed from the work by 12,000 miles, numerous time zones and a culture difference.

For better or worse, once you have entered into a relationship with an offshore vendor, you are likely to be more tightly coupled and for a longer period of time than you might be with a domestic services provider. Switching costs are simply higher. You can position yourself to manage this risk optimally through a robust selection process, but you may also opt to engage in certain activities prior to contract signature that in a domestic environment might normally not occur until after signing. Contact with operational personnel with whom you will ultimately be doing the work is critical, as is understanding the framework for managing challenges when they do arise. Detailing of this governance model discussed next is often best established prior to conclusion of the contract, since it will help to head off issues prior to their becoming problems.

	Offshore relationship attributes	
Area	Indicative of a need that can be met by a vendor.	Indicative of a need that can be met by a partner.
Skills	Skills can be readily found and assimilated.	Skills not easily found. Investment must be made in training.
Savings	Easily achieved by numerous providers for low complexity functions.	Significant learning curve required to get productivity to 100% requiring larger transition cost.
Process integration	Limited integration required to domestic client.	Complex integration required to develop the end product and for maximizing benefits.
Capital expenditures	Limited to no capital requirement.	Significant capital outlays required for infrastructure, training, and other integration and process areas.
Price of failure	Minimal long term impact to buyer if relationship is not successful.	Serious ramifications to the clients business or their customers.
Switching costs	Low to no switching costs.	Very high switching costs due to capital and complex process integration requirements.

Table 18: Need for Vendor versus Partner

Governance

Governance is defined broadly here as a set of activities to manage the formal reporting relationship, including fulfillment of specific contractual obligations and service levels as well as the operational interparty relationship that includes escalation and resolution of issues, joint planning and general communications. The right governance structure will speed decisions, increase visibility and ultimately reduce risk.

A number of specific actions promote good governance:

- **Steering committee**—Your executive review board should include representation from the partner. The better the partner understands the context of the overall initiative, the more able they will be to work toward your goals. This forum also gives them the opportunity to express their concerns in a nonoperational, and ideally nonconfrontational environment. This is a critical element to communications, particularly if the partner needs to deliver tough messages about your organization's own performance but is concerned about doing so with the line managers they interact with on a day-to-day basis.

- **Chain of command/escalation procedures**—Establish a clear understanding of the chain of command and the events that should trigger an escalation of issues. The goal should be to manage issues proactively prior to their becoming problems.

- **Key process gate reviews**—Use a metrics-driven process where possible and create enough gates to ensure quality and expectation alignment during the process, not only at the end of the process when opportunities for correction are limited.

- **Status meetings**—These should be held regularly at the project and program level and should be as brief and concise as possible. Establish firm schedules as well as records of attendance, discussion points, decisions made and follow-up actions mandated.

- **Quarterly and annual account reviews**—These should be highly scripted exercises that review operational and financial performance metrics along with outstanding issues. Beyond contractual obligation review, the general tone of the meeting should be kept at a strategic level, with a heavy focus on understanding structural impediments to future increased performance.

- **Joint goal setting**—The idea is to break down organizational barriers and to have everyone focus on the problem with the same level of intensity. Smoothing out hierarchical differences for this exercise is tricky and

requires cooperation at all levels. It is essential to create a structure of joint
accountability that does not leave room for finger pointing.

As with the discussion above on vendors versus partners, the governance
structure will depend heavily on an understanding of the relationship that you
need in order to be successful. What level of integration is required for the
success of your initiative? Does your operational model provide for sufficient
collaboration to focus both parties on achieving your objectives? Or does the
model simply focus on each party fulfilling checklists of obligations?

Planned and deliberate activities including communication and travel can have a
profound impact on the success of the governance model. The figure below
contrasts activity levels that we have observed in partner versus vendor
environments.

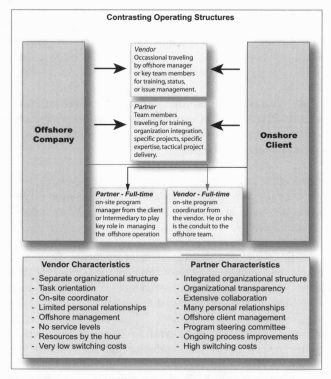

Figure 22: Vendor versus Partner: Contrasting Operating Approaches

Your Offsourcing Roadmap should identify a framework for the governance
model you'll require to keep the relationship on track. A curious contradiction is
that it will have the most value when you are at the lowest point in your
relationship.

One final note on governance: understand the offshore environment. If you are working with a partner, then by definition you have established the strategic, long-term or high-switching-cost nature of the relationship. In such a case, the lack of site visits may significantly impede your ability to help your partner help you to be successful. Invest the time to understand the local operating environment—its resources as well as constraints. Get to know the people, understand their culture and enjoy the relationship.

Communication

Communication is crucial; yet under even the best circumstances it can be fraught with problems. Add to that a separation of 12,000 miles, many time zones, different cultures and language barriers, the lack of gestures and facial cues, and you begin to get a picture of the offsourcing communications climate. You ask a series of questions over the phone, you get limited response, and at the end of the conversation the vendor says, "Yes, I can do that" or "Yes, I understand and it will be done by that date." But in fact the individual on the other end of the phone did not understand, expectations got completely out of sync, and as the date approaches the vendor is surprised at the customer's reaction when he or she learns that the deadline will not be met.

Adherence to some basic rules can help you to overcome the challenges:

- Document all requirements, actions and requests.
- Use instant communication mediums, including chat rooms, to allow staff to ask questions online in real time (however, be sure to follow up with an e-mail to confirm in writing whether decisions were made or key assumptions established).
- Use conference/video calls with key people.
- Hold face-to-face meetings.
- Practice extreme diligence on both sides of the ocean:
  o Offshore must be diligent and tenacious at follow-up and asking questions.
  o Onshore must be diligent and tenacious at follow-up and asking questions.
- Give the vendor permission to just say NO!
  o You must establish an environment in which the offshore personnel feel comfortable in challenging the prevailing wisdom of the onshore team.

Too often, partnerships disintegrate into vendor-like relationships as a result of neglected and insufficient communications. At the executive level, contact may occur only at the contract signing or as the offshore CEO passes through town on one of his or her US trips. The project managers will talk periodically depending on the complexity of the processes or, more likely, only as issues arise. The team leaders may also communicate periodically, but in the vendor relationship this seems to occur (too often) at the last minute. At the staff level, there may be little to no contact. Consider the possibilities if the Vendor Communications Patterns figure were to have black lines connecting the organizations at each level.

Success requires people at all levels and on both sides of the ocean to take responsibility for communicating. If there is a question, talk, send an e-mail and follow up diligently. Don't ever let the communication flow stop. Rework will diminish, quality will escalate, relationships will evolve and confidence will increase.

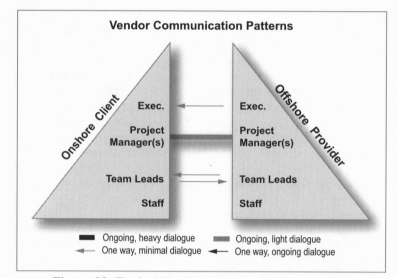

Figure 23: Typical Vendor Communication Patterns

Formal

Governance activities will account for the majority of formal communications. Be sure to keep a written record of the meetings along with any related artifacts for reference. The legal department will undoubtedly store the contracts, but we recommend that you keep a separate copy close to hand for reference. Consider building a taxonomy of working papers that can be accessed by the entire management team. These can be made available in electronic format through a collaborative management portal (see Chapter 18).

Escalation procedures in the operational environment and disaster recovery scenarios are especially important and should be reviewed on a periodic basis. Numbers change, personnel move on and the environment is modified to accommodate new requirements. Do not assume that the existing information is current. The offshore management portal is a great tool to allow role-restricted access to a centralized set of updated information.

Informal

Informal communications at a level that will help you understand personnel concerns and competencies in the vendor environment may be more challenging. If your partner is doing a good job of managing the process, deliverables and organization, then you may be given only limited unsupervised time to interact with your offshore team members—particularly if you have a senior position in the buyer organization. This is both natural and understandable since your partner will want to put their best foot forward. Allowing less experienced partner personnel to interact at length with you, as a client, creates the risk for the partner of someone wandering off script and raising unnecessary doubts.

The counter position is that if you want to understand the true nature of the offshore environment, you certainly won't get it by interviewing personnel with their boss or their boss's boss in the room. You must go directly to the source, but be cognizant of the challenges. You are a client asking in for perspectives not communicated to you through formal channels. Further you are asking for them from nonexecutives who probably come from a culture that values hierarchy and saving face. To get anywhere you must establish some baselines.

- **Confidentiality**—First and foremost you must establish and remain true to a policy that anything that you say or hear will be held in confidence. Call it the "Vegas" rules for relationship management.

> *Remember the Law of Reciprocity: To get information you must first give it.*

- **Informality**—Choose an environment that is relaxed and where the staff does not feel that they are under the spotlight. Don't bring individuals in one at a time to the office, where they are likely to feel intimidated. Consider ordering in some food or taking a group out to lunch where they can make a logical break from their professional surrounding.

- **Repetition**—You cannot expect to build trust overnight. You must make yourself available over a period of time, possibly constructing scenarios to make this happen: happy hours, food breaks and team presentations on areas of expertise all provide opportunities to establish informal communication with the rank and file of your partner.

Above all, remember the Law of Reciprocity: To get information you must first give it.[25] Expect that the cost of building trust is sharing information and your own perspectives.

Time Zones

Time zones often present interesting challenges for the onshore team. Their habits and schedules must change to reflect time zone differences, since the availability of offshore personnel may sometimes be restricted. Offshore personnel are accustomed to this, so their work patterns tend to include coming into the office later in the morning and staying later into the evenings. (Call centers are an exception, since these personnel work at night in the local geography to be available for business hours in the United States.) The figure below reflects the time variances between Dallas, Mumbai and Manila. As with other areas of the offshore paradigm, communication requires a little more planning and preparation; you can't just pick up the phone and call your offshore colleagues in the middle of the day (your time).

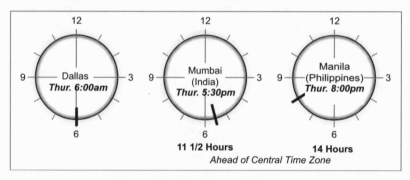

Figure 24: Time Zone Differences

This forces the onshore team to set clear agendas and meeting times, record attendance and discussion points and, frankly, do the things that we all should do anyway. Successful communication requires an increased level of discipline.

Service Level Agreements and Performance

Service level management is a field enormous in scope and highly specific in implementation. We will say only this: *Just as the vendor or partner must understand your business model, there is tremendous value and urgency in your understanding theirs.* If there are disputes over performance or the maintenance of service levels, the right contract will protect you; however, your knowledge of your partner's business can create potential win/win scenarios. Be creative about trading on those service level penalties to get things that add value to your organization but that, given seasonality, variance in client demand and other

---

[25] All graduates of Fernando Bartolome's (INSEAD) Managerial Behavior class are drilled on this concept.

factors, are part of a fixed cost for the vendor and therefore "less expensive" to offer to you.

Portal: Partner Management Scorecard

The portal, home to so many other initiatives, is also a great vehicle for keeping abreast of a partner's performance and helping them to manage themselves. Your metrics development exercise will undoubtedly have identified numerous areas where the vendor will be required to build and deliver metrics. The best place to present this data is through the collaborative management portal.

Consider dedicating a portion of your Portal Vision Workshop to looking at these partner requirements. Data that is aggregated automatically from their systems will help them to be a better partner and should lower their collection costs. If you dictate the method whereby your partner must present performance data to you, you will have the opportunity to defray some of the portal development costs. However, portrayed accurately as a way to help your partner, this tool should be something in which they have great incentive to invest.

Summary

One day not long after the contract has been signed, the honeymoon will be over and you will begin to feel the stresses of operational challenges. When that happens, will you be working with a vendor or a partner? Make that assessment before you get hitched, so that you can set your expectations appropriately. There is unlikely to be a stick big enough to get you what you want after the fact if there is no alignment between parties. Effective relationship management requires a mutual understanding of goals and incentives.

If your business plan requires a long-term relationship to achieve performance and quality objectives, then be prepared to work aggressively with your partner to set expectations, communicate early and often, and enable management with automated decision support systems. No contract can account for all potential situations, but a good governance structure can go far toward bridging the gaps.

Chapter 19 Summary
Managing Vendors, Building Partnerships

Chapter Theme

Isn't everyone a partner? They say that they are. Understanding whether the offsourced solution requires a vendor or partner seems subtle, but it can fundamentally change the effectiveness and efficiency of the offsourced operation. The authors articulate some of the differences.

❏ Vendor or partner
❏ Skill requirements
❏ Investment requirements
❏ Operating model
❏ Cultural alignment

Key Points

Determine your needs, vendor or partner, by understanding your switching costs and the complexity of the processes that you must build.

Build formal and informal communication bridges and opportunities, and recognize that the working hours and behavioral patterns of your onshore team must accommodate the new paradigm.

❏ Integrated teams
❏ Organization transparency
❏ Switching costs
❏ Onshore working hours
❏ Governance model

Reader Take-Away

You should have a thorough grounding in the characteristics of an environment that requires an offshore provider to step up in true partnership fashion. Your ability to perform this diagnostic will allow you to better focus on elements that you must secure during the contract negotiation process. In addition, you should have a baseline understanding of the governance model and actions required to effectively communicate at all levels of the organization in a partnership arrangement.

Questions for Consideration

❏ Does your organization require a vendor or a partner? Has this been considered?
❏ Has the governance model been developed, and how will it affect the provider?
❏ Is the function you are going to offsource a simple handoff: get the finished product back?
❏ What tools do you feel will be required for ongoing communications and collaboration?

Chapter 20

The Offsourcing Maturity Model

Overview

The Offsourcing Maturity Model is a roadmap and risk management framework for reinventing the IT function into a low-cost, high-service organization leveraging remote resources.

In Chapter 1 we introduced the stages of the IT-enabled services value chain that constitute the field of offsourcing. In this chapter we focus on a framework for reaching the maximum benefits that offsourcing has to offer using the application development areas of the IT-enabled services value chain to illustrate. We call this framework the Offsourcing Maturity Model.

The Offsourcing Maturity Model (OMM) was developed as a way of providing context for clients struggling to find a path forward in the offsourcing environment. It recognizes that even with cost savings, IT organizations will ultimately be measured by the industry based on the predictability and quality of their results. Execution, then, as well as cost savings must be the objective.

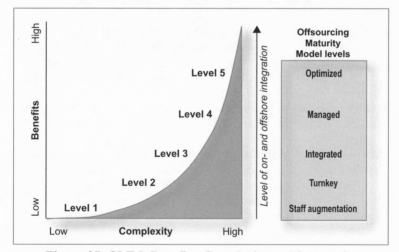

Figure 25: OMM: Benefits, Complexity and Integration

For organizations that have no offsourcing capability (internal or external), the question may be how or where to get started. Others may be enjoying success in some areas and looking to expand the benefits, while still others may be failing miserably with no clear understanding of what went wrong or how to improve the situation.

No matter your current level of activity, the OMM serves a number of purposes:

- **Diagnostic**—The model provides a baseline for diagnosing your organization's level of performance and ultimately provides a set of goals for you to achieve in order to improve your current operation—in other words, your organization's readiness for offsourcing and at what level of activity you can be expected to begin to see success.

- **Roadmap**—Based on the diagnostic and an understanding of where you currently fit in the overall maturity schema, next steps become more obvious. The goals and objectives are not the same for every organization, since risk profiles are different, but significant commonalities can be inferred.

- **Investment guide**—An overview of the personnel, processes and measurements to be successful at each level are presented. This creates a comprehensive overview of the investments required to support the transition.

- **Metrics guidance**—The model outlines the measurements that your organization needs to begin collecting so that you can effectively gain visibility and control and eventually manage problems proactively.

You will notice that there are similarities in some of the terminology discussed here and in reference to the Capability Maturity Model (CMM) as defined by the Software Engineering Institute. This is in part a reflection of the high regard in which we hold CMM as a software engineering management tool. It is also because many of the behavioral patterns discussed and the metrics identified in the CMM are necessary to be successful in moving application development into an offsourced model. However, the OMM and CMM are different.

The CMM strives to describe "the stages through which software organizations evolve as they define, implement, measure, control, and improve their software processes." Additionally it provides "a guide for selecting process improvement strategies by facilitating the determination of current process capabilities and the identification of the issues most critical to software quality and process improvement."[26]

The OMM provides an organizational framework at a higher level, one that is squarely focused on moving an organization up a learning curve to reinvent

---

[26] Addison Wesley, *The Capability Maturity Model: Guidelines for Improving the Software Process* (SEI, 1995).

itself globally to reduce costs and increase service levels. It focuses on the ability of highly distributed operations to work effectively together, whether as part of the same organization or in a buyer/partner relationship.

For illustrative purposes in this chapter, the OMM considers that a third party provides the remote services. It may be desirable for reasons discussed in Chapter 6 to choose a different legal relationship such as a joint venture or even a wholly owned subsidiary in achieving the maximum benefits for your organization.

Level 1: Staff Augmentation

At Level 1 of the OMM, the organization begins to foster relationships with an offsourcing partner to provide resources on site, on a time and materials basis. The relationship is marked by lower value–added activity. It is that of buyer/vendor, with the vendor limited in its ability to differentiate itself from its competitors beyond pricing and the skills of the specific resources in question.

Process plays a somewhat diminished role in the day-to-day management of the outputs of the third party, since they are providing technical skills in areas of limited scope or task orientation. They plug into the work plan like anyone else, have limited to no decision-making responsibility and have no responsibility for managing risk. Expectations are only managed upward toward their team leader or project manager.

Success of the engagement boils down to, "Did the resource create the specific deliverables or tasks that were asked of them and were they of high quality?"

Key characteristics of Level 1 are:

- **Personnel**—The quality of the service is only as good as the individual staff member providing it.

- **Process**—The vendor is not required to have any process, and the buyer simply needs to define a set of inputs, outputs and expected time frames.

- **Technology**—Technology risk is high in anything except the core skill set of the individual contractor.

- **Metrics**—Metrics are captured on a very limited basis, if at all.
  - o   Work units per hour
  - o   Defects per work unit

- **Vendor/partner relationship**—Arm's-length. Cost- and skills-based relationship.

- **Key learning focus**
  o   Initial vendor management
  o   Integration of nonemployees into the development team

Level 2: Turnkey

At Level 2 of the OMM, the organization takes on some degree of risk in the contracting arrangement. The third party is contracted to take a set of detailed specifications and turn them into a high-quality, tested deliverable.

Key characteristics of Level 2 are:

- **Personnel**—Project management experience, and probably some level of knowledge of the application architecture, is required in the vendor. At a minimum, an on-site and an offshore manager are required to funnel questions and answers back and forth. Reduction in personnel on site (and the associated change management issues that accompany this action) will be based on whether the buyer is seeking addition capacity or views the turnkey relationship as part of a long-term strategic direction.

- **Process**—The degree of difficulty in achieving Level 2 in the OMM is largely dictated by the size and complexity of the application. A relatively simple application may be shipped offshore; and with the usual management tools in place and regular access to the requirements manager, success is highly probable. A large project involving a complex service-based architecture requires significant process controls to meet the same expectation of success. Some key elements of process are:

  - Management
    o   Budgeting and time tracking
    o   Visibility to onshore configuration management
    o   Contract management
    o   Requirements clarification
  - Organizational
    o   Training on architecture to be used by developers as required
    o   Buyer resource dedicated to process management
    o   Vendor resource on site to manage interface with remote geography and provide visibility of management goals to remote team
  - Engineering
    o   Understanding and adherence to quality standards

  - **Technology**—Technology risk may be more insulated because more resources with a presumably broader set of skill sets are being leveraged in the third party.

- **Metrics**—Measurements of vendor performance and remote development productivity will be tracked. The focus is on validating vendor performance and when necessary using it as a negotiating tool.
  o   Work units per hour
  o   Defects per work unit

- **Vendor/partner relationship**—The relationship is still somewhat arm's-length since there is still a specified set of inputs and outputs. However, some up-front investment is required to understand the vendor's quality assurance process.

  o   Key buyer resources (or their 3rd party catalyst) should visit the offsourcing facility to gain a fuller appreciation of the cultural aspects of the relationship. A visit is also important for understanding the constraints under which the vendor is working with respect to onshore information and access to decision-making personnel.

Level 3: Integrated

At Level 3 of the OMM, the organization pushes additional development activity offshore including analysis and design, system testing and ongoing code fixes (maintenance). The delivery of quality product is truly an "integrated" experience with multiple cross-border activities.

Taking the step from Level 2 to Level 3 involves a significant evolution in the operating structure between onshore and offshore. A number of factors come into play:

> *Taking the step from Level 2 to Level 3 involves a significant evolution in the operating structure between onshore and offshore.*

- **Potential savings**—As the volume of work executed remotely increases, so too does the potential for cost savings. In an application development environment, we estimate that moving to Level 3 permits the organization to move 60% of the work offshore, up from 25% in Level 2. This has an enormous impact on the cost structure and the service levels that an IT organization can achieve. Assuming a development budget of $10 million that is now operating at Level 3, 50% savings on the 60% of work moved offshore results in a $3 million gain—*or* the capacity to complete 30% more projects.

- **Costs of failure**—The stakes are raised. At this level the organization is making a significant commitment to offsourcing as a part of its strategic direction (which may also be true at Level 2) since the cost of reversal is high when measured in time, personnel and ultimately money. Further, failure at this level may irreversibly damage the future prospects of using offsourcing as a means of improving the cost structure and service level of the IT organization.

- **Change management**—With the amount of work now being done in the remote geography, the skill mix onshore will change significantly and a restructuring of the development organization will be required. If offsourcing is used strictly as a cost-reduction tool, there are significant human resources and cultural impacts that must be managed proactively and aggressively to ensure that the transition is smooth and that individuals who do not possess the skills to move forward with the organization are either provided training or transitioned out of the organization with dignity and respect.

- **Vendor/partner relationship**—The cost of failure and the investment being made by the buyer will likely warrant a significant review of the relationship to ensure that it adequately protects the buyer from vendor-related risks. The buyer may wish to begin reviewing the legal structure of the relationship to gain long-term control of certain aspects of the process.

Key characteristics of Level 3 are:

- **Personnel**—Significant reduction of onshore headcount will occur and the profile of the remaining headcount may require change to reflect modified job responsibilities and a more complex work environment.

- **Process**
  - Management
    - Integrated management team
    - Daily (if not more frequent) structured conversations and other communications between onshore and offshore resources
  - Organizational
    - Process management resources required in both onshore and offshore environments
    - Team building and cross-cultural training required
    - Technology training required
  - Engineering
    - Process management

- **Technology**—Elements of the architecture are now being worked on and possibly investigated in the offshore environment while architectural vision and control remain in the onshore environment.

- **Metrics**—The amount of information being shared across the organization increases in correlation to the number of mutual dependencies that now exist between the onshore and offshore environments. We recommend that some metrics be tracked on items that require joint focus, thus reinforcing some of the communications requirements.

- **Vendor/partner relationship**—The relationship has changed from "them and us" to "we." Success is now completely dependent on joint efforts, with numerous critical dependencies between the onshore and offshore environments. As noted above, a review of the contract may be required for the organization to feel comfortable in making the commitment to move from Level 2 to Level 3.

  o Regular rotation of key individuals must occur in both directions. Line managers in the onshore operation must understand the visibility and constraints under which their teams and peers are working in the remote geography.

Level 4: Managed

At Level 4 of the OMM, a heavy focus is placed on the use of data to understand and regulate processes. At this stage, many aspects of the development capacity have been moved offshore and data is being collected consistently across the entire organization. This creates the opportunity to begin giving focus to consistently problematic areas.

The level of quantitative data and the transparency in the organization works well enough in both directions that management may feel comfortable taking the following two steps:

- **Removal of duplicate line management interfaces**—The model of on-site manager versus off-site management for specific areas of activity indicates two possible scenarios: 1) The activity is sufficiently complex that real-time guidance and feedback must be given for resources to perform effectively; or 2) goals are not sufficiently clear, work is not adequately structured and relationships are not sufficiently established for work to proceed without constant feedback. At Level 4, organizations should no longer need the crutch of an on-site manager to address the second scenario.

- **Delegation of responsibility to offshore environment**—The data is now in place to manage quantitatively, and objectives and goals are equally visible across both organizations. Issues are identified early and corrective action can be taken before serious problems occur. In this environment, it is appropriate to ask whether ownership of specific areas could be completely delegated to the offshore environment.

Key characteristics of Level 4 are:

- **Personnel**—Strong onshore managers have been put in position to manage activities remote to them. This can occur both ways with functions such as maintenance being managed offshore while more junior team members provide any necessary onshore presence.

- **Process**
  o Management
    ➤ Beyond the structured communication between onshore and offshore resources, informal communications are observed regularly and areas of mutual interest are explored.
    ➤ A significant number of offshore resources can expect to have performance evaluations written by onshore team members.
    ➤ Some activities may be managed in the reverse fashion.
  o Organizational
    ➤ Duplication of management resources on both sides of the offshore environment may no longer be required, as a culture of openness has been developed.
    ➤ Many onshore staff members will require training on managing personnel remotely.
  o Engineering
    ➤ Research and development is conducted with objectives being pushed offshore, and the remote team is left to determine the best approach to establish the working models

- **Technology**
  o Technology research priorities may begin to be determined for some areas in the remote geography.

- **Metrics**
  o Data is being used to focus attention and resources on problematic areas.

- **Vendor/partner relationship**—The contractual relationship may have now taken on more of an equity arrangement to recognize the risk that the organization is assuming by relying so heavily on the vendor/partner. As data is now being collected and analyzed for numerous areas of performance, the vendor/partner should be given an opportunity to share in the benefits of meeting specific performance criteria.

Level 5: Optimized

At Level 5 of the OMM, the organization is completely integrated and operates in a seamless fashion across geographies. Management is focused on moving as much work as possible to an offshore environment to take advantage of cost savings, greater capacity or time-to-market benefits. The organization is functioning as a single unit and is benefiting from reduced delivery times, better quality code and higher average salaries for its onshore workers, who now have higher value–added roles. The organization is self-teaching and so continues to tweak process and procedure in the pursuit of perfection.

In addition, the organization takes a different strategic perspective in Level 5 than at Level 4 with respect to two key elements:

- **Legal structure**—It is unlikely that Level 5 would be achieved without an accompanying joint legal investment relationship, given the need to retain key personnel and assure them of career growth. At this level, the buyer has made an enormous strategic commitment. It is easy to understand why they would want to have more than just contractual remedies to address issues if they arise.

- **Placement of key personnel**—The preoccupation about what to keep onshore versus offshore as a way of managing risks arising from issues of visibility and control is absent. Personnel decisions are based on a combination of skills, cost and efficiency.

Key characteristics of Level 5 are:

- **Personnel**—Location of personnel is no longer viewed as an impediment to performance of work except as it requires immediate and regular interaction with users and business sponsors.

- **Process**
  - Management
    - ➢ Offshore resources are part of the IT organization's executive team.
    - ➢ Process changes required as a result of inputs from data collection are documented, incorporated and communicated on an ongoing basis.
  - Organizational
    - ➢ Areas for additional IT-enabled offsourcing are being explored as part of an ongoing process of cost and service improvement.

- **Technology**—Technology is recommended and introduced as a result of investigation by both onshore and offshore resources.

- **Metrics**—Data is used as an input to making proactive improvements of the process.

- **Vendor/partner relationship**—The relationship is likely to be one of equity, with a minimum of joint ownership on the buyer's part.

Summary

The Offsourcing Maturity Model is a roadmap and risk management framework for reinventing the IT function into a low-cost, high-service organization leveraging remote or offsourced resources.

The OMM is imperfect and limited in that by standing alone it does not have the detail of process, templates and history that drive specific task-oriented actions on a day-to-day level. However, when used in conjunction with a commitment to deploy other domain-specific methodologies including the Capability Maturity Model, the OMM provides guidance and significant insight into managing risk in the new remote geographic environment. It assists you in focusing your efforts and in understanding the education, personnel and investments required to build a world-class distributed IT-enabled services organization.

| Activity | Offshore Maturity Model | | | | |
	Level 1 Staff Augmentation	Level 2 Turnkey	Level 3 Integrated	Level 4 Managed	Level 5 Optimized
Maximum offshore % of process	20%	40%	50%	60%	70%
Control	On	Split	Split	Split	Split
Vendor governance model	Yes	Yes	No	No	No
Partner governance model	No	No	Yes	Yes	Yes
Onshore staff alignment	No	No	Yes	Yes	Yes
Communications needs	Informal	Informal	Formal	Formal	Formal
Infrastructure needs	None	None	Yes	Yes	Yes
Metrics defined and captured	No	No	Yes	Yes	Yes

Table 19: OMM: Application Development Perspective

- This scenario reflects application development. Percentages will vary according to the risk that a client wishes to assume, and other IT-enabled services may require initiation at Level 2 with some type of turnkey project.

Chapter 20 Summary
The Offsourcing Maturity Model

Chapter Theme

The Offsourcing Maturity Model (OMM) is a roadmap and risk management framework for reinventing IT and repetitive process functions into a low-cost, high-service-level organization leveraging offshore resources. It delivers a macro context for planning process and infrastructure needs, training and metrics development.

- Staff augmentation
- Turnkey
- Integrated
- Managed
- Optimizing

Key Points

As you move up the OMM, the level of integration between on- and offshore components allows you to increase the percentage of work performed remotely and thus increase savings while maintaining or improving service levels. Levels of control, sophistication in communications, process maturity and other factors play into the defined levels.

- Process control
- Local presence
- Communications
- Training
- Process maturity
- Metrics maturity
- Quality assurance maturity

Reader Take-Away

You should have a strategic perspective on the evolution of offsourcing initiatives within your environment and an understanding of the mechanics required to be successful at ever greater levels of sophistication. You should be able to apply the OMM as a diagnostic to understand at a high level why some initiatives are failing given the absence of specific support mechanisms. You should also understand where to go next as you seek to increase the benefits of your initiatives.

Questions for Consideration

- Where does your organization currently fit within the OMM?
- Is there alignment between the level at which you are operating and the presence of underlying support structure including communications and metrics?
- If you are operating at Level 3 or above and are working with a vendor, have they stepped up to invest in process and long-range joint goal setting?
- Do you know the level of maturity required to meet your organization's goals?

Part V: Offshore Case Studies

Chapter 21

Case Study: Outbound Call Center

Overview

A large insurance marketing organization creating telemarketing leads sought to reduce its cost per lead while improving the quality of the output. The emergence of Internet customer acquisition as a viable and cost effective solution placed the long-term cost model of the telemarketing in question.

Environment

The insurance group was operating two domestic call centers to service lead orders from the field organization. The operation had been honed to a high level of efficiency over the preceding years through a combination of technology upgrades, process management and training. Incremental improvements in the operation would be minimal at best.

Turnover was running at approximately 300% on an annualized basis, and there were ongoing challenges with the quality of the diction and accent of agents working the phones.

Unique Challenges

Significant customization had been completed on the predictive dialer to accommodate lead objectives as related to geographic areas.

Scripts had to be modified and tested on a regular basis to respond to ongoing regulatory changes and to accommodate new campaigns.

Approach

A standardized approach to the solution development was adopted including:

- **Business Case**—The Business Case was developed with key stakeholders in validating the potential for cost savings. Conservative assumptions were made regarding the productivity of the agents.

- **Offsourcing Roadmap**—The planning exercise was conducted concurrently with a vendor selection process in which candidates from numerous geographies were interviewed. Vendor presentations were conducted by groups operating in the Caribbean, Philippines and India, with the latter two emerging as very strong players. As qualified vendors emerged, the Business Case was refined and the decision was taken to proceed with a pilot.

At this point, a broader set of personnel was brought into the initiative. The technology and process models for the pilot and implementation environments were developed. Focus was given to the pilot while the full implementation models were taken far enough to validate that the long-term target model could be achieved.

- **Pilot**—The vendor attended US-based training and the operator sent a senior management team to take charge of agent training and to ensure the process and technology environment during a two-and-a-half-week launch period. A 90-day pilot with 25 customer service agents is in process at press time with specified metrics and goals but is relying on some manual procedures to minimize technology investment during the trial. As initial results indicate favorable performance, investment in the full implementation technology environment is anticipated.

- **Full Implementation**—Subsequent to a favorable pilot the implementation is expected to scale into a full outsourcing relationship. At that time additional technology investments are anticipated to address automation requirements on the predictive dialer.

One of the domestic centers is anticipated to be kept online at reduced capacity to act as a backup and to operate as the hub for testing, new campaigns and other functions.

Benefits

The primary benefit expected is the reduction in lead generation costs of approximately 40%. Beyond that it is hoped that the yield rate on dialing files will improve, further enhancing the Business Case by reducing expenditures on calling lists.

Summary

The operator began the offshore process as "an academic exercise" but based upon favorable vendor interviews moved rapidly to an execution strategy. The most difficult decision in the process was to determine which geography to select: India or the Philippines. The due diligence indicated fewer accent challenges and a closer cultural affinity to the US in the Philippines, but an additional cost savings from India. The final selection hinged on the company's belief that their operation was simple enough not to be impeded by any perceived unfavorable comparisons in the Indian environment with that of the Philippines.

The company will continue to consider the Philippines as additional opportunities to move operations offshore emerge. They wish to take a long-term position of diversifying their geographic risk.

Chapter 22

Case Study: Software Company

Overview

A midmarket software company utilizing remote, nearshore and offshore development services in a traditional vendor relationship sought to take a more strategic approach to leveraging its offshore capability. The objective was to cut costs while increasing capacity and quality.

Environment

The organization was building a third generation Web based supply chain application with a team of 100+ developers. Remote, nearshore and offshore capabilities had been in place for a few months, with design, coding and testing distributed between three different locations. The offshore component was regarded within the organization as having minimal impact, questionable quality and little understanding of long-range requirements. The offshore environment was on the verge of being shut down, while the nearshore activities were being touted as the long-term solution. Team dynamics were such that belief in offshore was not evident and the consensus was a desire to increase local, remote and nearshore resources.

Challenges

Moving the integration of the offshore development capabilities beyond a simple "body shop" approach to reap maximum benefits required focus in a number of areas:

- **Division of labor**—Integration of the offshore component into the many other aspects of the project required looking at specific roles and responsibilities as far down as the team level.

- **Development methodology**—The process had not been adequately defined and was not being enforced among all locations. The requirements phase was very weak and followed an iterative, object-oriented development approach, and few gates had been established to formalize handoffs and common understandings across the team.

- **Communications and change management**—Management restructuring of the organization included understanding the required new working styles in a cross-cultural environment and appropriately communicating the goal state.

- **Quality control**—The complexity of the new environment added challenges to both metrics definition and capture, along with adding gates into the process to allow for quality reviews.

- **Infrastructure**—Additional network bandwidth was required to allow for videoconferencing and access to onshore applications along with reducing the cost of existing communications.

- **Visibility**—With a 12,000 mile barrier, visibility of day-to-day activity was a concern. An integrated program capable of permeating the cloud was required.

Approach

The organization launched the new offsourcing effort by eliminating the nearshore capability and committing to the offshore model. There was consensus that costs could be cut about 50% from internal loaded costs, but that this would require significant enhancements to methodology and infrastructure. The process described below was used to achieve these objectives:

- **Offsourcing Roadmap**—A comprehensive review of all aspects of the development organization, including personnel, process, architecture, vendor relationships and development schedules, was conducted. Findings were reviewed with executive management and a work plan was established with specific roles, responsibilities, milestones and deliverables.

- **Full Implementation**—The implementation of the target model was completed in two phases. During the first phase, the organization focused on improving communications, establishing baseline metrics and developing the required methodology enhancements. It also backtracked in a number of areas to establish working business process and development design models for use in delivering late releases of the software.

In the second phase, the target model was identified to have some analysis, all design, development, unit and integration testing offshore. This resulted in the following actions:

- **Organizational model**—The organization was significantly restructured based upon the target model:

  o **Larger offshore capacity**—The onshore development team reorganized with larger offshore development component. The offshore component eventually constituted 60% of all resources.

o **Management**—A US-based project manager was deployed to the offshore environment to work on the issues on an ongoing basis. The local offshore manager, perceived as a bottleneck to communications, was removed.

o **Joint goals**—Bicountry teams were developed with joint team goals and metrics.

o **Individual empowerment**—Team leaders were encouraged to work directly with offshore resources, circumventing the traditional "onshore manager" model. Most established daily early morning conference calls with their peers and direct reports in India.

- **Communications**—Enhancements were required in just about every area from written documentation to daily interaction and ongoing status checks.

o **Communications plan**—Daily calls and videoconference infrastructure were put in place. Weekly status meetings including the management team in both sites were established.

o **Data and training**—Cross-cultural management briefings and organizational development exercises were conducted employing the Birkman Method assessment tools. (See Chapter 17.)

- **Process**—A significant amount of time had already been invested in adapting the RUP methodology to the company's needs. This process was tweaked to reflect the program management ideas from CMM and the need to accommodate the onshore/offshore division of labor.

o **Methodology enhancement**—Enhancement of requirements documents was required to move significant analysis and design activities offshore, and procedures in every area had to be upgraded or refreshed.

o **CMM**—A program to install the Capability Maturity Model was established with a leader, support resource and clearly defined objectives and timelines.

o **Metrics**—A comprehensive set of project metrics was established and tracked. These metrics became an easy guide to tracking status at weekly project meetings.

- **Infrastructure**—A dedicated line between the offshore and the US locations replaced a satellite link to handle connectivity requirements for daily builds, testing, file transfers and overall communications. This had the added benefit of making videoconferencing, IP-based phone calls and regular backups much easier. The satellite link continued to provide a rapid backup in the event that the line was cut or experienced downtime.

Benefits

Benefits of the approach were identified and quantified in a number of areas:

- **Cost reduction**—There was significant impact on the hourly blended development rate: from $120 to transition included fully loaded, including consultants and ongoing travel. The second phase of transition through ongoing included the TCO on an hourly basis.

- **Increased capacity**—Budget flexibility created by cost reduction permitted an increase in development personnel. This was especially important in meeting client market demand.

- **Enhanced quality**—A focus on metrics permitted better understanding of issues and opportunities regardless of offshore operating model.

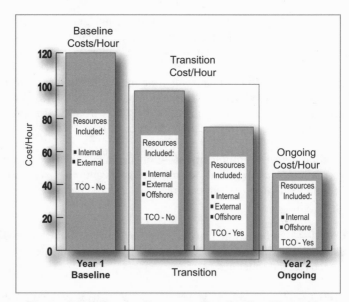

Figure 26: Software Company Hourly Cost Transition

Summary

The program outlined above required approximately 12 months to establish. During that time, the work process was streamlined from four locations to two and the average blended cost per hour dropped from $120 to $47. In addition to the activities described here, the vendor was required to upgrade certain areas of its own operations to accommodate the more strategic nature of the relationship—specifically in methodology training and the recruiting process, as workers were required to bring more significant architectural skills to bear. Finally, the work contract was negotiated under more favorable economic terms for the buyer that reflected its investment in process and skills and the ongoing commoditization of certain skill sets.

Chapter 23

Case Study: Joint Venture

Overview

A US-based high-end professional services company focused on technology and packaged solutions sought a large Indian incumbent partner to provide software development and other IT-enabled services. The goal was to provide clients with lower-cost back-end solutions attached to the high-value, domain-specific technology and management consulting services. At the same time the US provider wanted to minimize the time, cost and risk of building its own offshore capability.

Environment

The service provider had management consulting, package installation and custom development capabilities. As the market for services fell off in 2000 and 2001, management felt that when the market revived there would be pressure on margins and decided to implement a hybrid on-offshore business model. Given the pressure on the US provider's own financial situation, organic investment could not be justified, so it found a partner.

The offshore vendor sought approaches to create new distribution channels and to build credibility through domain knowledge. Partnering with an onshore domain expert created the opportunity to interact with clients of the onshore firm and prospects in the context of much higher value–added discussion.

Unique Challenges

Several organizational and operational difficulties were identified:

- **Contractual**—No two consulting engagements are exactly the same, regardless of a provider's best attempts to "productize" its offerings. How could the organizations craft a contract to accommodate all scenarios in advance of field experience?

- **Cultural**—The two entities had dramatically different operating styles regarding the customer value proposition. One was a more consultative approach focused on identifying problems and building solutions, while the other was a more resource-based, skill-driven environment.

- **Model overlap**—In the long term, the offshore vendor wanted to augment its value-add to the end customer through vertical and horizontal practices, while the US player believed that it must have an organic offshore capability to survive. Alternatively, it could simply scale down to become a niche management consultancy.

Approach

A lengthy contractual relationship was drawn up with a number of key provisions:

- **Investment**—The offshore provider committed to make a material cash investment in the US company and in exchange would receive exclusivity and a seat on the board.

- **Exclusivity**—The US organization agreed to work exclusively with the offshore provider.

- **Fee participation**—A fee schedule was recognized for margin on deals in which the respective companies introduced one another. The fees were rigid and at very high offshore retail rates, making the initial strategy of the US company out of sync with market realities.

- **Sales**—The sales model was assumed to be an integrated one where both sales teams shared and worked leads.

Benefits *Not* Realized

Minimal revenue was realized through this arrangement in the first 12 months after the contract was signed.

Specific failures resulted from:

- **Poor baseline pricing**—The resale pricing offered by the offshore vendor did not reflect market condition reality, making it difficult to compete in head-to-head opportunities. It also did not provide for pricing flexibility based on market conditions.

- **Lack of education/incentives**—The US sales force was not adequately educated on the offshore capabilities, selling approaches and value proposition. In addition the compensation plans did not provide sufficient incentive for them to change their sales strategy. This problem extended to both parties.

- **Service line development**—The US marketing arm did not integrate the offshore capability into the "go to market" service offerings, and vice versa.

This limited the sales vehicle and made it impossible for the combined on- and offshore entities to speak with one voice.

- **Operational capabilities**—Only a couple of individuals in the US organization had experience in the offshore environment, making it difficult for the provider to position itself correctly and to speak from experience in customer dialogues.

Summary

The message of this case study is not that joint ventures are impossible or that "co-opetition" (competing in some markets and cooperating in others) by companies with overlapping capabilities is not the right approach in the offshore environment. It is that US service providers that attempt to change or augment their business model to accommodate and capitalize on the coming wave of offshore activity must commit to the new paradigm. They must:

- **Plan rigorously**—The planning process must identify organizational handshakes, education, client value propositions and contractual components that must be fluid in response to market conditions. In short, an abbreviated Business Case with a full Offsourcing Roadmap should be conducted.

- **Engage at all levels**—The offshore exercise is not simply another piece of paper reflected on the Web site with a logo in the alliances section. It involves a fundamental change in the way that solutions will be sold and provisioned for end customers. This transformation implies involvement of a multidisciplinary team from sales, marketing, operations, legal and human resources.

Despite the size of many of the offshore incumbents, there is still time for US service providers to excel in the new world of offering hybrid on- and offshore solutions. Established providers enjoy strong barriers to entry, including long-standing relationships, deep domain expertise and local knowledge. Now is the time to press the advantage.

Part VI: Offsourcing Summary

Chapter 24

Key Messages

Overview

The tremendous benefits of migrating IT-enabled services offshore are within your reach if you approach your offsourcing initiative with a rigorous planning process and the appropriate operational model. Early adopters will benefit from freeing operational dollars for market growth activities like sales, marketing or new product development at the expense of their competition. Meanwhile as the adoption of offsourcing spreads beyond the Fortune 500, this once mysterious activity will become increasingly crucial for all companies with high IT expenditures or manually intensive processes to compete in an economy that knows no geographic boundaries.

Offsourcing is not a silver bullet, although it can dramatically help companies to reduce their cost structures while maintaining functional equivalence. Success requires commitment, focus and, often, difficult decisions about good people who are doing good work. But when it is executed well, offsourcing offers tremendous gains. In this book we've endeavored to demystify the steps to achieving rapid benefits and to increasing them over time. We hope that we've also communicated a palpable sense that offsourcing can be a core and highly manageable component of your long-term operational model.

This chapter summarizes a few of the areas explained in more detail in other parts of the book. The figure below reviews key points and considerations in offsourcing. It illustrates the stages and processes that must be implemented in order to achieve a successful transition from onshore to a hybrid onshore/offshore offsourcing implementation. The key elements in the each of

> *Offsourcing requires commitment, focus and difficult decisions about good people who are doing good work.*

the major phases below are a) education, b) commitment, c) process, d) communication and e) change management.

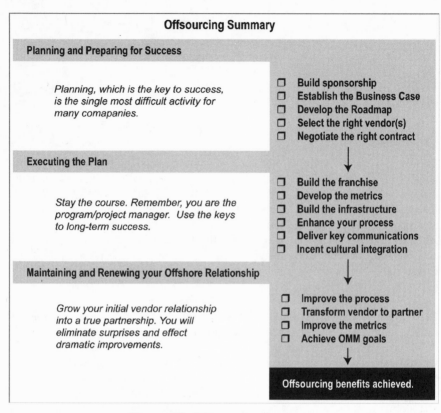

Figure 27: Offsourcing Summary

Planning and Preparing for Success

The first step is often the most difficult. Organizational inertia can be a terrible thing to overcome, so take stock of your own span of control, the characteristics of the organization's life cycle and the disposition of your colleagues. The time will come when bullheaded commitment to overcome all obstacles may be necessary, but your goal here should initially be to educate, inform and seek commitment to conduct a Business Case leading to an Offsourcing Roadmap. This Business Case will go a long way toward building the sponsorship required to accelerate the initiative through the full planning exercise. What may begin as an academic exercise on the part of some individuals has the potential to rapidly expand into a strategic and potentially business model–altering initiative. Be open to deploying external expertise to speed up and refine your process.

Executing the Plan

Implementations are challenging under even the most controlled circumstances because of the many variables that can affect success. Offsourcing entails a different, yet extreme set of the same challenges. A full grounding in the disciplines and elements upon which the initiative rests, including change management, methodology, infrastructure, communications and cultural integration, will allow you to see cause/effect triggers within the bigger picture. Identifying key resources as early as possible and bringing them along from planning into the execution phase will provide continuity and help to establish a sense of inevitability about the success of the initiative.

Maintaining and Renewing Your Offsourcing Initiative

Early results often hold significant potential for improvement, so be prepared to keep pushing hard to reach the theoretical limits of the new paradigm. Expansion and fierce monitoring of metrics are an excellent way to focus the organization's attention on specific areas for improvement. If you are working with another party, understand the nature of the business relationship you require for optimal success: vendor or partner. If a partnership is required, be prepared to invest time and resources in maturing the relationship, and use the Offsourcing Maturity Model (see Chapter 20) as a reference point for understanding your current position vis-à-vis your potential to create a self-improving system.

Other Key Messages

Education

The economics of the offshore experience are compelling, but there are so many unknown variables for a first-timer that the practical application may seem very improbable indeed. As a sponsor or influencer you must build your case for change by focusing on a variety of areas:

- **Competition**—Understand what your current competition is doing offshore and determine how that will impact your long-term business. Identify new threats from offshore that may erode your market share or reduce your margins over time. Expose the areas where you believe your organization could be at risk and then share the information with your colleagues and executive team.

- **Buying trends**—Research the growth of the offshore markets and identify the primary buyers of the services. Be able to offer tangible examples of brand name companies that are operating and expanding overseas to take advantage of the offshore wave. Consider the lead time to become operational and take that into account when planning for the future.

- **Hard numbers**—Be prepared to get specific in your assessment of offshore savings, but equally be fluent in expressing how those savings may be translated into additional capacity or higher service levels, new product development or R&D, additional marketing or sales dollars that can focus on new revenue opportunities.

Executive Commitment

Always remember that *executive commitment remains the single most important factor in achieving success in offshore solutions.* Understand and communicate internally that going offshore requires commitment to be successful. Executive management is likely to be the easiest to get onboard once the numbers have been fleshed out. Line managers will likely have the greatest reservations, so be sure to include them in your education and planning process. No one likes to be brought in at the end when there is a perception that all the decisions have already been made and any questions are simply delaying the inevitable.

Involving stakeholders from across various disciplines as you move into the Offsourcing Roadmap will enhance the quality of your analysis, planning and ultimately your solution execution. If done with sufficient education and sensitivity to concerned parties, involvement of the additional resources can also expedite your planning process.

Finally, be prepared to personally step up to a leadership role when the call comes for someone to take this initiative forward.

Planning and Process

It is no accident that the discussion of the Offsourcing Roadmap was the longest in the text. The detailed information gathering, analysis and planning that it requires are fundamental to positioning for a successful implementation. Poor information gathering and inadequate planning usually lead to poor decision making and failed implementation. That said, offsourcing initiatives are equally vulnerable to "paralysis through analysis," an unending revisiting and reconfiguration of the facts with no end in sight.

Make a commitment to a defined process in your offshore planning and implementation.

The approaches we recommend in this book incorporate the following elements:

- **Business Case**—This opportunity-identification, prioritization and financial modeling exercise relies on a small executive or senior management level team.

- **Offsourcing Roadmap**—This planning exercise translates identified opportunities into concrete implementation plans with a set of business owners and a clear understanding of potential vendor involvement.

- **Pilot**—During a testing period, the opportunity is taken through the paces to confirm operational viability and the precision of the Business Case. The pilot is typically completed within a 90-day period, with specific metrics and a more limited size and scope than in a full implementation.

- **Full implementation and ongoing improvement**—Work toward the same type of closed-loop, metrics-driven process that you would in your regular operations. The offshore move will give you a productivity boost, but you will soon be on the hunt for more improvements. Build the metrics in at the outset while they seem cheap to deliver, so that you will have them when they're needed later.

Other process considerations at an operation level include the need and the opportunity to:

- **Modify your methodology**—The handshakes and transitions between various groups are likely to be different in the offshore environment. Budget the requisite time to reflect these approaches in the new operating environment.

- **Adopt best practices**—As you are planning the go-forward business process, look for opportunities to improve your existing process as opposed to simply replicating it in an offshore environment. You may decide to invest some of your anticipated savings in improving the technology base, so that your end solution can benefit from a combination of automating technology and lower cost labor.

A framework for conceptualizing the evolution of your offsourcing activities is the **Offsourcing Maturity Model** (OMM), a roadmap and risk management framework for reinventing the IT-enabled service functions into a low-cost, high-quality service organization leveraging remote resources. It is also a framework for considering the way in which you set goals, operationalize and manage your offsourcing activity.

Communication and Change Management

Communicate, communicate and then over communicate. Your communication strategy should incorporate a variety of constituencies internally and externally. Each will have a preferred method of assimilating and digesting the information, so in the best consultative fashion you must be prepared to meet their needs if you are to ensure that your message is heard.

In many cases you will be prepared to communicate the same data in a variety of formats including narratives, financial models and presentations. Make sure that your team has the skills to communicate effectively in different formats or your progress will be slowed by redundant questions and objections.

In many scenarios, the offshore option will result in the loss of personnel in your domestic operations. These individuals will reenter the job market with skills that are increasingly commoditized and available offshore. Treat them with respect and integrity. Challenge your executive team to make this transition as smooth as possible, to offer retraining to the extent feasible and to bring along as many on the team as you can. They possess valuable context and information on clients that will take time to rebuild. Remember always to consult your human resources department regarding all personnel actions.

Offshore Model

The figure below illustrates elements of the operational model required for your offsourcing initiative. The multidimensional aspect of the environment, with each element relating to every other element, means that root cause analysis of issues can be challenging. Enhance cultural integration and project management may improve. Ignore change management and operational efficiency will be put at risk. The issues are nearly always manageable and often even predictable as the organization matures its offshore capability.

One element highlighted in the model that is particularly important in a vendor/partner

> *Active engagement by the buyer in building the governance model, establishing the correct metrics and establishing an open spirit of cooperation will preclude many expectation related conflicts.*

environment is expectation management. Trust, the cornerstone of a strong long-term partnership, is impossible to build and maintain without proper expectation setting and management. Anecdotal history suggests that some offshore vendors have fallen short in the area of expectation management. This has been ascribed to training and governance, but is often simply a result of cultural reservations about giving bad news. Active engagement by the buyer in building the governance model, establishing the correct metrics and working in an open spirit of cooperation will preclude many expectation-related conflicts.

Figure : Balanced Offsourcing Model

Summary

Offsourcing provides real competitive advantage: quality and productivity at low cost. However, it's different—very different—from the status quo. You will need more than the usual executive commitment, change management, program and project management, process formality and especially communications to succeed. But the benefits are extraordinary, and they are within your grasp.

You will also need to become a guide for your organization or find someone with a compass. Offsourcing will not just happen—it represents a change of culture, and sometimes a threat, and it is a daunting task to accomplish.

In this book we have tried to cover a broad spectrum of topics from the practitioner's perspective. Whether you are just beginning to consider offshore IT-enabled services or have programs under way, we hope that we have been able to provide direction on the issues and challenges that you will face in an area that is soon to become a dominant factor in the provisioning of IT-enabled services.

We wish you every success.

Chapter 25

A Look at the Future

Overview

As this book aims to be the *Lonely Planet*[27] of the IT-enabled services industry, the focus remains on the operational and implementation issues of offsourcing. To the extent that self-control permits, we have avoided abstract discussions of the looming macro changes that can be expected in the services industries of the US and other developed Western economies as a consequence of the coming offshore services migration. However, we have provided some context here since it may prove beneficial in building your case for change, a necessary step in your Offsourcing Roadmap.

A Butterfly's Wings

Offshore maintenance and development capabilities have been around for almost 30 years. Call centers have existed in mainstream areas probably three to five years and various groups with business process outsourcing capabilities for the same time or less.

Some of the incumbents have achieved significant scale and a few have employee bases over 20,000. A visit to some of the campuses in Bangalore with their many buildings and futuristic designs is apt to evoke comparisons with the infrastructure in Redmond or Redwood City. These operations have not only hit "scale," but they have also demonstrated that they can continue to scale further. The talent pool is vast and growing while the infrastructure and traditionally difficult-to-find skill sets continue to become more widely available. Investment banking reports on the industry indicate numerous deals in the works with lifetime contract values in excess of $100 million. Governments are allocating billions to enhance their infrastructures and venture capitalists and parent companies are investing the same to aggressively attack the IT-enabled services business including the latest push around BPO operations.

> *Anything that could be shipped on a plane could and would be commoditized to a lower-cost operator in a remote environment. It so happens that people fit on planes.*

---

[27] For those unfamiliar with Lonely Planet "travel survival kits", they are detailed travel reference books written with substantial contributions from real travelers (not marketing agents) covering often less-traveled geographies.

And yet, the current service providers are in their infancy from the perspective of the market penetration that they have achieved in the United States and Western Europe. Chapter 2 highlights the many variables that are coalescing to accelerate the adoption of the offshore environment, but it does not tell the story of the macro impact on your industry or business, in part because the story has yet to play out. But it will, in the very near future.

We recall reading an analyst piece four or five years ago sounding a warning about the commoditizing affects of the Internet. The researcher suggested that anything that could be shipped on a plane could and would be commoditized to a lower-cost operator in a remote environment. It so happens that people fit on planes. In fact Airbus is working hard to fit more of them, eight hundred to be specific, on a single flight.

Tsunami

The standard metaphor used to describe chaos theory is of a butterfly's wings setting in motion of a chain of events resulting in a tsunami, an event of no small consequence for those in its path. The butterflies have taken flight in India and the Philippines, and are preparing for take-off in China. What happens when the tsunami hits? Here are a few thoughts:

- **Rate and wage deflation**—The bursting of the tech bubble in early 2000 has had a profound impact on fee structures and wages in many areas of IT-enabled services. Every quarter, we hear new stories about companies buying services for as little as 50% of the going rate two years ago. The retail price reduction will continuously cause wage deflation as service companies struggle to stay alive in the current economy.

- **Displacement of current domestic service providers**—Some of the current service providers will not survive the new onslaught. They will act halfheartedly or too late to develop an offshore capability. When they finally wake up to smell the butterflies it will be too late. They will have minimal margins on a reduced client base and will not be able to turn the corner. Staff augmentation companies today are dealing with thin margins and tremendous competition from offshore providers. Project-based IT service firms have growing benches and shrinking margins in the face of competition from the larger offshore players.

- **Consolidation of current offshore service providers**—Many of the current offshore service providers will be consolidated into fewer, but larger companies as the market matures. Once again using India as a reference point, there are over 900 IT-enabled service providers. Not all will survive. Some will go out of business due to inadequate scale or limited US/Western European sales and marketing. Others will have the right plan but insufficient capital, and still others will be acquired by larger entities in their respective countries or by US and European players seeking to jump-start their own offshore delivery capabilities. Mergers and acquisitions teams should be kept busy in this sector in the coming years.

- **Political activism**—Silicon Valley and the tech sector as a whole have been notoriously silent in political circles. This may be a reflection of the schizophrenic nature of the business: maverick geniuses with passion for community and social causes on the left and hard-core venture capitalists with a ruthless focus on the numbers on the right. Perhaps they have simply cancelled each other's votes out. More likely, a combination of the white collar nature of the jobs, the inexorable growth of the industry and the difficulty inherent in regulating any industry whose rate of change seems only to accelerate is the root cause. However, offshore development with the resultant loss of domestic jobs is likely to create some grassroots movement to stem the tide in some fashion. This influence may take the form of regulation, taxation and certainly increased spending on job training.

The Case Against Outsourcing

One piece of speculation that we will allow ourselves in this book is the impact that the offshore markets will have on outsourcing trends in the United States. Companies generally outsource for one of the following reasons:

- **Focus**—The outsourcing company has decided that some repetitive activity is not core to the business.

- **Skill / Best Practices**—The outsourcing company will be able to take advantage of the skills that the outsourcer maintains in sufficient depth that may be either difficult to find or retain internally.   Alternatively, the outsourcing company may want to take advantage of best practices and rigid process to gain a level of sophistication and efficiency difficult to achieve internally.

- **Scale**—or put another way, cost. The vendor has sufficient scale in its operations that the unit cost of providing its service even with its premium for return on investment is lower than the cost of a company building its own operation.

The second point, skill, in some cases might also be considered from the point of view of cost, since with a less constricted budget specialists might be kept on staff to address infrequent or only periodically occurring issues.

As outsourcing in its various forms and niches has become mainstream, CFO's have come under pressure to take advantage of the cost savings that their competition enjoys. This occurs even as CFOs understand that for all the cost savings, outsourcing some functions may constrain the business in outlying years. Changes to service levels, modifications to processes and exceptions to negotiated clauses are expensive, often prohibitively so.

So what is the prediction? Low-cost offshore capabilities represent a 5–10 year window (possibly longer) for large companies to lower their internal costs without resorting to outsourcing. As CFOs and CIOs weigh their alternatives, more and more will begin to take at look at the offshore model as an approach to stemming the onslaught of outsourcing deals.

Naturally, the outsourcing community will not sit idly by for long, but as of early 2003 very few have significant presences in the offshore markets. EDS, the grandfather of them all, is reported to have had only 600 employees in India as of 2001 and a target of 5,000 for 2005. The 5,00 represents less than 5% of EDS total workforce and won't put a dent in their cost structure so the question is when will they really add scale offshore?

It is tough to get to the new world when you have an infrastructure and operational model built around the old. The outsourcing community is no different from anyone else when it comes to struggling with next steps.

The outsourcers that embrace the new model will further enhance their value. Meanwhile the window is sufficiently large for fast-moving companies to capitalize on the time available to make decisions that best suit their need for flexibility in the coming years.

New Business Models

The economist Joseph Schumpeter described capitalism as a form of "creative destruction," with one form of business emerging in a fit of creative genius to consume and destroy another. The emergence of offshore, nearshore and hybrid onshore/offshore models in the coming years will create a "fit" of new business models.

Some of these new businesses will deliver the same services as current service models only differently: they will have a significant offshore component to the work done onshore. Other businesses will flourish to support this service delivery model including:

- **Telecommunications**—Think videoconferencing saves money on domestic flights? How about business class seats to India at $5,000 to $7,000 a shot? And what about all the "dark" fiber that has been laid that will be filled up with data making the 12,000 mile trek from servers to your desktop?

- **Training**—This market is huge, varied and growing. Have you heard of the Institute for American Accent Training? You might if you were building an outbound call center that required workers with neutral voice modulation.

- **Change management**—Organizations will have enormous change management and cultural training needs in the coming years as they build truly global, blended teams to achieve maximum effectiveness with maximum economic efficiency.

- **Offshore program management**—Value-added third parties (described in Chapter 7) can bring expertise in managing cross-cultural and remotely located delivery environments.

Talking about new business models is a bit like trying to predict the future: you are bound to be wrong even with the best of data. What is certain is that step function changes like the offshore evolution create enormous opportunities. Nature abhors a vacuum, and into these new spaces are bound to slip a myriad of US-based creative, entrepreneurial thinkers with opportunities of which we cannot currently conceive.

Summary

How can you be best prepared for the changes coming? Share this book with your colleagues, check out the references and educate yourself on the types of services that are likely to become commoditized. Just as the US did not wake up to a manufacturing sector moving overseas overnight, it will not wake up to an IT-enabled services sector that moves overseas overnight either.

The US continues to have a vibrant manufacturing sector and always will. The difference between now and 25 years ago is the productivity levels required for the work to be remain economical enough to stay onshore. In spite of the calamitous calls for intervention, protectionism and the like, the US economy has remained the most robust in the world in no small part due to the continued commitment to allow free markets to determine the ultimate allocation of resources.

The IT-enabled services sector is no different in this regard. There will undoubtedly be terrific dislocation pain felt by those that are affected by the loss of jobs, but the jobs that remain will reflect higher levels of productivity. In place of those jobs that move offshore we shall see a slew of new opportunities as yet unimagined as this market continues to evolve and mature. The US, with its culture of entrepreneurism and persistence, will weather this storm, emerging stronger, more efficient and solidly in a position of leadership in technological, IT-enabled services innovation.

Part VII: Appendices

Appendix A: Notes on Travel to India

Overview

As with most endeavors, proper preparation leads to a more productive experience. Travel to your offshore destination is no exception. This chapter contains a few notes on travel to India with basic information for the business traveler. It is recommended that you purchase a travel guide and speak to a travel agent that specializes in traveling to India (or any other offshore destination) in order to get the latest information.

Getting There

Travel to India can be punishing, entailing a minimum of two long flights to get in country. The eastern route requires a stop somewhere in Europe (London, Amsterdam, Paris or Frankfurt). You leave the US in the afternoon or evening, arrive early the next morning in Europe, typically depart again later in the morning and arrive in Bombay in the very early hours of the following day. Some direct flights are also available from Europe into Bangalore and likely more will be available once the new international airport comes online. The total air journey, assuming no delays, is between 21 and 25 hours depending on your departure point in the US. The total travel time, depending on connections, can be between 28 and 32 hours.

The westward route to India is longer and may require an additional hop. The route will take you through a US West Coast gateway (Los Angeles or San Francisco) and then on to possibly Seoul, Tokyo or Kuala Lumpur. This second leg may last up to 14 hours, and you will still require a lengthy third flight to reach Bombay. You can add another 4 to 8 hours to the eastern route to get the estimated travel time.

Bombay has two major airports, one for international flights and the other for domestic connections. Commuting between the two is a simple affair requiring a few dollars and 30 minutes, but there is always the possibility of traffic problems. Be sure to allow plenty of time between connecting flights, since you will have to transfer your luggage yourself

Most of the airlines now have power for your PCs assuming you have a travel adapter. We have found that some of the older 747 jets may not have available power, so you may need to bring a couple of additional batteries or be prepared to read and watch movies.

Taking your PC into the Country

You will have to declare your PC and any other electronic equipment that you bring into the country. For specific rules and processes along with baggage rules in general, go to www.indianconsultate-sf.org/ for further information.

Getting Around

By Plane

India is a large country with numerous centers of IT-enabled services activity. More than likely you will fly between your in-country destinations. We highly recommend the staff and professionalism of Jet Airways—a kind of Continental Airlines and Southwest Airlines rolled into one. Security is typically tight, so you should arrive at the airport at least 90 minutes before your flight is scheduled to take off.

By Car

If you don't have a driver waiting for you at the airport in Bombay, you will use a taxi service into the city. (Expect to pay a little extra for air conditioning.) Once ensconced in your five-star hotel, you will have need of ground transportation. In Bombay you are likely to take any of the thousands of available taxis with their rather fashionable retro look of the Ambassador model.

Outside Bombay, you will probably want to have a car and driver arranged for you. They are on call 24 hours a day, and if you require it you can even book one for your entire stay. The cost is quite reasonable, very similar to renting a car in the US. We have found that tipping the drivers each day ensures that extra level of service. For the more adventurous, a ride on a motorized rickshaw is an inexpensive and fun (if hair-raising) way to get around the city, at least for short trips.

Car travel is not recommended for business travel between major cities as the distances are large and the infrastructure is not yet sufficiently well developed.

By Train

Trains provide an option for some tourist excursions but are not recommended for in country business travel.

Visas

Visas into and out of India continue to be relatively straightforward, even with the current environment of heightened security.

US Citizens

US citizens require a visa to travel to India. Business visas are generally easily acquired and are good for either six months or a year for multiple entries. You need only demonstrate the following:

- **US Passport**

- **Letter of introduction**—This should come from the company with whom you are conducting business. It should be signed, dated and business purpose defined.

Check with your local consulate or passport agency for assistance on expediting the visa.

Vaccinations

Your local county health department should be equipped to tell you what vaccinations are required for the duration of your stay. Colleagues in the past have received shots for:

- Hepatitis A
- Hepatitis B (a three-shot series requiring a minimum of one month)
- Hepatitis C
- Polio
- Typhoid

An additional vaccination for rabies was also strongly recommended for those staying for extended periods or planning a safari or visit to a rural area.

Malaria is also a health concern. A couple of different types of medications can be taken as a preventative. The standard protocol is to take one pill per week beginning two weeks before your trip and continuing for two weeks after. The two weeks prior is not a loading dose, but is instead recommended to ascertain in a controlled environment whether you are going to have a reaction to the medication. If you take ill during this two-week trial, you have time to switch to a different type of medication.

Emergencies

Health Care Facilities

Your hotel will have detailed information on health care facilities. Here are a couple of facilities to keep in your travel file:

Mumbai
Bombay Hospital
Telephone: 91-22-206 7676

Bangalore
Mailya Hospital
Telephone: 91-80-227 7979/227 7990

Foreign Exchange

The major hotels that we have listed all will exchange foreign currency. You can use American Express, Visa and MasterCard credit cards in most hotels, restaurants and shops. You will want to carry rupees for tips and small purchases.

US Embassy and Consulates

Mumbai
Lincoln House
78 Bhulabhai Desai Road
Mumbai – 400 026
Telephone: (22) 363 3611
Fax: (22) 363 0350

Calcutta
5/1, Ho Chi Minh Sarani
Calcutta – 700 071
Telephone: (33) 242 3611 – 15
Fax: (33) 242 2335

New Delhi
Shanthipath
Chanakyapuri
New Delhi – 110 021
Telephone: (11) 688 9033
Fax: (11) 419 0015

Local Services

Hotels

The best hotels in India are among the finest in the world. Chains like Oberoi, Taj and Leela are all first class,

> *The best hotels in India are among the finest in the world.*

offering impeccable service, excellent facilities and staffs that will attend to your smallest need. The occupancy rates of many of these institutions have fluctuated significantly over the past couple of years. No doubt your travel agent will find a reasonable (by US standards) rate, but if you are prepared to call and negotiate, you may find that you can find a "best" rate for your stay. You should be able to get a rate between $80 and $175 per night depending on the city, hotel, duration of stay and time of year. Mumbai is much more expensive than Bangalore, Calcutta, New Delhi and Chennai.

Tourism

India boasts many fascinating destinations for business travelers, including some of the world's great treasures like the Taj Mahal. If you want the ocean and excellent nightlife, go to Goa, which is easily accessible by airplane from any major city. The locals are used to having visitors and are always accommodating, but be aware this is not like tourism in Europe. The amenities can be sparse and the food may be unfamiliar, although it is generally excellent.

References

It sounds like a cliché, but your local travel agent can be an excellent source of information.

Indian National Holidays

Holiday	India Holiday Schedule	
New Year	Wednesday	1/Jan/03
Makar Sankranti	Tuesday	14/Jan/03
Republic Day	Sunday	26/Jan/03
Bakri-Id (Id ul zuha)	Thursday	13/Feb/03
Shi vaji Jayanti	Wednesday	19/Feb/03
Mahashivratri	Saturday	1/Mar/03
Holi	Tuesday	18/Mar/03
Gudi Padwa	Wednesday	1/Apr/03
Ambedkar Jayanti	Monday	14/Apr/03
Mahavir Jayanti	Tuesday	15/Apr/03
Good Friday	Friday	18/Apr/03
International Labour Day	Thursday	1/May/03
Id-E-Mikad	Thursday	14/May/03
Independence Day	Friday	15/Aug/03
Raksha Bandhan	Tuesday	12/Aug/03
Pateti	Thursday	21/Aug/03
Ganesh Chaturthi	Sunday	31/Aug/03
Anant Chaturdashi	Tuesday	9/Sept/03
Gandhi Jayanti	Thursday	2/Oct/03
Dashera	Saturday	4/Oct/03
Laxmi Pooja	Saturday	25/Oct/03
Balipratipada/Bhau Beej	Sunday	26/Oct/03
Gurunanak Jayanti	Saturday	8/Nov/03
Ramzan Id	Wednesday	26/Nov/03

Table 20: Indian National Holidays

Overview

Earlier in the text, we noted the strategic selling that must go on within an organization to get to the point of considering offsourcing activities. Given that the goal of this book is to make these offshore initiatives successful, we include a few notes to address some of the ongoing provider challenges that are occasionally the result of the initial and on-going selling process in the offshore environment. We believe some offshore service providers must address these issues if they are to enhance their customer retention rate and fully achieve their long-term growth potential.

The Offshore Providers' Dilemma

A theme that we hope resonates through the body of this text is the need for buyer organizations to fully commit to and engage in their offshore initiatives if they are to be successful. We hear repeatedly about the benefits achieved when buyers take an active role and the challenges and missed expectations that are manifest when they stand on the sidelines with a wait-and-see disposition or assume that everything is being taken care of for them. That said, experience suggests that clients are not always as involved as they might be due to the selling process that they move through. What does this mean?

Domestic service providers in the US and Western Europe do not have to address nearly the number of buyer objections to which offshore providers must respond. It may take an offshore group six months to sufficiently educate a customer about the communications infrastructure, disaster recover planning, accent quality, operational responsiveness, etc. to get to the point that they even have the opportunity to discuss how they are going to solve a client's problems through a service offering. Once that point is reached, it would seem suicidal from a selling perspective to now challenge a customer regarding their need to commit to have executives play an oversight role, key managers to travel and teams to overhaul existing processes and methodologies in certain areas. After all, a significant amount of time, effort and money have just been invested in creating the perspective of the ease with which these offshore initiatives can be conducted.

> Domestic service providers in the US and Western Europe do not have to address nearly the number of buyer objections to which offshore providers must respond.

The problem is that within the context of long-term and large scale initiatives, many difficult areas must eventually be addressed for optimal performance to be achieved. There can be a tendency to downplay the operational challenges while intending only to demonstrate that the solutions are entirely viable. As the market for offshore services continues to become more competitive and as buyers become increasingly savvy, the switching costs for many initiatives will go down. When this occurs, providers that have not adequately structured the engagements, established open dialogue at the outset and committed to a partner-oriented relationship in which demands are made from both sides in the spirit of reaching the best solution, may find that customers meeting with only limited benefits are prepared to make investments elsewhere.

Obviously there is no easy answer to the scenario posed. There is a fine line to be played between being seen as a "safe" choice, one that can render tremendous benefits with the appropriate level of planning and resourcing, versus an option that is apt to create operational problems larger than the financial ones that it solves. That is why it is called a dilemma. A couple approaches, however, do seem to be gaining traction.

First, the extensive use of pilots creates the opportunity to demonstrate execution capability and build credibility in a highly controlled environment that requires limited investment by the buyer. The implied rationale being that as this threshold is crossed, the provider then has the opportunity to revisit long-term critical success factors within the context of the negotiation for the full implementation. A happy prospect that has now internalized the possibilities can be expected to be more open about making the required adjustments to its operations.

> There is a fine line to be played between being seen as a "safe" choice, one that can render tremendous benefits with the appropriate level of planning and resourcing, versus an option that is apt to create more potential problems than it solves.

Second, we see offshore providers increasingly making use of professional sales and marketing people that have their primary training experience in the local market in which they are hired to sell. This is akin to the way in which companies like EDS achieved critical mass as they moved outside the US. These individuals have the benefit of a broad set of relationships and more importantly often have the advantage of local experience in conveying difficult messages to their peers about buyer objections as simply part of the offshore structuring process.

The Vendor Trap

Sometimes the failure to establish the need for client involvement up front also impacts the perception of organization and its ability to be considered as a long-term partner.

Consider the relationship indicators in Figure 29 within the context of an initiative that was positioned with strong expectations of involvement from the client-within an initiative with low expectations of involvement.

If you find yourself more often than not on the right-hand side of the illustration, then you are probably stuck in a relationship perceived to be of minimal value. At a minimum you are open to pressure from your client on discussions about pricing since you are probably perceived as vendor with limited differentiation from other providers. Just as important, you may be missing potential opportunities to win additional business, crucial given the lower cost of sales in existing accounts than for new ones.

Relationship Indicators Diagnostic	
Positive - moving forward ...	**Issues - unknown destination ...**
Make recommendations	*Justifying what has been done*
Very open and honest dialogue	*Avoid tough issues*
Use the phone to communicate	*Written, formal communications*
Show appreciation	*Discuss the last misunderstanding*
Make proactive service suggestions	*Respond to service requests*
Use the "we" problem-solving language	*If "you" would only outsource ...*
Openly discuss issues and challenges	*Discuss the latest surprise*
Accept responsibility, work it out	*Deny accountability; 'you' need to ...*
Discuss the future in positive terms	*Discuss the past and how "it will improve"*
Working toward a business relationship	*Continually dealing with T&Cs*
Executives have an open dialogue	*Executives met at contract signing*
Executive meet to discuss ideas	*Executives discuss contract issues*
Sharing of information	*Information is difficult to obtain*
Collaborate on ideas	*Constantly trying to sell*
Proactive "I was glad to see ..."	*"Where is the ... that you promised ..."*
'this person' can help you do that ...	*... that 'company' may be able to help you ...*

Figure 29: Provider/Client Relationship Indicators

What Does It Take to Become a Partner?

What then is required of a break-out strategy to move from being considered a vendor to a partner? From a short-term service provider to a long-term ally?

Becoming a partner requires that you provide a high value–added service with a high level of organizational transparency. You must establish a reputation through regular sessions with all levels of the client organization focusing not on simply selling, but on trying to improve processes or other aspects of the operation. Your goal must be to be viewed as an extension of the client organization, not as an arms-length processor simply providing transaction services.

Changing a perception of your entity as a vendor is challenging and difficult, but not insurmountable. Focus on areas including:

- **Business value**—You will have truly arrived as a trusted partner with the client if you can make it through a discussion without discussing technology. This implies that you are now involved in solving business issues and that the technology capabilities that your organization represents are a fact no longer in need of questioning. Focus on understanding the client's business and building sufficient domain expertise to speak to the issues and make the connection between these issues and the services you offer.

- **Internal sales support**—As you establish credibility with the business issues, you will now be in a position to assist your sponsor with selling solutions internally, something beneficial to both parties. Except for the most demanding of functions, experience suggests that technical prowess is rarely the differentiating feature of one selling effort over another. Understanding of the business domain issues, appreciation of the risk management required, effective communications and a track record will carry the day.

- **Formal status**—Too often status is expressed in a haphazard and perfunctory manner. Do not understand estimate the risk management and selling opportunity that you have with a carefully delivered status. A common complaint that we hear from clients is that their offshore providers do not notify them of bad news until it is too late to take corrective action, something clients are usually happy to do given the alternative of missed deadlines.

  On a selling note, if you downplay the challenges that you are managing for the client, then they will be perceived as minor issues, with limited value. If the client does truly appreciate the complexity, as you manage it on their behalf overtime, don't be shy about continually and professionally informing the client of the terrific work that you are doing, you have an opportunity to cast the work and therefore the relationship in a more strategically positive light. You will delay the inevitable discussion they will want to have regarding pricing.

- **Selective billing**—Clients have a way of wanting everything, and at a minimal cost. As you negotiate your contract, push to win allowances for items not yet discovered, so that as new items emerge you can avoid having to go back with multiple requests for budget increases. The ideal scenario should involve change orders funded by these allowances. If you do have to go back for additional money to fund requests, be selective. If there are five items on the table and only two carry material financial implications, then give away the other three and trumpet what a good "partner" you are.

- **Bench resources**—If you have resources on the bench that are not otherwise billing, identify whether they can perform value-added services for valued customers.

- **Intellectual property**—Work diligently to build domain knowledge of your customer's business, so that you can engage in strategic (as opposed to tactical) discussions. This may mean slowing the rotation of your own personnel, so that they can achieve a level of competency that matches the client's own, but it creates a powerful lock-in factor.

- **Attachment to revenue**—Except for a few call center solutions, as a service provider you are likely to be viewed as a cost

> By attaching yourself to the client's revenue, you help to shift the long-term dynamic from spending the minimum on you to spending more, since the more that is spent in this context, the greater the client revenues will be.

center. After the honeymoon of savings from the initial offshore boost, the discussion will inevitably return to more cost savings. However, the maturity of the offshore market and the programs that many clients have in place mean that there might be areas where you can help clients provision their own customers. As you establish trust with your client, work to understand if there are areas where you can add value, either through higher margins or unique skills, in servicing their own customer base. By attaching yourself to the client's revenue, you help to shift the long-term dynamic from spending the minimum on you to spending more, since the more that is spent in this context, the greater the client revenues will be.

You must boost your client's view of your capabilities and earn the right to compete for other opportunities where you can add more value and over time become a true partner. You'll need strong leadership, desire, commitment and (yes) investment to make this happen. In many cases your current project managers or sales staff must move aside in favor of much more experienced program management that understands the vertical business of the client and can establish more value-added executive relationships over the long term.

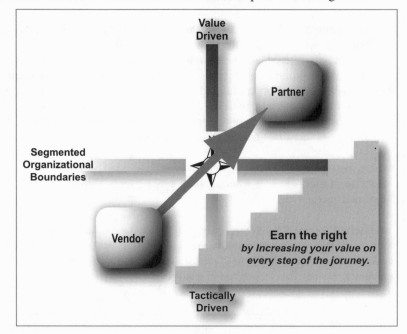

Figure 30: Transition from Vendor to Partner

Summary

Technology-related professional services seem to be under the constant threat of commoditization. This is no where more true than in the offshore markets where the over-riding value proposition has traditionally been cost savings. In such an environment it is difficult to both survive and to differentiate one's organization from other providers by focusing a client's attention on the total cost of offsourcing. And yet, many organizations are achieving this by evolving their sales forces and working hard to position themselves away from pure technology and rate-based discussions. They are having candid discussions with clients about the need for commitment and the benefits that can accrue to those buyers that truly internalize and commit to the new paradigm. As the offshore markets continue to grow and mature, these value-focused service leaders who have cracked the providers' dilemma will become the aggregators and survivors who dominate the landscape of tomorrow.

Appendix C: Other Sources of Information

Organizations

A significant component of the barrier to entry of offsourcing is the relatively sparse amount of information in the public domain. This is changing as the adoption of offsourcing solutions increases dramatically. Below we list a number of organizations and Web sites that pertain to specific countries or regions, with descriptions from their sites.

CISA—"The Information Service Industry Association represents Taiwan's representative body of information service industries. Founded in 1983, CISA is one of the most time-honored hi-tech associations in Taiwan."
http://www.cisanet.org.tw/

IASH—"Founded in 1982, the Israeli Association of Software Houses (IASH) is the umbrella organization for Israeli software and IT companies, representing the common interests of its member companies. The more than 100 members of IASH are a mixture of mature and leading companies as well as young and innovative ones."
http://www.iash.org.il/Content/Organization/Organization.asp

ISA—"The Irish Software Association (ISA) is a dynamic association which represents an ever-increasing number of Irish and multi-national software and computing services companies."
http://www.software.ie/

NASSCOM—"The National Association of Software & Service Companies is the industry clearing house for the Indian IT-enabled service industry. Through wide sponsorship it maintains among other things a comprehensive listing of providers."
www.nasscom.org

NSDA—"Offshore software development market in Russia has recently enjoyed a surge in interest and activity. From the bottom up these include favorable demographics and labor costs, competent technical education facilities in national university systems, a well established presence of leading hardware and software platform manufacturers."
http://www.nsda.net

RUSSOFT—"The association of the leading companies in the field of Software Development from Russia and Belarus. Currently RUSSOFT consists of more than 50 companies with 6000 highly qualified software developers who are experienced across a broad range of applications and technical platforms."
http://www.russoft.com

WITSA "is a consortium of information technology industry associations from countries around the world. Information is available on information technology providers and solutions along with some geographic information."
http://www.witsa.org

SBPOA "merges with *akris.com* to form the world's largest community of shared services and business process outsourcing professionals. The SBPOA will combine its online presence with *akris.com*, to provide the single largest base of knowledge on shared services and BPO, to a community of close to 100,000 professionals worldwide."
http://www.sharedxpertise.org

Sourcing Interests Group "assists members in learning from each other's experiences in outsourcing, alliances, procurement, E-Commerce and shared services. Interest areas include Information Technology, Corporate Support Services, Business Processes and Supply Chain."
http://www.sourcinginterests.org/

ITAP—"The Information Technology Association of the Philippines is a group of leading IT solutions providers in the country."
http://www.itaphil.org/

ITAC—"ITAC is the voice of the Canadian information technology industry. Together with its partner organizations across the country, the association represents 1300 companies in the computing and telecommunications hardware, software, services, and electronic content sectors."
http://www.itac.ca/

Glossary

Bench—Billable resources that are not currently on active revenue-producing assignments.

Best Alternative to Negotiated Agreement (BATNA)—Negotiation strategy that involves the creation of as an attractive-as-possible fallback position in the event that you are unable to come to terms with your negotiating partner. It is a strategy that increases negotiation leverage during the negotiation.

Birkman Method—A noncritical assessment tool designed to help an individual identify his or her own likes, needs and reactions to stress. Can be deployed to identify norms in multicultural environments as part of a comprehensive change management program.

Branch office—Limited operation in offshore geography through which a parent company negotiates and manages local vendors.

Build, operate & transfer (BOT)—Contractual arrangement whereby an organization contracts with a vendor to create an offshore capability, run it for some period of time and eventually transfer complete control to the buyer.

Business Case—A financially driven conceptual model and justification for the investment in offsourcing practices.

Business process outsourcing (BPO)—Contracting of an external service provider to operate repetitive, often manually intensive processes. The provider is able to offer lower unit costs as a result of scale or favorable geographic operating model.

Call Center Association of the Philippines (CCAP)—Philippines-based industry association promoting high standards and best practices in the Filipino call center industry.

Capability Maturity Model (CMM)—An industry-recognized standard for the development of quality software, it is a "model for judging the maturity of the software processes of an organization and for identifying the key practices that are required to increase the maturity of those processes."[28]

Chaos theory—A set of ideas and principles attempting to explain the unpredictable nature of complex systems. A fundamental tenet is that seemingly small events can trigger other, much larger ones.

---

[28] http://www.sei.cmu.edu/cmm/cmm.html

Cost of failure—Enormous economic loss resulting from lost potential savings, inability to compete with low-cost competition and rival business models as a result of ineffectual or incomplete adoption of offsourcing solutions.

Disaster recovery plan (DRP)—A set of policies and procedures intended to provide an organization with business continuity in the event of a major disruption.

Division of labor—Separation of work between onshore, offshore and nearshore elements of the business process.

Exit clause—Contractual language defining the terms and process of unwinding a relationship.

Follow the sun—An approach to work practices intended to minimize time-to-solution by handing off work between onshore and offshore personnel to take advantage of different time zones.

Fear, uncertainty & doubt (FUD)—A very human reaction to new and unknown environments.

Governance model—A framework for managing oversight of offsourcing programs and initiatives. Should be developed as part of the Offsourcing Roadmap.

International Standards Organization (ISO)—Geneva-based, nonprofit group promoting global standardization of practices.

Joint venture—A corporate entity having equity ownership by two or more parties. In the offshore environment this often involves the pairing of a well-established offshore provider with a US or Western European service company that acts as a demand creation engine.

Law of Reciprocity—States that you must first give information to receive it.

Metric—(usually plural) Aggregation of data used to provide evidence of underlying activity or the absence thereof. When deployed in conjunction with a repeatable process, it can provide guidance to management for operating and improving a business.

National Association of Software & Services Companies (NASSCOM)—India-based industry association promoting high standards and best practices in the India IT services and IT-enabled services industries.

Nearshore—Refers to "remote" geographies that are relatively close to the base operating environment of a company. Example: Mexico has nearshore capabilities for US companies.

Offsourcing—The contracting of IT-enabled services internally or externally from a remote geography to take advantage of lower costs and better availability of specialized skill sets.

Offsourcing Roadmap—A detailed plan for moving the organization's IT-enabled services into an offshore environment. It includes risk management, change management, communications, infrastructure, organization, process and change control plans. It also includes a detailed refinement of the Business Case based upon the confirmed target operating model.

Ostrich syndrome—The tendency of unenlightened management to stick their collective heads in the sand and pretend that it is business as usual even as disruptive technologies and business models lay siege to their livelihoods and personnel.

Pilot—Implementation of limited scope (and usually limited duration) intended to prove the feasibility and benefits of a target operating model.

Portal—A flexible, Web-based application providing users with a collaborative workspace to achieve specific business purposes. Built well it will provide access to data from multiple sources in a personalized fashion. Also referred as **collaborative management portal**.

Portal Vision Workshop (PVW)—A time-boxed, facilitated exercise intended to rapidly drive out portal requirements, priorities, technical issues and a consensus on the ergonomics in the target solution.

Project Management Institute (PMI)—A nonprofit group that promotes good project management practices.

Rational Unified Process (RUP)—Enterprise software development process.

Reduction in force (RIF)—Termination of employment for a group of individuals as a result of a restructuring event.

Request for information (RFI)—Basic vendor inquiry for background data including size, services capabilities, experience and skill sets.

Request for proposal (RFP)—Detailed solicitation of vendor bids. Should include requirements, schedules, timeline for bidding process and all other relevant expectations.

Six Sigma—A management discipline intended to benefit the organization through a reduction in the variability of processes.

Switching cost—Incremental expense (time, money, resources) required of an organization to change strategies or vendors once a path has been executed.

Technology park—Usually a government-sponsored physical location in an offshore geography with superior infrastructure to attract IT-enabled service operators.

Total cost of offsourcing (TCO)—Comprehensive cost to move operation(s) offshore, including labor, travel, management, overhead, communications and other factors.

Index

Notes

Notes

Notes

Order Information

Mail to:

We encourage you to share the insights that you have gained from reading *Offshore Ready* by giving a copy to a friend or colleague.

ISANI Press
4625 Manor Way
Suite 100
Flower Mound, Texas 75028

Telephone: 713-256-7584
Fax: 817-464-2312
e-mail: order@offshoreready.com

Price: $39.95 plus tax and shipping

Name: _____

Title: _____

Company Name: _____

Address: _____

Address: _____

City/State/Zip Code: _____

Telephone: _____

e-mail address: _____

☐ Visa

☐ Mastercard

Card number: _____

Expiration date: _____

Signature: _____

Discounts:

1-9 copies:	$39.95
10-20 copies:	$35.95
21+ copies:	$31.95

Quantity: _____

Price: _____

Tax (8.25%): _____

Shipping: _____

Total: _____

Shipping Costs

1 book - $5.00

each additional book. $2.00

Ground shipping 3-7 business days in the US.

Call for International shipping costs.